Where Do We Go From Here?

A Guidebook for the
Cell Group Church

Where Do We Go From Here?

A Guidebook for the
Cell Group Church

REVISED EDITION

RALPH W. NEIGHBOUR, JR.

TOUCH PUBLICATIONS
Houston, Texas, U.S.A.

Published by TOUCH® Publications, Inc.
P.O. Box 7847
Houston, Texas, 77270, U.S.A.
1-800-735-5865

Cover design by Don Bleyl
Text design by Rick Chandler
Editing by Scott Boren

International Standard Book Number: 1-880828-17-0

TOUCH® Publications is the book-publishing division
of TOUCH® Outreach Ministries, a resource and consulting
non-profit organization for churches with a vision for cell-based
local church structure. TOUCH® = Transforming Others Under
Christ's Hand®

For more information on other fine
TOUCH® Publications, call 1-800-735-5865
or find us on the web:
http://www.touchusa.org

To my wife RUTH

In all the years we have shared,
she has never failed to exalt her Lord.

Contents

Foreword to the Revised Edition

On election night in 1992, God spoke to me clearly and told me: *Two things are coming in America: Harvest and Hostility. Your church is not prepared for either of them. I will show you something soon that will prepare you for what is coming upon the earth.* I spent November contemplating the impressions of that election night, calling out to God to give me more insight.

My prayer was answered within the month when a pastor friend who shared with me how his church was making the transition to becoming a cell church. He gave me a copy of Dr. Ralph Neighbour's book *Where Do We Go From Here?*, and I spent the next month or so reading the book, nearly infuriated by its message. I was frankly outraged at how easily Dr. Neighbour disposed of the traditional American church and described a new paradigm of church structure called the "cell church."

Gradually, my anger turned to intrigue as the book explained how the principles of the early church in Acts have birthed huge cell churches throughout the world today. My anger and doubt gave way to a soft reverence for something I saw as awesome and supernatural.

I caught the vision and was able to impart it to our staff and church. We took the plunge and transitioned to a cell church, beginning in April 1993 with 54 cells. Since then, our church has grown both numerically and spiritually. Presently, we now have over 600 cell groups, and ministry has never been more exciting. God has indeed given the church today a blue print to returning us to our New Testament roots — in community, structure, discipleship, body ministry, and evangelism.

I owe a great debt of gratitude to Ralph Neighbour as one of the pioneers in the cell church movement. His heart has yearned to see the Church all over the world embrace a New Testament model of ministry which equips and empowers believers to do the work of ministry. I am eternally grateful for the impact *Where Do We Go From Here?* has had on my ministry and the church I pastor. I pray as you read this book, you too will be open to the Holy Spirit doing a new thing in you and in your church.

Larry Stockstill, Senior Pastor
Bethany World Prayer Center

Foreword to the First Edition

This book may be the second most important book you have ever read. That doesn't mean it will be easy to read. Quite the contrary!

I'm not referring to the writing style. It's well written, often captivating. But to some, it will be difficult to read because of our excess baggage of tradition and culture.

Let me make a suggestion: before you begin this book, agree with me to do four things:

First, lay the book aside and pray the Holy Spirit will guide and instruct you according to His will. Certainly, we can all agree this is a fair and non-threatening request.

Second, deposit the baggage of your church's tradition and your cultural heritage at the end of the book. You may reclaim it when you arrive there. Some of that baggage is good, and some is excess weight that will burden your spiritual journey. Let the sole measure and authority for your evaluation of this book be according to God's Word under the tutelage of the Holy Spirit.

Third, agree to read the entire book.

A majority of the readers will find sections that will take them out of their present "comfort zones." Those at either end of the theological poles may find passages that will raise questions for them. Don't stop — to understand the book, you must finish it.

Pastors of traditional churches may be offended at some points. If you are one of them and fail to capture the spirit of love that the author has for you — read on! Leaders of churches who are not doing any evangelism may be overwhelmed — but read on!

You don't have to agree with everything written here in order to benefit from the book. There are some points made where I am still unsure and searching. But, I challenge you: if you disagree, use scriptural exegesis as your basis for disagreement, rather than your tradition and heritage.

Fourth, when you reclaim your baggage at the end, don't just pick up your bags and walk on. Open your luggage and examine it. See if there are any items you may no longer need — items that will just add to your burden and make your journey more difficult. Lighten your load! Consider where you are going, and move on to the fulfillment of the task God has called you to complete.

I hope your curiosity has been aroused. I don't think you will be disappointed. This may be the second most important book you will ever read.

Now, put the book down for a moment and prayerfully prepare yourself to read it!

Dr. David Finnell, Professor of Evangelism
Columbia International University

Introduction
to the Revised Edition

I wrote the first edition of this book in 1989. It was a lonely time for me! Back then, the cell church movement did not exist. It was only a dream.

I had left the traditional church 20 years earlier, seeking to find a more effective and biblical model for church life. Our move to Houston in 1969 was a "back to the future" journey to form an "experimental church." *What would a New Testament church look like in our generation?* Most of my pastor friends treated me like I had just run off with the organist. They thought I was crazy to leave behind the security of a denominational post to experiment with alternate forms of church life.

I bought a picture painted by Fred Machetanz, the artist laureate of Alaska. It shows an Eskimo with his dogsled, the lead dog sitting pensively beside his master. The man had ventured onto new ice on the edge of the rocks to hunt seals. The ice has cracked from the shoreline and a great gap of icy water is now between him and the shoreline. He is drifting away from the land, unable to return. The picture is titled, "What Every Hunter Fears!" I really identified with that Eskimo.

During the 1980's, I tried hard to convince pastors and churches and even denominations that the future of the local church would require transitioning to a cell-based structure. I taught classes in several seminaries, held hundreds of seminars, consulted with dozens of churches. I even briefly joined the staff of a "megachurch" whose pastor promised me he was willing to transition but later reneged, deciding he would continue to dance with traditional structures, a safer option for him.

It didn't seem that Christian workers were as tired as I was with "business as usual." The pastors I tutored met with stiff opposition from "Church Pillars" who saw their positions of prestige threatened by the theology that taught all believers were ministers.

As I mentioned in the first edition of this book, there came that final phone call from another dear pastor in California telling me he had just been sacked for trying to transition his church. With great pain, I decided it was not worth it to crusade further for change in American churchianity.

I now publicly repent from the caustic comment I made in the first edition that the new wineskin could never exist in American churches. Time has demonstrated I was wrong about that. But I have come to some conclusions about why it seems to be so difficult in the United States for the cell church movement to take hold. I am now preparing a companion book to this one which will be titled *Never Ask A Fish What Water Is Like.* I will deal with this issue in depth in that volume.

Let me bring you up to date about what has happened since the first edition was released.

A New Opportunity

The story begins with the renewing of a broken friendship. Back in the 1970's, I served briefly in Singapore as a missionary planting "house churches." At that time, I was greatly impressed with a young college graduate, Lawrence Khong, who had more potential than any pastor I met there. Soon after I returned to pastor *The People Who Care* in Houston, he came to the United States with his new bride to attend seminary. I brought him to serve on my staff as a pastor intern working with youth cells for a summer. We were quite close until he began to accept the seminary's teaching that all the gifts of the Holy Spirit had ceased with the passing of the original disciples. While I do not consider myself a Pentecostal, my own journey into cell church life confirmed that the proper use of spiritual gifts is mandatory for edification and for evangelism. As a result, our friendship cooled.

My friend returned to Singapore and began to grow a very large Baptist church. Imagine his shock when, without any exposure to the charismatic movement, he broke out in a prayer language while alone in his study. It scared him to death! He immediately began to "test the spirits" by saying, "Jesus is Lord!"

In purity of heart, he drew together the deacons and explained to them that his theology did not match either his experience or his further examination of Scripture. They did the only Christian thing to do: they summarily fired him!

As I was writing the first edition of this book, he called me and explained what had taken place. He asked for my advice. I said, "This is good news! Now that you have realized that spiritual gifts exist, it is time for you to start a cell church." He agreed, but insisted I should come over to meet with him and his staff of five pastors. Thus, I found myself back in Singapore consulting with a 600-member split of a traditional church.

Using a pure cell base, they quickly grew to 1,000, then 1,500. Commuting back and forth did not make sense. I agreed to become the "guru" for this congregation, a "pure" cell church from the start.

As soon as I could arrange my affairs, I resigned from teaching at Columbia Biblical Seminary, gave away KEYY radio station in Provo, Utah to a missionary organization working among the Mormons, turned TOUCH Outreach Ministries over to a fine young man and moved to Singapore.

The next four years were the most exciting and productive in my entire life. Here was a pastor who would not drag his feet when I proposed what should be done. His brilliance in the pulpit and in management, along with the experience I brought to the table from years of testing the cell models, provided a perfect environment to fine-tune the equipping of converts and the training of pastors.

Nearly all I had learned about cell life proved to be effective when tested in Singapore. The pastoral staff was committed to win the lost and develop a pure cell church. We spent endless hours brainstorming and planning, skipping more lunches than I care to remember.

Even more importantly, I found myself in an environment where I could focus on one of the greatest flaws in traditional church life: *equipping every single believer to become an effective minister.*

Equipping Every Believer

From the beginning of my journey into the cell church movement, I had struggled with the problem of discipleship materials that were not functional. The traditional church pastors were not able to prepare each

Christian for ministry. Their focus was on training 10 to 15% of the members to fill the positions needed to conduct church programs. There was training to teach Sunday School, sing in the choir, serve on the budget committee, etc., but equipping every believer for service was placed on the back burner. I had dabbled in this field and had seen massive use of my booklet *A Survival Kit For New Christians*. However, a full journey into ministry had not yet been written.

At that time, nothing was in print to walk a new convert through the steps of moving from a "little child" to a "young man" to a "father" (1 John 2:12-14). My skills in writing programmed learning materials, developed under the tutoring of Avery Willis years before, motivated me to write *The Year of Equipping* modules. Everything I wrote was carefully tested over four years through several generations of converts, revised after each cycle. It is the most important contribution I will ever make to the cell church movement.

We eliminated weekly training classes to be held in a traditional way in a church building, Instead, the *Daily Growth Guides* I prepared in *The Year of Equipping* modules were combined with weekly mentoring by a "Sponsor." We also added exciting weekends for bonding cell members together: the *Spiritual Formation Weekend*, the *Spiritual Victory Weekend*, the *Touching Hearts Weekend*, and the training for "Fathers" to develop Share and Target Groups in the *Opening Hearts Weekend*.

Of great importance was helping the "little child" become a "young man" by learning how to deal with the "evil one." Inner strongholds and soul ties that were dragged into the new life like grave clothes had to be removed. For this, a careful blending of materials in *The New Believer's Station* and *The Arrival Kit* prepared the convert for the deliverance received in the *Spiritual Victory Weekend*.

Since writing the first edition, I have not only developed *The Year of Equipping* for Cell Members, but I have completed training tracks for all levels of leadership. I called it the TOUCH Equipping Stations. My experience in Singapore gave me the opportunity to structure equipping tracks for Cell Leaders, Zone Supervisors and Zone Pastors. From this base, many models are now being developed and distributed.

It is a delight to see the many adjustments that have been made to it to fit different environments. For the illiterate Causas in South Africa, one pastor took my materials and tape-recorded the materials so his members could listen to audiotapes. Another man, working with a tribe in the east of the country, drew stick figures on one side of a piece of paper and wrote a few simple words on the back side for the "trainer" to remember what to say about the illustrations.

A Great Harvest

It became obvious to us that as new converts came to Christ, their *oikoses* became ripe harvest fields. Thus, we began to structure an annual calendar that had three cycles of sowing, cultivating, and finally reaping. We incorporated *Harvest Events*, three in number: *Let's Celebrate Christmas!*, an event that drew 48,000 to the Singapore Indoor Stadium; *Let's Have A Good Friday!*, a luncheon where cell groups invited unbelievers into their homes for a special Easter meal; and a drama presentation in July/August where cells would bring guests for a powerful presentation of the Christian life.

It was thrilling to see the results of equipping every believer. The receptionist had a board behind her desk with the words HEARTS OPENED. Numbered cards were changed through the day to show the total figure of conversions since the first of the year. Cell members were encouraged to phone in a report of each new convert by the hour. Thus, as I would pass through the lobby it was thrilling to see the number of conversions recorded increase by the hour. We averaged five new conversions a day, 365 days a year. I would repeat to myself as I looked at the report board, *"And the Lord added daily to the church those who were saved!"*

Never in America had I seen mass baptisms, but we did in Singapore. Cell leaders and Zone Supervisors did the baptizing. A part of the training of all cell leaders was to learn how to baptize converts. This was usually done in a hotel swimming pool during their weekend of orientation. Cell members with cameras would photograph their friends at baptismal services, jamming close to the water to get close-ups.

Touching the World

Singapore was not the only place where the cell church movement was taking hold. A 1990 trip to Hong Kong caused me to meet a long-haired "hippie" type of pastor named Ben Wong. He had just completed his training at a seminary and was specializing in reaching "grass roots" people. Ben followed me around, picking my brain, begging me for my books. He was one of several men who formed cell-based churches. Soon his Shepherd Community grew to several hundred and launched a training center for potential cell pastors. He translated many of my books into Chinese. Repeated trips back to Hong Kong to do seminars organized by him for other pastors generated a transition of dozens of traditional churches. At present, over 168 churches in Hong Kong are all linked together across denominational barriers, and there is a new 14 story building to house their training events.

Back in 1990, Japan's churches typically numbered 11 to 15 people. As one worker said, "In our country, 29 members makes a *megachurch!*" Several trips there to hold seminars brought the cell vision to the pastors of that nation. My equipping track was translated into Japanese. Now there are dozens of cell churches in Japan, many of them exceeding 250 members.

We went to Russia to hold seminars in Moscow that drew hundreds of pastors. The launching of the cell movement there was picked up by Chuck Squeri, a Christian worker from Ohio, who has now graduated over 1,000 pastors and has held seminars all over the CIS.

Kazakestan's first seminar on the cell church was held in Almaty. While some of the old traditional pastors were insulting to us, the new converts from the post-Perestroika era soaked up all we taught. Later visits to Almaty astonished me: virtually every church in the city is now a pure cell-based structure. One week I taught over 500 cell leaders in a church formed by a Korean Pastor. The final evening God met us in a dramatic outpouring of His Spirit I had never before experienced.

Trips to Taiwan brought the entire church community there to consider the cell church model, and many of the largest congregations adopted the New Testament pattern of Basic Christian Communities.

Annual International Cell Church Conferences were held in Singapore, with over 23 nations attending. The American delegations included pastor Larry Stockstill and some of his team. Walking through the offices of our Zone Pastors, seeing all the charts of cell attendance and conversions, Pastor Larry caught the vision. Later he brought a team from Singapore to speak in his church in Baker, Louisiana. Other key pastors from America also visited us and strong bonds were formed. Among them, Gerald Martin from Cornerstone in Virginia quickly grasped the concepts and applied them in the Shenandoah Valley.

The Next Step

As 1994 came to an end, I realized the "guru" was no longer needed in Singapore. I had completed the TOUCH Equipping Stations System (TESS) in 1990 and had by then graduated several hundred students who took our one year internal training course. Many of them were now on the staff as Zone Pastors. There was a feeling in my heart that staying too long would smother the creativity of the team there. Paul would plant and leave, deliberately getting out of the way so local leadership could develop. So it was that God moved me to another challenge even greater than the first one.

In South Africa, *apartheid* was drawing to a close. With the election of Mandela, the nation faced a paradigm shift in government, culture, and also church life. God arranged an invitation to lead five seminars in different locations in late 1994. I was stunned to discover the huge crowds that attended these three-day seminars: in the Johannesburg area, we had over 3,500 attend. It was a *kairos* moment in the history of that nation. One courageous pastor returned to his pulpit in Blomfontein and said, "I have just come from a cell conference. All positions of leadership in this church are dissolved! If you want to be part of the new leadership, you must begin a cell group!"

The zeal without knowledge of these pastors frightened me! The Lord brought to my mind the many visits I had enjoyed with an American missionary who was planting cell churches in the villages of India. He had seen several thousand new churches born by bringing in the pastor/evangelists to a central training time every three months. This week of instruction would then be applied as they returned to their fields. I realized this would work in South Africa. Thus, *The Year of Transition* was born. As I moved back to Houston, I began to commute to South Africa every three months to train pastors there. The response was great. Hundreds of pastors came to the seminars held in Johannesburg, Capetown, and Durban. The IFCC, a fellowship of charismatic churches, adopted the training immediately. Other pastors from the Presbyterian, Dutch Reformed, Methodist, and Rhema groups attended.

One Dutch Reformed Church in Ermelo developed 90 cells in their first year of transition.

Meanwhile, my friend Dion Robert came to minister with me in Zambia and Zimbabwe. My visits to his church included teaching over 3,000 of his cell leaders in a lovely government auditorium in Yammasukro during the week of a stadium crusade that saw many thousands come to Christ.

The devotion of the Christians in his church in Abidjan is best illustrated by an event that took place in the summer of 1997. A crusade had been set to take place in a stadium in Bouake, the second largest city in the Ivory Coast. It is also the stronghold of a Rosicrucian cult. Word was sent to Pastor Dion that his crusade was under a curse, and he had better think twice about coming there. He had hundreds of Abidjan cell leaders who were transported by buses and vans to Bouake to help with the counseling of converts. On the way, a lumber truck plummeted into the oncoming traffic and sheared the cab of a bus from the frame. It rolled down a steep embankment with 28 cell leaders in it — all were killed! At the end of the procession, Pastor Dion came upon the scene of the recent tragedy. He slid down the bank, saw the bodies, clambered back up to his own vehicle and gave instructions to some of his pastors about what to do. He went directly to the crusade and preached. Thousands were converted. An American pastor present went to him after the service and said, "I don't know how you could get up like that and preach after coming through the shock of the deaths of your cell leaders!" Pastor Dion put his thumb into the chest of the American pastor and said, "That's the difference between the kind of Christianity you have in America and the kind we have here. For you, there is black and white and a lot of gray in between. You are so confused by the gray, and think that some of the events of life do not have to do with the battle between God and evil. For we Christians in Africa, there is no gray area. There is only the power of God and the presence of Satan and his evil deeds. I am a general, and I led my soldiers into a battle. I knew in advance the enemy would seek to destroy us. I have lost some soldiers, but look at the thousands of conversions — the enemy lost far more than we did!"

In Russia, Pat Robertson drew over 12 million letters when he transmitted a prime time series explaining the gospel. From that correspondence, 800,000 requested Bibles and a study book. I was then asked to come to Kiev and make a proposal for how to conserve the results where people could not find a church to attend. I wrote a 16 page booklet explaining what a cell group was ("Basic Christian Community") and how to form a cell with friends. I included 10 weeks of curriculum. As a result, tens of thousands of cells have been formed. An appeal to South African pastors to come and follow up these cells is presently taking place.

In Brazil, Roberto Lay has established TOUCH BRAZIL and is in the second year of teaching *The Year of Transition*, now called "ACT." In April of 1999 I had the joy of training 964 people in the launch of the second cycle of training.

Back in 1980, a denominational executive said to me, "Ralph, you're just ahead of your time. I suggest you hibernate by teaching in a seminary and 20 years from now, the church might be ready for you." He was a prophet. In 1999, the International Mission Board of the Southern Baptist Convention blessed me with an opportunity to explain the cell church movement to church planting missionaries in Brazil, Paraguay, Uruguay, and to teach key missionaries from every major city in South and Central America in a Mexico City conference.

The Journey Ahead

As we enter the next century, the cell church movement will have a profound impact on traditional church life. More and more pastors are fed up with "business as usual." Many new church plants are starting fresh with cell structures. Joel Comiskey's material on the "Groups of Twelve" model, originated by Cesar Castellanos in Bogota, will be pivotal in forming the way cell churches organize themselves.

Here are some reflections for those who will be leading the movement in the next generations:
1. There must be a balance between basic Christian communities and the gatherings for celebration and worship.
2. The harvesting of unbelievers is best done through "body life" evangelism, where the unbeliever observes the life of Christ in the cell and confesses, "God is certainly among you!"
3. Far more emphasis is needed to stress that a cell embodies the literal incarnation of the Spirit of Christ. To say it another way, a true cell is the Body of Christ.

4. While men may think they can form a cell, the Scripture plainly teaches in 1 Corinthians 12 that it is the work of the Holy Spirit to baptize all men into the Body of Christ. We have not yet grasped that if all are ministers, then all are to be called by the Holy Spirit into the area of ministry where they serve. The more we can keep our hands out of organizing people, the more the Holy Spirit can freely call each person to the appropriate ministry.

5. There is no further excuse for delaying the militant equipping of every saint for the work of his or her ministry. Pastors who tolerate "sit and soak" Christians deserve what they get!

6. People do not change value systems by listening to sermons and lectures. They revise their values and habits through experiences. Also, we must remember it takes *six experiences* to make an impression on a life.

7. It is now time for the networking of cell churches around the world to develop. Watch for men who are Kingdom builders and not Castle builders to protect the movement from carnal leadership.

I pray that this new edition will advance the kingdom of God. Much has happened over the last 10 years in the cell church movement. I have updated crucial points in this new edition. Specifically, I have included new information on cell structures in chapter 14. My finalized equipping track for every member is fully explained in a new chapter. I inserted a new chapter on how to design harvest events in the cell church. And the new information on transitioning a church to cells will be much more helpful.

With Dr. Lorna Jenkins' permission, I took out the chapters on children in the cell church. She has since written many excellent tools that surpass the introductory survey of the first edition. I encourage you to read them.

I conclude with the trilogy I have lived by during these years:

1. It is the task of a servant to obey his Master.
2. It is the obligation of the Master to provide for that servant.
3. Therefore, the servant must never be afraid!

Introduction
to the First Edition

I am convinced that the traditional church worldwide is being slowly replaced by an act of God. Developments taking place today are as powerful as the upheaval in 1517 during the time of Martin Luther. One cannot say that Luther caused the first Reformation. He was only the tinder that lit the fire; the dead wood was ready to burn.

Historians have examined the forces which came into play at that moment of time. The development of the printing press, the seething impatience with the greed of Rome, the growing disillusionment about philosophical systems, the emergence of scientific methods, all made that century a time of transition. The church was reformed by the hand of God to prepare it for the new world that was about to exist.

The Catholicism of the Dark Ages was simply incompetent to cope with the new environment. The reformed church was a child of its time. It faced each new event with power from above. To be sure, it didn't come out of the old mold far enough — and the more conservative branches retained enough of the old ways to burn at the stake those who did go farther out.

The styles of church life so appropriate for the Reformation period are now impotent. The church is impotent. It cannot reproduce unless it first physically fathers new children. I have roamed this earth since 1974, and the impotence is widespread.

It is time for the second Reformation. The people of earth have moved into a new era, one which never existed before in all the history of man. Change comes faster and faster, and the church becomes more and more irrelevant to cope with the changes.

I pen these words on my way back to the United States from Singapore. Just a speedboat ride away from that modern world class city is the Indonesian island of Batam. It's not large — about double the size of Singapore. I met a Muslim man there who was over one hundred years old, and who had never seen the opposite side of the jungle-covered island.

The peace and quiet of fishing villages that have existed for a century is about to disappear. The local inhabitants are being given $75 for each shack in their kampong and 50¢ for each coconut tree and told to move out to make way for resort hotels to be constructed. Both Singapore and Indonesia are sinking a billion dollars each into the development of Batam. All the land has been gobbled up by speculators. By 2000 A.D., the entire island will become a teeming city!

Cities of a million people will spring up during the next 20 years all over the earth. How can they be reached for Christ? Most certainly, not through planting existing church forms in them! That's why God is quietly ignoring religious power structures and those who make their living from preserving them.

I am going on 62 as I write, and I have felt for years like those old men in the Gospels who wanted to live long enough to see the Messiah with their own eyes. I have longed to see the new church in all its glory before I go to Glory. Praise God, it's here! He has launched a new form of church life called the "cell group church." At this stage, it's still pure enough to reach the exploding population of our day. This book is all about what I have seen and learned in the last 25 years concerning this new form of church.

The chapters will describe the problem with the old and will prepare the reader for the new by first discussing the theology of the cell group structure. Finally, I will tell everything I can think of which might help those who are ready to journey into the second Reformation — concepts which have been gleaned from many men and many groups in many nations.

Spare me the phone calls that begin, "Where is a cell group church in my area?" If there's one near you, you already know about it. Its detractors delight in slinging mud at it, and its members delight in harvesting the unchurched. If there's not one near you, take a trip. Visit one of the churches mentioned in this book, or better yet, start one yourself!

I had men come to see my experimental church in Houston by the droves. Most successful churches do what I did: they hold Pastors' Conferences to satisfy the curious. However, few men whom I have spent precious hours talking to or holding seminars for have ever done anything with what they learned. On the other hand, I have asked every cell group pastor I have met on my journeys, "When you started, did you make a trip to see a model of what you have here? Did you attend someone's seminar before you started?" In each and every case, the answer has been "No. I went to my knees and got marching orders from my Lord. I had no choice. He taught me as I went along."

After you have some battle scars, take that trip! Like those veteran missionaries who return to Columbia Biblical Seminary on furloughs, you will know what you're looking for is worth the investment of time you will require. I'm thinking just now of Jim Romaine, one of my doctoral students. With 15 tough years in Turkey under his belt, he drilled and grilled me in every class. How I love him! His new insights into God's activity in forming cell group churches will guide his coming years there, and I will avidly read his newsletters.

There are other materials you will want to peruse when you finish reading this book. You can find these on our website: www.touchusa.org.

Let's covenant now to pray for each other. The first birds in the air fly alone, and I can testify that it has been lonely up there. Drop a letter to the address on the copyright page, and let me know what the Lord is doing to you on the journey.

A Look at the
Current Situation

Part 1

The Journey into New Church Life

Before we begin our journey together, let me give you the conclusion. With great love and affection, we shall examine the lifestyle of traditional church structures we have all known since childhood, and we shall find them wanting. Or, to put it more clearly, the Holy Spirit is finding them wanting. I repeat: we make this examination with sensitivity and compassion, in the same way a doctor examines an old friend who has a terminal disease. Sadly, I weep within as did Jeremiah over his beloved Israel as I write about the traditional church. I also seek to withdraw from those who are filled with anger and criticism of it. Such negative spirits never become a part of what this book is about. Their motives are not pure enough for the Spirit of God to bless them.

As I have looked within the traditional church, I have at the same time sought a better way, a way that we shall find in the pages of the New Testament. This way will serve as a yardstick to evaluate today's congregations. In so doing, we will see how far we have strayed from where we started. This study will also explain why today's "churchianity" is slowly dying from its own terminal disease, diagnosed as the deadly "Program Base Design." A report has just been released that 70% of Southern Baptist churches are either declining or stagnant. We are at the end of an era. The church as we have experienced it is shrinking.

We are going to observe what the Holy Spirit is beginning to do in our generation to raise up the beautiful Bride of Christ in a more appropriate form — one with the ability to harvest the billions of newborns of this generation. To distinguish between the traditional church as we have known it and these new life forms, we shall call them the "cell group churches."

They are growing like mushrooms in the rich soil of a dark night. A recent estimate by a Nashville church-watcher puts the number of new, innovative cell group churches in America alone in the thousands. Only a few of them existed in 1979. They are a recent activity of the Spirit. They are new wineskins, and they hold a new wine — the wine of God's activity in a world we must bring to Jesus' feet as we minister to this generation.

The Awesome Population Explosion and the Church

As we enter the new millennium, the world's population has crossed over the six billion barrier, and it will increase to eight billion by the year 2025. The preponderance of that growth will occur in the developing countries. The Director of the U.N. Centre for Human Settlements in Nairobi writes:

> The urban share of total world population, which was estimated at less than 30 percent in 1950, had steady growth to 36.9 percent in 1970 and 41.6 percent in 1985. Now it is projected to surpass the 50 percent mark just after the turn of the century and to approach 60 percent in the year 2025 . . . in 1950, four out of the five largest urban agglomerations were located in the industrialized world . . . today, of the world's 10 largest urban agglomerations, only two — Tokyo/Yokohama and New York/Northeastern New Jersey — are situated in a developed region . . . at the top of the list are . . . Mexico City, with 26.3 million; Sao Paolo, with 24 million; Calcutta, with 16.6; Greater Bombay, with 16; Seoul and Shanghai, with 13.5 million each; and not much further behind will be Rio de Janeiro, Delhi, Greater Buenos Aires, Cairo/Giza/Imbaba, Jakarta, Baghdad, Teheran, Karachi, Istanbul, Dacca, Manila, Beijing, all with populations between 10 and 13 million people.[1]

It is hard to believe the rate at which cities are growing. In 1970, there were only three cities of 10 million. Now there are over 18. By 2015, it is projected by the United Nations Population Division that there will be over 26 cities of 10 million or more. Only two of these cities will be in North America.[2]

As we observe this explosion and implosion of people, it becomes quickly obvious that the world is being impacted by young people. In Asian cities like Singapore, people below 15 years of age form 23.4 per cent of the population while those above 60 comprise 8.1 percent.[3]

All this points to an important fact. The population explosion is taking place in the non-Christian world. We are not alone in seeking to reach these exploding metropolises. Other world religions are alert to the importance of these days and are hard at work making converts. In Abidjan, Ivory Coast, it is reported Muslims are greeting incoming buses and trains, snagging rural people coming to live in the city. They are offered food, shelter, and assistance in getting a job. As a result, thousands are being snatched away from the message of Christ within minutes of their arrival. In South Africa, the new government has kicked the Christian church services broadcast nationwide on Sundays and has replaced them with Muslim teachers explaining the Koran. We have entered an era of history when evangelism must be sharpened and honed to cut into the darkness of a burgeoning non-Christian world.

Our evangelism must take new forms and shapes if it is to keep up with the needs of our day! The crusades, the evangelistic preaching activities of local churches, must not slow down. But we must add another dimension if we are to keep up with the exploding population. We must plant a new type of church that can think in terms of multiplication, not addition.

NET ADDITIONS TO WORLD POPULATION
AT 25 YEAR INTERVALS, 1900-2100

Source: Population Division, United Nations

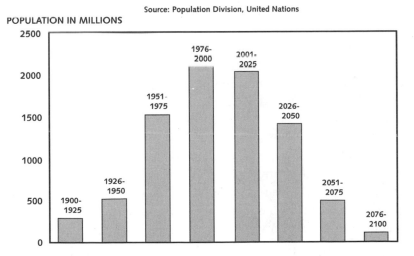

This graph shares the alarming situation. Never before in history —
and never again before 2100 A.D. — will the earth's population grow so
fast! The church as we know it is simply not capable of harvesting such
an increase.

Church Structures Are Woefully Inadequate

In the light of this population explosion in
the world, we must question whether
traditional methods of church planting
will keep up. There are several reasons we
should call these methods into question:

5%
OVER 350
MEMBERS

29%
151-350
MEMBERS

33%
UNDER 50
MEMBERS

33%
51-150
MEMBERS

1. The form of church planting we are
   now using in major urban centers is
   taken from a rural concept of church life.
   It is not appropriate for urban structures. The
   kaleidoscope of cultures which intertwine in the cities requires an
   urban form for church life.
2. We cannot afford to continue planting congregations in urban areas
   which are limited by parish boundaries or "church fields." This is a
   rural mind set, inappropriate for world class cities. (See graph on next
   page.)
3. We cannot afford to continue erecting church buildings in small
   districts of world class cities. We must find an alternative to spending
   huge amounts for land and for the construction of "starter buildings"
   every few miles.
4. The traditional church, consisting of a church building, a pastor, and
   a flock gathered from the "parish area," has specific growth limits.
   Each church will plateau at certain points. One third of all traditional
   churches in the world today plateau at 50 members. Another third
   quit growing when there are 150 members. Twenty-nine per cent will
   stop growing when there are 350 members. Only five per cent grow
   larger than this, and most plateau at 1,000 or 2,000.[4] It is sad, but
   true: the church structure we have duplicated over and over in this
   century is shockingly inefficient! The buildings are empty for most of
   the week. The members aren't equipped to minister to hurting people.
   Everything centers on activities within the church buildings.

5. We have entered the Age of the Internet. With traffic problems exploding and people spending more and more time at home, the internet must be used for both evangelism and equipping. A new form of "basic Christian communities" is needed that includes modern communication structures.

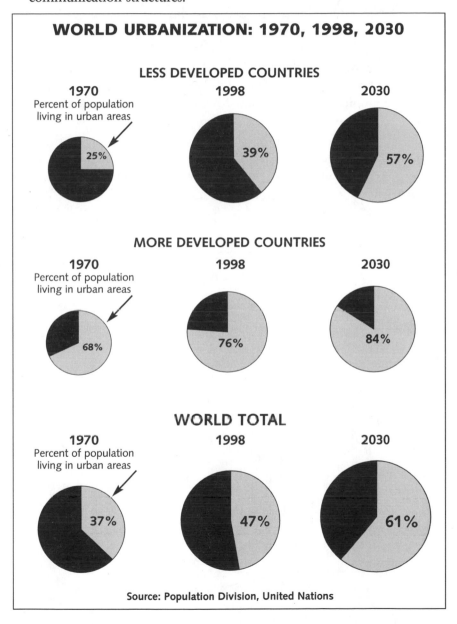

WORLD URBANIZATION: 1970, 1998, 2030

LESS DEVELOPED COUNTRIES

1970 — Percent of population living in urban areas — 25%

1998 — 39%

2030 — 57%

MORE DEVELOPED COUNTRIES

1970 — Percent of population living in urban areas — 68%

1998 — 76%

2030 — 84%

WORLD TOTAL

1970 — Percent of population living in urban areas — 37%

1998 — 47%

2030 — 61%

Source: Population Division, United Nations

American Churches Are in Deep Recession

According to The Gallup Organization, four adults out of every ten Americans (40%) attended a church or synagogue in a typical week in 1999. In 1958, that figure was 49%.[5] The average for the nation is skewed by the larger church attendance in the smaller communities. *The Houston Chronicle* has estimated that only 30% of Houstonians darken the door of a church on an average Sunday.

At the same time, the average weekly attendance in the American church has decreased by 7% since 1987 even though the average pastor *thinks* his attendance is increasing.[6] While we might think things are getting better, the statistics reveal otherwise.

Sunday School, the highly touted "arm of evangelism" of the local church, is no longer impacting the society. Many churches today are registering larger attendance in their worship services than in their Sunday Schools — a clear reversal for evangelicals.

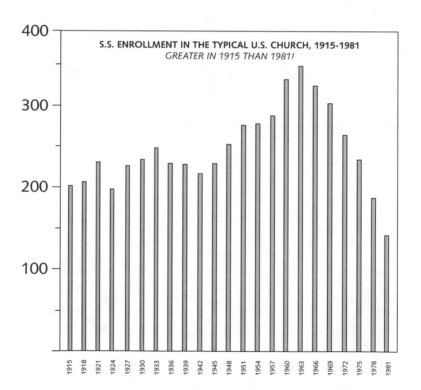

S.S. ENROLLMENT IN THE TYPICAL U.S. CHURCH, 1915-1981
GREATER IN 1915 THAN 1981!

What happened to it? *In Growth, a New Vision for the Sunday School,* Donald MaGavran and Win Arn provided us with these insights in the early eighties:

> The focus of the Sunday School changed from those "outside" to those "inside" . . . . Leadership of the Sunday School shifted from the laity to professionals . . . . There developed a loss of community and sense of belonging . . . . The Sunday School became less and less of a priority for the church.[7]

The graph on page 34 is taken from this book, and clearly documents the inability of Sunday School to remain relevant to the changing American society at the end of the century. As we enter the year 2000 the effectiveness of Sunday School has continued to decline.

Along with the decline of the backbone of the church program, the evangelistic thrust subtly changed. With little to offer the unbeliever in the "here and now," the most popular programs for training Christians to evangelize clearly emphasized that the advantages of becoming a

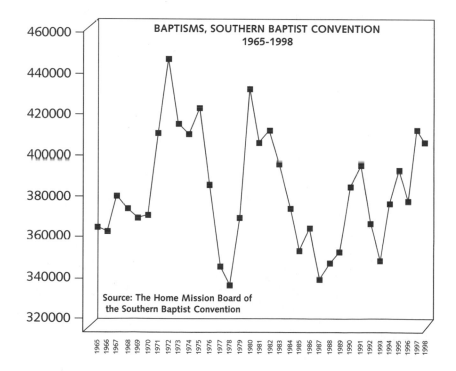

BAPTISMS, SOUTHERN BAPTIST CONVENTION
1965-1998

Source: The Home Mission Board of the Southern Baptist Convention

Christian *comes* after you die: "If you were to die today and God were to say, 'Why should I let you into my heaven,' what would your answer be?" Have we nothing to offer between now and then? Unfortunately, this isn't appropriate for a generation more interested in how to "live it up" than how eternity will be spent. Our loss of converts is shown by the decline in annual baptisms within the most evangelistic denomination in the nation.

The church in America has spent so much time discipling itself that it has become an ignored appendage to a large portion of the nation's population. To forecast just how a society can look at irrelevant religion, one should examine New Zealand and Australia, where no more than 10% of the citizens attend church, or England, where hundreds of church buildings stand unused.[8]

Televangelists Disgraced, Pastors Fired

Emerging Trends indicates that public opinion of television evangelists in general is at an all-time low. 65% of viewers feel these men have "no special relationship with God," and nearly 70% feel they are "insincere." It is too soon to measure the damage these men have done to the future of organized religion in America, but it is already affirmed that contributions to many valid Christian causes have been severely damaged.[9]

Bruce Grubbs of the Southern Baptist Sunday School Board reports that over an 18-month period that ended in early 1989, more than 2,100 Southern Baptist ministers were dismissed, a 31% increase over a similar period that ended in early 1985.[10] So many clergy are being released by frustrated congregations that special non-credit schools are being set up to reequip the wounded. T. D. Hall of Fort Worth had over 80 applicants for his Emmaus Road school when it opened — mostly pastors who simply could not please their churches.

Some want to explain away these dismissals as the fault of exceptional preachers who reach church members through the media, making the local pastor's preaching and teaching look shabby in comparison. *The Emerging Trends* poll doesn't bear this out. A more realistic evaluation may simply be that the old ways of "doing church" in the next millennium neither satisfies those who are inside nor outside the structures.

Most popular of all forms of traditional church life just now are the "Megachurches." These city-wide congregations have bled the life out of neighborhood churches in the same way that grocery chains drove the "Mom and Pop" corner stores out of business 30 years ago. Plush, ornate auditoriums and subsidized ski trips for the Yuppies appeal to the social side of Americans, but do little to touch the broken lives of the unchurched. These churches attract some who desire to "get lost" in the largeness, and their Sunday Schools are filled with members who average a twice-a-month attendance. Since their activities are extremely building-centered, they choke off growth by growing large enough that they can no longer afford to add further space to their facilities. Few options remain for the American church!

God's Solution: A New Lifestyle for the Church

There *is* a more effective pattern in our world today than planting traditional churches. The Holy Spirit is the author of this pattern, and it has sprouted up like mushrooms all over the globe. It is called the "cell group church."

While cell group churches also develop successfully in towns and villages, they grow most rapidly when used in an urban context. Given the proper soil to take root, they are capable of exploding to astonishing sizes. The entire Christian world is aware that the Yoido Full Gospel Church surpassed the 800,000 member level. How many know, however, that the largest Presbyterian and Methodist churches in the world are also cell group churches located in Seoul? In fact, 19 out of the 20 largest churches in the world are cell churches.

Harvesting in World Class Cities

Why are cell group churches more appropriate for world class cities? Why do they grow so much faster? There are several reasons:
1. They are more efficient than traditional churches. In the traditional church, only ten to fifteen per cent of the membership is engaged in the tasks required to make the church function. After the teachers, administrators, musicians, etc., have been culled out of the total membership, the rest are expected to be faithful members. If an automobile engine were rated at fifteen per cent efficiency, it would

never see the light of day. The contrast between this misuse of Christians and the New Testament church, where one hundred per cent were involved, is scandalous.[11]

2. They are based on the scriptural concept of community. The essence of community is a sense of belonging.[12] There is a powerful Christian camaraderie established when people belong to each other in a cell group. It cannot be equaled in a church which assembles people only in large groups. Some have adopted the term "Basic Christian Community" to describe the cells of this new style of church. People look after one another, and they share the ministry of reaching the unconverted as a community task.

3. They focus on the importance of prayer for their ministries. Half nights of prayer are commonplace among cell groups. As much as one third to one half of the time spent in their gatherings is devoted to prayer. Because they expect God to answer prayer, they often experience healing of bodies and the restoration of broken lives in their gatherings.

4. They penetrate deeply into the structures of the city, reaching people in a more personal way than the traditional church will ever be able to do. While the traditional church compresses as much as ninety per cent of all service to the Lord into the church buildings, the statistic is exactly reversed in the cell group church. The life of the church is to be found in the home meetings, which typically move from one residence to another on a weekly basis.

5. When one reads church history, the term "movement" is often used. It is the only proper word to use when describing a global phenomenon. A worldwide movement has been launched by the Holy Spirit, and He is paying no attention to denominational lines. Instead, He is finding those who are not imprisoned by the past, who have a hot heart for reaching the lost, and who are ready to acknowledge every Christian is a minister! Unlike those traditions which commission missionaries to *establish* a certain type of church, cell group churches are truly *planted*. They are indigenous to their soils in a manner that has caused them to be bitterly criticized by many missionaries and pastors, who view them from without as a threat to the status quo. In reality, they are exactly that. They are not only the new wine, but the new wineskins. There are vast differences, as well as striking similarities, between the cell group churches of the earth. Their structures are truly flexible, able to

adapt to their environment. Each one has had to be shaped within its special culture impacted by history, economics, and political situations. All of them in the third world are truly indigenous, unlike the more traditional churches which have always exported, intact, the Reformation rituals of Europe and England, or the program-based styles developed in America. They have a vision for reaching the entire city, not just one part of it. The term "movement" is continually heard when interviewing church planters who are committed to the cell group church. There are no parish boundaries, no delimiting "church fields." A cell group church sees the entire metropolis as an area teeming with unreached people, and they seek to insert a cell in every neighborhood within it.

6. They are not circumscribed by the size of a church building. It is obvious that most traditional churches are limited by the size of their buildings. For some, the original edifice is used for generations. For others, a spurt of growth requires a massive building fund drive and a small addition of space. The success of the church is measured by how packed the auditorium is, rather than by the number of people who are brought to personal faith. When cell group churches do construct space, it is clearly created for the purpose of equipping, and not for attracting, members.

7. Their evangelism includes the powerful witness of Christ working within His body, beyond the traditional, cognitive presentation of the plan of salvation. The "ungifted" and the "unbelievers" of 1 Corinthians 14:24-26 are once again, as in the early church, exposed to the amazing power of the body of Christ, where all are involved in the process of edification. Once again, it has become commonplace for these seekers to fall on their faces and say, "Surely God is among you!" This "new" form of evangelism is as old as the book of Acts!

The Answer to Non-Christian Cultures

It is important to recognize that the cell groups of the earth have developed most rapidly in a non-Christian context. Why has this form of church life been so powerful in such an environment?

1. Because of its ability to deeply penetrate pagan communities. Instead of one church building in an area of a city, the cell group church has scores of "points of light" within the neighborhoods. These are often

viewed with curiosity by nearby dwellers. For example, when I served as a missionary in Viet Nam, we had only to begin singing in one of the member's homes to fill the room with curious neighbors. Their observation of our lifestyle was a powerful testimony, drawing them to listen as the Bible exposed them to the Light of the World.

2. Because the gospel is offered by non-professional hands, the hands of friends or neighbors, not outsiders. Suspicion of the Christian clergy is not present when people in the community are the bearers of the gospel. It is not uncommon for cells to see conversions on a weekly basis.

3. Because the cell groups are battlefields where people are set free from strongholds. It is commonplace for a cell group meeting to focus on a biblical teaching related to a life problem. Whereas the traditional church would focus on this with a sermon and an admonition, the cells call each member to be accountable. As in the days of Wesley's class meetings, it is commonplace for the cell leader to ask each person present, "What is the state of your life concerning this issue?" In the intimacy of the cell, people can wrestle with personal sin, long-standing habits, and find release. Personal victory spawns deeper awareness of God's power and reality.

4. Because it can powerfully meet the needs of pagans. Indeed, it focuses on needs as the key method of making contacts with the unreached. One of my students from India, Dr. Samuel Raj, told me the first thing he does when he enters an unevangelized Hindu area is to seek out a family where someone is sick or demented. He teaches and prays in that home until the power of God sets the prisoner free. The impact on the neighbors causes the first cell group to develop, and the new work is on its way to being solidly established.

Examples of Cell Group Churches: Korea

The Buddhist world of Korea has a centuries-old commitment to Buddhism. Massive statues of the Buddha are found throughout the land. Tens of thousands have journeyed to mountain areas where shrines have been erected. A little over a hundred years ago, the first missionaries arrived to evangelize this country. While the land responded to the Christian message, the growth was slow. Then the cell group church movement came to invade the strongholds of paganism. The growth among the non-

Christian community by cell group churches has been breathtaking!

The largest single local church in the history of Christianity exists in this land. It is the Yoido Full Gospel Church in Seoul, Korea.[13] It has grown from five people who gathered in a tent in 1958, to a congregation of over 800,000 in 1999. After spurts of growth using more traditional church methodology, Dr. Cho instituted cell groups in 1964. In the first five years, without cells, the congregation grew to about 3,800 people. By September, 1980, the congregation had 141,000 members.[14] The church has averaged a growth of 140 members every single day. In a personal interview with Dr. Cho in 1984, he explained he was seeking to curb the growth of the congregation by selecting capable men from his pastoral staff and giving them 5,000 members to launch a new church. The church's Prayer Mountain now registers over two and a half million people each year.[15] The amount of time spent in prayer by this congregation exceeds any other single activity of their weekly schedule.

If this church were the only cell group congregation showing such growth in Seoul, it might be ignored as the fruit of a dynamic pastor's personality, but this is not the case. There are dozens of other churches using the cell group pattern, and all are growing at an amazing rate. Today, the world's two largest Presbyterian churches, along with the largest Methodist church, are cell group congregations in Seoul. All are multiplying at a rate which far outstrips sister Korean churches who do not take advantage of a cell group structure.

Seoul's skyline after dark is filled with neon crosses, mounted on the tops of buildings where a church exists. There are literally hundreds of them! A Presbyterian pastor said to me, "Most of those crosses mark small churches with fewer than fifty members. They never seem to grow beyond that figure." Those who seek to discount the amazing growth of the cell group churches in Korea must understand not all their churches are growing at the same rate. The difference is quite clear: *when all the believers are equipped and involved in ministry, there is a radical difference between them and traditional churches nearby.*

Examples of Cell Group Churches: Japan

Strongly resistant to the Christian message, the Japanese have not accepted the traditional Christian church. The teachings of Shintoism and Buddhism are well woven into the culture. The powerful control of the "web society" in this land strangles the individual Japanese who tries to break out of the life of the community, school, family, and nation. The concept of a building, a pastor, and programs conducted in the name of Jesus has been seen as "Western."

For many years, missionaries working in Japan have concluded the culture will not support large churches. As a result, some church planters did not even expect a church to grow larger than twenty people. As one Japanese student said to me recently, "In my country, a thirty-member congregation is considered a megachurch."

That was before the introduction of the cell group church movement! It is now evident that these older patterns have been out of tune with the Japanese situation, and the new cell group pattern fits it perfectly.

Datin Solhein has said: ". . . home churches, cell groups, and other patterns seemingly must be developed, for these have often been the key to the growth of new religions."[16]

An illustration of what can happen is reported by Pat Hansen, Church Planter in Tokyo. After this American appointee finished his language study, he was seconded to a fellow OMF missionary for a three year apprenticeship. His mentor was a newly appointed Korean pastor with vast experience in developing cell group churches. Pat discovered the lifestyle of his equipper would require significant changes in his own life as a cell group church planter.

First of all, he had to adjust his prayer life. He began to share in a weekly schedule that included hours and hours of prayer, including all-night sessions. Second, he observed how his Korean associate made contacts for the new cell group church. His home was filled night and day with Japanese unbelievers. He contacted them in the neighborhoods, at the shops, in nearby eating houses, and invited them to his home. (Japanese prejudice against Koreans is so strong it took weeks for this pastor to find a place to rent!) Soon, merely curious Japanese became interested seekers for Christ. Bible studies developed in the rooms of the Korean couple. As the first converts were established, the first cell group was formed. It was followed by a second, a third, a fourth, a fifth, and a sixth. In about 35 months, the newly planted cell group church saw over sixty conversions and is now on its way to having hundreds in the fold. Recently, this Korean pastor took Japanese pastors to Korea to see the cell group churches there.

Yonggi Cho sent a Korean woman to plant the first cell group church in Japan just a few years ago. From that humble beginning, the cells have grown and grown. Peter Wagner has viewed Cho's strategy of penetration and is convinced it will succeed.[17] In any culture — every culture — there is both a need and a desire in the hearts of people to live in a community of love and acceptance.

The significance of the cell group as an indigenous church planting method is the use of *hoza* in the rapidly expanding *Rissho Koseikai* religion. Masao Takenaka, Professor of Sociology of Religion at Doshisha University writes:

> *Hoza* is a kind of informal discussion and dialogue circle which takes place daily . . . It provides an opportunity for the believers not only to know each other but to share one another's burdens and personal problems. This indicates that in modern society where people have left the homeland of traditional religion, they need a common ground to share their own problems. It clearly indicates that such a small circle of sharing each other's problems is one of the most important functions of religion in modern society.[18]

Thus, the potential of Christianity spreading into the Japanese culture is greatly enhanced by restructuring the life of the church to be relational, small group, and home centered. Sadly, *Sokka Gakkai* did after World War 2 what the church could have done, harvesting millions.

Examples of Cell Group Churches: Thailand

Into this powerful core of Buddhism came a young professor who had been converted while studying for his Ph.D. in Economics in Melbourne. Chareonwonsak Kriengsak returned to Bangkok with a vision of reaching the entire nation for Christ through cell groups.[19] He formed a movement called the "Hope of God" and established one small cell in his own residence. Soon, the "Hope of Bangkok" church had exploded across the city. Literally hundreds were converted in a few months of time. Kriengsak eventually left his teaching post at the university to shepherd the hundreds of cells. On Sunday, hundreds of cell group leaders stand in line to turn in their reports and offerings before attending one of the multiple worship services held in a leased shopping center. The congregation has recently paid cash for a choice piece of land in Bangkok for the erection of a praise center, astonishing everyone by raising the millions required in just one short week.

Although jealous traditional pastors in the community accuse him of being a cult or growing only by robbing their memberships, his actual statistics demonstrate that over eighty-five per cent of his cell group members are composed of converts. His movement has now passed the 5,000 mark in Bangkok, only a handful of years after it was launched.

The "Hope of God" movement has now opened new work in many other Thai cities. It openly seeks to involve existing Christians in these new works, thus drawing bitter criticism from churches in the area.

Such criticism is heard from traditional pastors in every area where a thriving cell group church exists. In Seoul, the Assemblies of God pastors severed fellowship with Cho, accusing him of doctrinal error. The same thing has happened in the Ivory Coast, in Togo, in Singapore, in Brisbane and London.

This accusation can only be understood by recognizing that churches, numbering 30 or 40 members, which have been in existence for years and which have failed to reach the lost, do not instill vision in members who truly want to serve the Lord and not just support a preacher. "Rescuing" them from stagnant situations has been understandably unpopular with traditional church workers, but it has resulted in rapidly growing cell groups who reach the lost in unprecedented numbers. This conflict is probably going to become more and more severe in the years ahead as the new structures replace the old. The cell church will always be seen as competitive, and its gains will be viewed as a loss to others. This is particularly true when a single church becomes so large that it equals the total memberships of all other churches in a city. (The fact that those other churches are still in existence, in spite of the growth, should make it obvious that only a few of the sheep have moved to the new pasture.)

Examples of Cell Group Churches: Mainland China

The expansion of the church under the persecution of the Communist regime in China has been through the use of cells. Recent reports indicate the movement is still expanding, still underground, still cynical of the government and unwilling to "go public." Yonggi Cho is scheduled to preach in China, the Lord willing. He told me his reports reveal there are between fifty and seventy-five million people meeting in these small groups at the present time. Mainland China is living proof of the way the church must exist under adverse circumstances. From century to century, the cell group church has preserved the Christian community from those who would oppress it. China is the contemporary illustration that it still works.

Dramatic stories have been reported by men who have the trust of these groups and move among them when visiting the mainland. One report is of a cave in the side of a mountain used for the clustering of one hundred and fifty cell group members to hear the teaching of the Scriptures. One cell group community sent one of its members from a small village to a large city a hundred miles away to pick up a cache of Bibles which had been smuggled in from Hong Kong. Upon returning to the village, he was caught by the police with them in his possession. The villagers were ordered to bring their honey buckets full of human urine to a horse trough in the center of the community. The man was then immersed in the fluid until he was nearly drowned. As frantic relatives sought to revive him, the political leaders warned the unknown cell group members that if they attempted such a thing again, the person so caught would be put to death. Such persecution has only served to strengthen the commitment of precious Christians who can only meet in the secrecy of their cell group meetings.

Reports from the cell churches include stories of many miracles which are taking place, including a well documented statement about the raising of a cell group member from death while the members circled his coffin, earnestly praying for his recovery. The small village was so stunned by the miracle that nearly every person made a commitment to follow Christ.

Examples of Cell Group Churches: Macau

Pastor Samuel Lam wears two hats. He is attached to Campus Crusade for Christ, and he also pastors a cell group church of 2,000 members. This Godly man struggles in a mobile society where there is a constant turnover of those arriving from China, departing for permanent residency overseas in a year or two. His pattern is to guide the cells into a full year of evangelism, followed by a full year of equipping the converts. Before they depart, they are able to win enough new people to

Christ to cause the cells to multiply. Traditional churches in Macau struggle to gather 50 to 75 members, and the turnover of pastors and missionaries using the traditional church forms is horrendous.

Examples of Cell Group Churches: Hong Kong

In 1989, I was teaching at the China Graduate School of Theology and I met Ben Wong and Tony Chan. They were taking classes while they were struggling to build cell groups in their church. In 1987, they began Shepherd Community Church with a vision to reach the unreached people of Hong Kong. They had seen success in evangelism, but little success in building a church.

I left them with my book, *The Shepherd's Guidebook*, and went back to Singapore. That year they started with two groups and it has now grown to 110 groups and 1200 people attending their worship services. Much of the success of Shepherd Community is a result of their Sponsor/Sponsee relationships in the Cell groups. They place a high value on mentoring every member into maturity. This value starts with the pastor and is passed down to the newest believer.

Yet the influence of this church stretches far beyond their own cell groups. Ben and Tony devoted the first few years of their ministry to their church. They declined every invitation to speak at other churches or conferences. They wanted to make the cells work. Then in 1994 they had their first cell church conference and had over 600 in attendance.

This propelled them even further as they looked ahead to July 1, 1997, the date Hong Kong would be returned to Chinese authority. They had to prepare for the worst — churches being closed and pastors imprisoned. They knew that most churches would not survive as they were. Therefore they developed the Hong Kong Cell Church Network. This network now consists of 168 churches from 20 different denominational traditions. They have bound together in a loose affiliation to help one another transition into cells. The Network runs a Ministry Training College, and it has facilitated the sending of people into the 10/40 window for missions. Last summer over 200 people joined the trips to help plant churches with unreached people. Recently the Lord provided the Network with a 14-story building complete with classrooms and apartments. Nev Chamberlain from New Zealand coordinates the training and sending of cell groups to go to other nations on short-term cell church planting assignments.[20]

Examples of Cell Group Churches: Ivory Coast

The *Eglise Protestante Baptiste Œuvres et Mission* is now in its twenty-fifth year of life. It is headquartered in Abidjan, Ivory Coast and has expanded into every major city and villages within the nation. The ministry was launched in 1975, but it was not until 1983 that the pastor, Dion Robert, fully developed a cell group pattern for growth. He had been struggling with how to use cells in his church from the very beginning, but only traditional church models surrounded him. When he finally developed the pattern, he grew from 638 to 23,000 in only eight years.[21]

As in all other effective cell group churches, there were several ingredients which caused this church to grow so rapidly. One ingredient was the amazing commitment to the vision by the pastor. Another was his determination to make the cell groups the heart and soul of church life, instead of a "holding tank" for people gathered by other means. A third was instilling a value system that calls for complete surrender to the Lordship of Christ.

Finally, a carefully developed organizational structure was put into place to provide ministries through the cells. This included outreach ministries which could be performed by cell members, putting them in contact with many different groups within the community. (A later chapter is devoted to explaining more about this structure.)

I first visited this work in Easter of 1988 to serve as one of the preachers at the annual "Retreat" held in one of the largest stadiums in Abidjan. The total estimated audience for the five services held over three days was 80,000 people. In preparation for this evangelistic harvesting event, the cells had been divided in half to make room for the expected conversions. Ninety-nine percent of those who attended were cell group members and unbelievers they had been cultivating for weeks or months.

Thousands of conversions were recorded. The harvest was handled by the carefully trained cell group members who did all the counseling and enrolled new believers in their groups.

This is a totally indigenous church which has none of the flavor instilled in African churches by Western missionaries. At the same time, it is uncanny to see the way it has developed a similar lifestyle to other cell groups located on other continents half a world away. This church has now established cell church extensions in several other African nations and even works in Paris with Francophone Africans who have migrated there.

Examples of Cell Group Churches: South Africa

With the demise of *Apartheid* in 1993, the alienated pastors of South Africa were opened for the first time to the cell church movement. The late Ed Roebert had installed a cell system in his huge church in Pretoria. When he received a copy of *Where Do We Go From Here?* from a friend, he held it up as he spoke to the hundreds of pastors in the International Fellowship of Charismatic Churches and said, "This book will change my church and our nation!" I was invited to conduct three-day seminars in seven areas of the nation and was stunned by the response. Thousands attended in each place. One pastor in Blomfontein, Pastor Boshoff, returned to his pulpit and announced that all offices in the church were declared vacant, and every person desiring to share in leadership would have to launch a cell group!

Alarmed that hundreds of pastors were about to transition into cell life with only three days of training, I designed *"The Year of Transition"* materials to prepare pastors for the journey into cell life. This was a one-week course taught in four parts, with a three month gap between each module. I had picked up this pattern for mentoring from an American missionary in India who had planted cell churches in hundreds of villages by training pastors for a week and then sending them back to apply what they had been taught.

Over 900 pastors were trained in this way in the first cycle. The identical material was presented in Johannesburg, Cape Town, and Durban. Suddenly even the Dutch Reformed Church began to experience cell churches exploding in their parishes.

The Apostolic Faith Mission, founded about 1907 by John G. Lake, had about 1.5 million members. Their president, Dr. Isak Berger, arranged for me to provide a four-day orientation for the leadership of the denomination, including the presidents of their seminary and two colleges. They unanimously voted to endorse the cell church model to all their churches. Thus, I repeated the training in 1995 for hundreds of their pastors. This is, as far as I know, the first denomination in the world to officially adopt the cell church model. It has turned around a declining church that was losing about 7% of its constituency every 10 years.

All of the materials I had written for training cell members, called *The Year of Equipping*, was translated and published into Afrikaans during this time. Today, the cell church movement in South Africa is guided by Pastor Harold Weitz, who has successfully transitioned his own church and now has hundreds of cell groups. The AFM denomination now has a pastor responsible for further guiding the transition into cell church life. Annual conferences are held and several men are still moving about the nation providing transition training.[22]

Examples of Cell Group Churches: Russia/Ukraine

When Communism fell in Russia, many Christian ministries seized the opportunity to reap a large harvest. They saw vast numbers of converts, but shamefully, these ministries left with stories of many converts without many churches. Miraculously, God raised up pastors with no training. Once while I was teaching, I met a woman who by default was overseeing a church numbering in the hundreds. To say the least, she was hungry for direction.

A major impact has been made by a Godly man from Ohio who has invested hundreds of thousands of dollars in training pastors all over Russia. He has arranged for all my equipping Daily Growth Guides to be published and distributed in Russia and has graduated hundreds of pastors from *The Year of Transition*. He has even published a special Russian version of the *CellChurch Magazine!*

Another church, which I will leave unnamed, in a city about 120 miles from Moscow, has served as a center for the cell church movement in Russia. The senior pastor learned of cells in 1992 and started doing them without practical guidance. In 1996, he came to visit Bethany World Prayer Center. They now have hosted *The Year of Transition* which was attended by over 1000 pastors from all over Russia.

This church, in a city of over 700,000 people, has 2000 attending and about 170 cells. They have cell groups in each of the five geographic zones of the city and they continue to gain strength as the door closes again to outside Christian influence.

It is unwise to publish the information about the vast networks of hundreds of cell churches inside the CIS. The *Duma* has made illegal all new church starts. However, their new law allows private groups to worship in homes — and thus the cell church movement is about the only way the Gospel can be spread.

Kazakestan is filled with cell churches. Some are the result of church planting done there by Swedes, others by Koreans or Singaporeans. I trained 500 cell leaders for a week in Almaty who are pastored by a Korean. Youth With A Mission has helped to plant cell churches there as well. In nearby satellite nations referred to as "RAN's" (Restricted Access Nations), many overseas missionaries are quietly planting cell churches.

In the Ukraine there is a Bible School training cell church planters. Publication of my equipping materials has been a project of CBN's ministry there. A pastor from Zurich has mentored dozens of Ukranian pastors and has even brought them at his own expense to see his cell church in action.

Examples of Cell Group Churches: Colombia

Much has been said about the now popular International Charismatic Mission in Bogota, Colombia.[23] Pastors Cesar and Claudia Castellanos began this church in 1983 and it quickly grew to 3,000 people. Then in 1986, Pastor Castellanos implemented the Korean model of cells. He copied Cho's model as much as he could but found it wanting. He hit a ceiling at 70 cells.

Then the Lord gave him the *Groups of 12* strategy. (More about the strategy in chapter 14.) After adopting this strategy, ICM no longer counts the size of its church by the number of people. They only count cell groups. From 1991 to 1994 the cells grew from 70 to 1200. Growth really took off at this point. At the end of 1999, they have over 20,000 cell groups and they are expanding their influence all over South America.

I visited ICM in 1997 along with Larry Stockstill. Both our lives were forever changed by the experience! The G-12 pattern is a powerful strategy for raising up leaders and multiplying groups. In consulting with transitioning churches in Toronto and Little Rock, I have seen how the cell church principles are maturing as more churches apply them.[24]

Examples of Cell Group Churches: El Salvador

I visited the Elim cell church in El Salvador in 1993. This is another story about a pastor who started with Yonggi Cho's model and adapted it to the culture of his nation. Using the "5 X 5" management model, this church has two cell meetings weekly: one to nurture Christians, and one for evangelizing. It exploded to become one of the largest cell churches in the world. It is interesting to note that it has survived the default of the founding pastor and has continued to grow under his replacement — which says a lot about the effectiveness of a church that is built around the ministries of cell leaders instead of a single leader!

In Miami a few years ago I conducted a cell seminar and shared the platform with the present pastor of the church. He told me he had visited England and was invited to meet a London pastor who serves one of the larger evangelical churches there. When asked by him, "What is the size of your church?" he replied, "About 118,000." A surprised look in the English pastor's face was accompanied by, "I didn't ask you what the population of your country was, but what the size of your *church* is?" He was invited to come and see for himself, with a guarantee that if this was an exaggeration the Elim church would pay for the plane ticket![25]

Examples of Cell Group Churches: Australia

A decade after the first edition of this book was released, many streams of the cell church movement have developed "Down Under." Many seminars, the constant teaching of the *Year of Transition* materials, and the development of networks of cell churches like *Ruach* in Sydney and elsewhere has firmly planted the cell model in this nation's churches. From Perth to Brisbane, the cell model has been utilized not only by Aussies but by ethnic congregations, including the Chinese. It is a natural "fit" for a culture that honors the relationships formed between "mates."

Examples of Cell Group Churches: South America

One of the most exciting areas for the growth of the cell church movement is the nation of Brazil. In Curitiba, Roberto Lay not only established a strong cell church but also launched *The Year of Transition* for pastors. In April of 1999, I taught 964 registered pastors and Christian workers the first module. This was the second cycle of the training in that nation. The complete *Year of Equipping* materials have been published in Portuguese and are widely distributed into many denominations.

Also significant is the invitation which came to share with the entire missionary family of the International Mission Board (Southern Baptist Convention) in Brazil, Paraguay, and Uruguay the way to plant cell churches. This was endorsed as a major focus for the next century in those nations. There followed an opportunity to meet in Mexico City with key missionary leaders from the IMB from all the nations of Central and South America. We spent a week discussing the importantance of planting cell-based churches in the place of traditional ones.

Ecuador has many burgeoning cell churches. One in Ecuador, mentored by missionary Jerry Smith, has several thousand cells. The Republic Church in Quito, Ecuador has grown from a new church plant to over 250 cells. Joel Comiskey is a part of the Republic Church team and is taking the cell vision all over the world with his excellent books and conferences.

Guatemala has at least four movements of cell based churches. In Guatemala City alone, there are several large cell churches representing slightly different doctrinal views. In smaller towns the cells seem to fit the relational culture of this nation better than the traditional church style. Often the cells are being called *Grupos De Amor* (Groups of Love) in the Spanish culture.

It is impossible to visit any major city in South America and not find at least one large and exploding cell church! It is easy in the cultures where people are relational to plant this model.

Examples of Cell Group Churches: The United States

In 1993, Pastor Larry Stockstill of Bethany World Prayer Center attended the International Conference on the Cell Church in Singapore. While viewing the cell offices at FCBC, he caught the vision and the strategy for cells. After that, this successful church in Baton Rouge, LA began 54 cells comprised of 500 prayer warriors. From there they have now grown to be the premier cell model in the United States with over 600 cells. During this time their celebration attendance has nearly doubled. He is now forming a network of cell churches, produces a monthly tape, and provides consultants who hold seminars on their pattern for developing cells. Attendance at his annual seminar continues to grow. The very spirit of the church is so anointed that those who visit there can never be the same. Attached to the church is a special one or two-year training for cell pastors guided by Tony Foster, who has successfully planted a cell church in Russia.[26]

After we released the second issue of *CellChurch Magazine*, a kind lady from Pennsylvania called our offices and told us that we might be interested in talking with her pastor. She informed us that they had been a cell church from the start and had grown to over 2000 people in rural Pennsylvania. In the late 1970's, Pastor Larry Kreider of DOVE Christian Fellowship had been given a vision by God to start an underground church. He did this without any of the current knowledge of cell groups and found great success. Now they have an entire network of churches that they are helping transition into cell groups. He has a training center and has written many equipping materials.[27]

Other churches like Long Reach Church of God in Columbia, MD have grown to over 100 cell groups since transitioning. Dr. Robert Davis, the Senior Pastor, conducts a special cell seminar for African American pastors annually and is forming a network with them across the nation.[28]

Colonial Hills Baptist Church in Southaven, MS adopted cell groups after they moved into a brand new facility and found it filled to capacity in the first week. They knew that they could not build more buildings so they had to find a better means for reaching the lost. This Southern Baptist church is a fully developed cell church model and is always among the top two or three churches in the state in reporting conversions. Many Baptist churches look to this fine group of Christians for guidance.[29]

Churches across the United States and Canada have moved boldly into the cell church lifestyle. Large and small churches, of all denominations and of all nationalities have embraced the cell church paradigm and are taking cities for Christ. Our office in Houston receives daily calls for help and advice from pastors and church members who are forming cell group churches.

Cell Group Churches and "Third Wave" Theology

The significance of cell group churches has, in the minds of many evangelicals, been downgraded because of the close alignment between cell group churches and what is popularly called the "signs and wonders" movement. This is, indeed, unfortunate. For those whose church life is formed around meeting in church buildings, there seems to be a limited vision of what is needed to bring the unreached to saving faith.

Many who scoff at manifestations of the power of God do not have unchurched friends. The more one leaves the insulation of the church office, the books, and the churched, the more the need for the power of God to do the work of God is recognized.

Physical, emotional, and spiritual healing is constantly experienced by those who live together in the cell group church. Building up one another through the manifestation of spiritual gifts is their lifestyle. Without the real power of God, a ministry to the abused, the abandoned, and the possessed is a farce. Cell group churches are not to be seen as Pentecostal or charismatic, but as *biblical.*

I submit we should confess that the traditional church has little need for the power required when assaulting the gates of hell. However, when cells begin to invade Satan's territories, they discover that evil forces are real! Peter Wagner writes,

> The most typical reaction of non-Pentecostals to spiritism has been one of polemics, and the kind of polemics which indicates that they do not take the validity of spiritism very seriously. . . . Spiritism is not simply ignorance, superstition and chicanery. A Christianity which does not recognize it as a manifestation of the powers of darkness will continue to be impotent in this particular field of evangelism.[30]

Dr. Charles H. Kraft has written *Christianity With Power* to plead with evangelicals to rethink their cognitive views of how ministry is to be done. He explains,

> . . . I am writing as an Evangelical to Evangelicals about a new understanding and experience of Christianity. I have long been part of a branch of Christianity that I feel has believed correctly

and accomplished much for God in nearly all areas except that of spiritual power. So I am not about to give up the good things that have been a part of my own Evangelical Christian experience for nearly half a century. Indeed, these good things are more meaningful to me than ever before. But I have now experienced more of what Jesus expected of us than my Evangelical heritage had provided for me.[31]

Spiritual power is the birthright of believers — all believers, from the most mature to the most recent convert. Jesus' ministry would have been impossible without constant manifestations of power from on high. In the Great Commission, He began by saying, "all power is given unto me," and ended by saying, "I am with you always . . ." Cell churches are constantly touching the evil within their world and constantly needing spiritual power.

Conclusions

1. We must recognize the activity of the Holy Spirit in the cell group movement and seek to use it for the harvest of precious souls. No other form of church life promises to harvest at the same rate the population is growing.
2. We must allow new missionaries, new pastors, and new churches to experiment with the creation of cell group churches. Many traditional denominational structures and mission boards are not open to the experimentation required to develop new concepts. Most pastors have too vested an interest in their careers, their incomes, and their reputations to participate in this new form of church life. They are to be excused with love from being participants — but respectfully asked to refrain from vilifying what the Holy Spirit is doing! They are reminded of Gamaliel's words about the young church in the book of Acts: if it's of the Lord, it can't be stopped, and if it's not, why bother to fight it?
3. We must realize that restructuring a stagnant church around cell church principles is neither easy nor painless. But it is not impossible, though it will require more dependance on God than we have ever known. This very dependance is what will make a church blossom. Cell group churches grow because God flows through them. God is

not interested in making grand church structures or pretty wineskins. He seeks to pour new wine into His people. As the church prepares the new wineskin, the Lord will pour out the new wine.

2

A Better Way!

Many of God's people are sincerely seeking a better way to experience church life. They are recognizing they have not found it in the traditional church structure. I believe we are now in a transitional period in the life of the people of God. It's the beginning of the Second Reformation, and it will go on for a long time to come.

Current Attempts at New Structures

Other more traditional church styles are being tested in this period of unrest. The "Megachurch" has become the contemporary "supermarket" for churchgoers. Other groups are seeking their destiny in the "Praise Churches," which provide overhead projectors to display the newest in worship songs. There are the "Restoration Churches," seeking to provide people with a more personal experience of the Holy Spirit's activity. Blends of the older charismatic churches continue to crop up. It's all a part of the contemporary search for spirituality among the people of God. With each new experiment, the traditional church loses ground.

In all of these attempts, a basic flaw in church life is still evident: *they're all "large group" structures.* In every case, the members still drive to the meeting place from their homes. When these churches use small groups, they use them as "holding tanks" for members. As one pastor ruefully said to me, "There are 22,000 'cruisematics' in this city, bouncing among the churches. Each Sunday, they attend the one with the most exciting guest speaker or singer. I'm using small groups to hang on to my share of them."

Such use of groups by pastors is theologically evil. These groups develop into navel-gazing clusters of impotent Christians who "Bible study" themselves to death, ignoring the cry of unreached persons. In examining these groups, I frequently hear the comment, "We have so many needs among ourselves! There just isn't time to reach out to new people." In the background, I can hear Beelzebub snickering! God must have something better for His church.

None of these models recognizes the basic flaw in a church lifestyle built upon a "Program Base Design," a term we shall refer to as "P.B.D." The term describes a structure of church life that is neither biblical nor efficient. It's used by nearly one hundred percent of all traditional churches today, whether they are Evangelical, Liturgical, Pentecostal, or "Fullness" in their theology.

"Program Base Design" churches rightly acknowledge that the foundation of their church is Jesus Christ. What they build upon that foundation is incomplete. To reveal the weakness of P.B.D. structures, we shall first view the church in its purest form as revealed in the New Testament.

The Early Church

In the Old Testament, the Tabernacle and the Temple were both referred to as "the house of God" (cf. 1 Chronicles 6:48, 25:6, Ezra 5:2, 15). In the New Testament, the concept of "house of God" radically changes. Peter sees believers as "living stones" that are being built up as a "spiritual house" (1 Peter 2:5). Thus, "the house of God" is no longer seen as an edifice made by joining stones, but by joining human lives. Further, the builder of the house is Jesus Himself, who said in Matthew 16:18, "I will build my church." This construction is not to be the work of skilled specialists as was the case in the erection of the Tabernacle. The Lord Himself is to become the builder. The stones He will select for the walls are called *ecclesia*.

The Foundation of the Church Is Christ; The Walls Are Formed from the Living Stones

A significant word appears in Jesus' teaching. The Greek word for "build" used in Matthew 16:18 is *oikodomeo*. It is frequently used as a verb to describe the construction of an edifice (Matthew 23:29, 26:61), or, used as a noun, as the building itself (Matthew 24:1). However, it refers most often to construction using material called "living stones." In 1 Corinthians 3:9 Paul says, ". . . you are . . . God's building." In Acts 20:32, Paul uses the verb form to say that God is the One "who can build you up . . ." Ephesians 2:21 tells us "In him the whole building is joined together and rises to become a holy temple in the Lord." Hebrews 3:6 says, "But Christ is faithful as a son over God's house. And we are his house, if we hold on to our courage and the hope of which we boast."

As we shall see, *oikodomeo* also describes the main work of the living stones themselves: "Therefore encourage one another and build each other up, just as in fact you are doing" (1 Thessalonians 5:11); "From him the whole body, joined and held together by every supporting ligament, grows and builds itself up in love, as each part does its work" (Ephesians 4:12).

It is obvious that Jesus intended to be the builder of the church, but just as obvious that the "living stones" were to be empowered by Him to share in the building up, or edifying, of all nearby stones. Consider the lifestyle of such a church: a tight relationship exists between every "living stone" and each contiguous stone. United by the cement of love, the stones know the life of Christ flowing His grace-gifts into them, empowering them to continually build up one another.

The Church Is a Body, Christ Is the Head

Another picture of the church likens it to the human body. Christ now becomes the head, the *ecclesia* the body parts. The Holy Spirit immerses each new believer into the body, properly connected at conversion as a working, functional member. Paul explains in 1 Corinthians 12:14-19 that the unity of this body is such that one body part never says, "I have no need of you" to another member. As the hand and foot and stomach must interact, even so the members of the body of Christ must live in intimacy. The members are united into a whole. There is freedom from diversity, a oneness of mind or feeling, exactly like that of a human body. Once again, the concept of bodily parts being responsible for building up *(oikodomeo)* one another becomes the focus of their lifestyle (Ephesians 4:15-16).

The Greek word *katartizo* used in Mark 1:19 for mending nets is translated "equipping" in Ephesians 4:12: each body member is to participate in helping other body members be repaired for service. In Galatians 6:1, the "spiritual ones" are again described as mending other body parts that are damaged, restoring them for ministry.

In a study of the early church, one observes that this is theory which was put into practice without a great amount of instruction. Paul describes the mutual building up of believers in 1 Corinthians 14. His order is for every single Christian to use spiritual gifts for the purpose of building up the church. He scoffs at the idea of exercising gifts for personal enjoyment. The word *oikodomeo* appears six times in his teaching (verses 3, 4, 5, 12, 17, 26) as he bears down on the fact that each one (absolutely no exceptions!) is to participate in the ministry of building the body: "When you assemble, each one has a psalm, has a teaching, has a revelation, has a tongue, has an interpretation. Let all things be done for edification (building up)." The word for "each one" used here does not mean, "each one of you who desires to enter into ministry," but "every single person in the group is to be a participant in the building up." Neither physical nor spiritual youthfulness are to be reasons for exempting Christians from participating. All are to exercise spiritual gifts to edify the others.

The early church did exactly that! Recognizing there cannot be total participation by every member when the gatherings are only made up of large, impersonal groups, the people of God moved from house to house in small groups. By moving among their residences, they became intimately acquainted with each person's surroundings.

Excavations in Jerusalem reflect that only the wealthy had homes with second-floor "Upper Rooms." For the rest, residences would usually not accommodate more than ten to twelve persons. Meeting in small cells — without seasoned leaders — these groups built up one another through mutual ministries.

These house churches functioned from their inception as the nucleus of the Christian community. The Lord of the church intended it to be that way; if He had desired it to be otherwise, He could have shaped its lifestyle differently. There were many organizations in His culture that assembled members into halls or specially constructed auditoriums. Guilds had their own edifices. Synagogues had dotted the countryside for generations, gathering members in impersonal large groups. Pagan temples were also common. Nevertheless, Jesus shaped the church to meet in homes. His own disciples were gathered together with Him in a home setting when He served them their last supper together.

The Home Ministry of Jesus

It's significant that in Jesus' ministry he operated out of homes, not formal buildings. He often taught his disciples in houses (Mark 2:1; 7:14-27; 9:33; 10:2-12; Matthew 13:36). We frequently see Him in the homes of others, including Peter, Matthew, a ruler, Simon the leper, Simon and Andrew, Levi, a pharisee, Jairus, Zacchaeus, and Martha. He referred to the owner of a large home in Jerusalem who would consider his upper room Jesus' "guest room" (Mark 14:14).

While "the Son of man had no place to lay His head," at the same time He taught in Mark 10:29-30 that "no one who has left home or brothers or sisters or mother or father or children or fields for me and the gospel will fail to receive a hundred times as much in this present age (homes, brothers, sisters, mothers, children and fields . . .)."

His itinerant servants took this literally. They lived with families in homes wherever they went. In fact, living in a home was a prime strategy for bringing people to personal faith. In Luke 10, Jesus assigned the 70 disciples to go to Perea to enter homes, offering peace to all who lived within. When they found a "man of peace" (one desiring to find peace), they remained in that home, eating and drinking whatever was set before them. In this way, a household would be converted to Christ — and another house church would be formed.

Peter's vision came at the house of Simon in Joppa. It was in the house of Mary the mother of John that Christians gathered to pray. Paul's conversion took place in the house of Judas, as Ananias prayed with him. We see him staying in homes wherever he served, including the house of Jason — who, as host, had to pay his bail when he was jailed. He lived in the house of Lydia after her household had been converted and ate in the jailer's house after his whole family had come to believe in God. There are many more who hosted the Apostle, including Titius Justus, Crispus, Philip, Gaius, Aquila and Priscilla.

There is a very important reason for the early church to be shaped in homes. *It is in this location that values are shared.* It may be possible to transmit information in a neutral building, but few values are implanted there. Value systems are ingrained through living together in a household. Something stirs deep within when life is shared between the young and old, the strong and the weak, the wise and the foolish. In the house groups, all participated and all were impacted by the values of the others as Christ lived within them.

The Impact of House Groups

The lifestyle of the first Christians meeting in house groups was so powerful that daily conversions took place. The total involvement of Christians in house groups overwhelmed outsiders: "But if all prophesy, and an unbeliever or an ungifted man enters, he is convicted by all; he is called to account by all; the secrets of his heart are disclosed; and so he will fall on his face and worship God, declaring that God is certainly among you" (1 Corinthians 14:24-25). This may be termed "Body Life Evangelism." The simple witness of the life of Jesus, observed as it flowed in His body with power and reality, caused the most hardened skeptics to confess Him as their Lord.

In that early church, there were no specialists. Apart from the teaching of the apostles, leadership was not emphasized to any great extent. Details were handled by those who were closest at hand as needs arose.

Our Lord knows there are two factors in spiritual growth. One is receiving His power; the other is becoming the channel of it. Maturity only occurs when both are experienced. The greatest men and women among the house churches were those who served, not those who led.

Every household had a "father," a man respected and obeyed. At the same time, a good father would encourage the development of all within the household. He would not be a tyrant in it. Only at the end of the New Testament era do we find a house church with a petty dictator, and he is soundly rebuked by John (3 John 9-11). The domination of one person over others limits the possibility of growth. This was not permitted in the early church. It is important to realize that cults universally control their members, while the true body of Christ desires to see each member grow into wholeness of life.

The house groups were not independent from one another. They networked together from the first hour of their existence. This city-wide federation shows that the "house churches" combined to form a "local church." Paul twice refers to "the church of God which is in Corinth"

(1 Corinthians 1:2 and 2 Corinthians 1:1), indicating a general relationship existed between all the believers there. Again, he speaks of the "church of the Thessalonians" (1 Thessalonians 1:1 and 2 Thessalonians 1:1). He also refers to "the whole church" in Romans 16:23. In 1 Corinthians 11, the city-wide gathering of the house groups created a scandal of lovelessness. In Acts 20:6-12, Paul's visit to Troas occasioned a gathering of all the house groups to break bread and hear the Apostle teach them.

The Church's Servants

As the movement developed, equippers of the saints for the work of their ministry arose from within the house groups. Ephesians 4:11-12 specifically states that Christ Himself "gave some to be apostles, some to be prophets, some to be evangelists, and some to be pastors and teachers, to prepare God's people for works of service, so that the body of Christ may be built up . . ." Nothing is ever said about Paul or anyone else in the church appointing any of these men. This silence is significant. These men earned their positions by demonstrating the anointing of God on their equipping ministries.

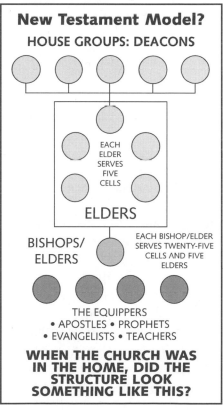

The first task of an "equipper" is to model the lifestyle that is to be transferred to members of the body. Thus, Paul's comments about bishops/elders and deacons dealt with their characters, not their duties.

In all probability, the role of "deacon" was assigned by the home group itself to one in their midst who modeled a servant life. This man (or woman, as in the case of Phoebe in Cenchrea) has no job description in all of Scripture. When one discards the clutter of ecclesiasticism developed

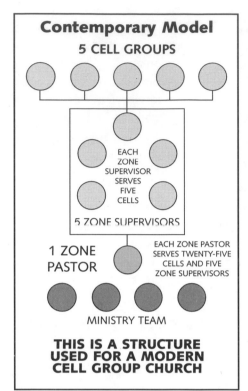

Contemporary Model

5 CELL GROUPS

EACH ZONE SUPERVISOR SERVES FIVE CELLS

5 ZONE SUPERVISORS

1 ZONE PASTOR

EACH ZONE PASTOR SERVES TWENTY-FIVE CELLS AND FIVE ZONE SUPERVISORS

MINISTRY TEAM

THIS IS A STRUCTURE USED FOR A MODERN CELL GROUP CHURCH

through the centuries, the reason for the lack of a job description becomes clear. When house groups met, they shared the Love Feast. "Deacon" means literally, "one who waits on tables." Had not Jesus said, "The greatest among you is the one who serves"? Had He Himself not washed feet at the last supper? Clearly, the godly man or woman in the midst of the house group was awarded this title, and respectfully permitted to serve the Lord's Supper, perhaps the entire meal, to the rest.

As we examine the life of current cell church structures around the world, we can reflect some practical light on the tasks of the offices mentioned in the New Testament. These cell group churches share common church structures needed for their celebrations. Each cell has a servant-leader. For every five cells, there is a pastoral figure (often called a "Zone Supervisor" or "Coach") to counsel and guide the ministries. For every 25 cells and five Zone Supervisors, there must be a person to shepherd this flock of two to three hundred (often called a "Zone Pastor"). Working with the entire city-wide local church, men who are recognized as equippers provide guidance, teaching, and equipping to all the cells, called the "Ministry Team."

While it is a matter of speculation, we may well consider the offices mentioned by Paul in the light of the universal pattern for churches in his day. In each area, the church originated when home groups clustered to form local churches. In the light of this, how would the offices be structured? If they were even close to the way current cell group leadership is arranged, this illustration may explain the function of a church life that had no hierarchy.

The deacon serves the house group. Since an elder (also called "bishop") requires experience in the developing and multiplying of house groups, it would take about two years before he or she would be prepared to assume responsibility for several of them. Thus, Paul would rightly tell Timothy to appoint elders when returning to churches after an absence of a couple of years. Those to be appointed as elders would be easily recognized after such a length of time. Note that in this interim no "Senior Pastor" (to use a modern term) or "elder" existed. Until the house groups proliferated, there was no need for these workers. If such an office existed, Timothy would not have had the freedom to direct the internal affairs of the local church. Church planters in the book of Acts were circumspect about interfering in the churches after they were launched.

There is both biblical and extra-biblical evidence that some apostles, prophets, evangelists, and teachers were itinerant servants who traveled between the local churches. These titles refer to offices within church life. *They founded churches, taught and equipped members, transmitted divine revelations, and expounded Scripture.* They were links between the house churches and their assembled local church structure and also between all the cities where churches existed.

This, then, is the "People Base Design" of the church as it is supposed to be. Contrast it now with the "Program Base Design" ("P.B.D.") of today's church life.

Today's "Program Base Design" Church

Before I present these thoughts, I want to express my love and affection for the precious men and women who serve their Lord so faithfully in P.B.D. structures. Their love for Christ and their sacrificial service is not to be despised or ridiculed. They often labor 70 or 80 hours a week for their Lord and are sometimes scandalously underpaid. I am not criticizing anyone who serves the Lord with all they have. They are sincerely seeking to do the work of the Lord.

I also want to express my thanks for what God has done through P.B.D. structures. Many have been saved through this structure that we call "the church." Many have experienced God and have heard His call in this structure. Many have seen the power of God change them and change others. I am grateful for what the Lord has done through these P.B.D. churches. But at that same time, the church can be much more, so much more. We do not have to settle for what we have known.

In a sentence, the P.B.D. concept doesn't build people on the foundation of Christ; it is designed to build programs. The assumption is that the programs are necessary to build the people, but it just doesn't achieve this goal! In other words, the P.B.D. structure is designed to develop programs and keep them running. It is not designed to develop people through relationships. No matter how hard someone tries to develop people, the P.B.D. system will in the end work against it because the goals of the programs get in the way.

The first thing a P.B.D. church looks for are Specialists to direct the different programs of the church. Even the smallest group will seek for a Pastor-Specialist who can come and preach, teach, counsel, raise the budget, administer its spending, win the lost, and effectively manage the church schedule. He is not particularly seen as an "equipper of the saints for the work of ministry;" instead, he is The Minister. He does the things that professional clergymen do. He preaches, marries, buries, visits the sick in the hospitals, pays courtesy calls to the elderly, consults with the deacons or elders, and — if the church can afford it — supervises the staff. He is the primary victim of P.B.D. church life. He will move his family to new "church fields" on a regular basis, always seeking a more responsive group of church members to fulfill his desire to reach the lost.

Yet, while he desires to reach the lost, he doesn't have time to know many of them. Less than five out of a hundred P.B.D. pastors (or missionaries overseas) have as many as three gold plated, certified, hell-raising unbelievers numbered among their close friends. There isn't enough time in their busy week to know the unconverted. The entire congregation can thus assume that cultivating unreached persons is not a high priority for the Christian life, since their leader never produces a convert apart from his pulpit ministry. Within such a model, the core leadership fill their lives with church tasks sacrificing evangelism.

The larger P.B.D. church will seek for other Specialists to work on the church staff. Typically, it is felt these people must come from outside the congregation. Thus, endless webs of "search committees" and "pulpit committees" scout out the best Specialists they can afford to hire. They arrive from Chicago or Memphis, Atlanta or Phoenix, move into their offices and begin to develop their specialty.

For example, the Minister of Education will scour the church roll for those who can teach or serve administratively in a Sunday School department. He will faithfully fill vacancies with the best workers he can find and form classes to train new workers for the future growth he anticipates. These times of equipping focus on the needs of the program, not the needs of the unconverted community or the personal ministry of the trainee apart from the Sunday School. The structure demands the maintenance of the program.

The Minister of Music will find those who can sing, play instruments, or lead a children's choir. He, too, will offer only the training required to develop his specialty within the life of the church. This is what the structure demands of him.

Other P.B.D. Specialists may include the Minister of Children, the Minister of Youth, the Minister of Singles, the Minister of Young Adults, the Minister of Median Adults, the Minister of Older Adults, the Business Manager, etc., etc. *In each case, they have a vertical vision of church life.*

Smaller churches fill these same Specialist positions with volunteers. These are the precious saints who have many stars in their crowns! Unlike full-time church staffers, they must juggle employment with their church work in a limited time frame. Sometimes their families suffer terribly because of the demands made on them by the church. Surveys of heavily involved volunteer church workers in P.B.D. structures show they burn out after two or three years. Furthermore, it's shocking to find a large number of them among the ranks of those who no longer regularly attend church.

With few exceptions, the Specialists involve no more than 15% of the total members as working volunteers. The balance of the members are expected to attend the many functions which have been arranged for them. In large churches, this may involve as many as one hundred meetings a month!

That brings up the next P.B.D. problem: inactives typically number from 40% to 50% of the church membership. In spite of the many meetings scheduled, simply being a passive participant loses its flavor after a time. Half of the inactives attend about once a month, and the other half don't come at all.

The mismatch of Christians with church tasks they perform is heart breaking. When the Program needs a warm body, people are enlisted regardless of their gifts (which are frequently ignored) or their abilities (which are frequently underutilized). Thousands more are not used at all — they are not deemed suitable for the vacancies to be filled. Few

opportunities exist for the discovery of spiritual gifts. The work of the P.B.D. church doesn't need them very often or for very long at a time. The God-given calling of every believer to be involved in building up others in the body of Christ is seldom developed even though many highly value this claim. This is true of the charismatic or Pentecostal groups as well as the Evangelicals. They have yet to develop a structure or system that will facilitate this calling.

Consider the inefficiency of the P.B.D. church: buildings stand empty except for a handful of hours a week; the Specialists service the members only to expand their specialty; only one-eighth of the members are involved in P.B.D. tasks; a massive group of hopeless inactives exists; and, last but not least, the entire church has little contact with the unreached community! Can we do any better than this?

How can this be reconciled with the intention of Christ to "seek and to save that which was lost?" Jesus said in John 12:26, "Whoever serves me must follow me; and where I am, my servant also will be." Apart from a few contacts with the synagogues and the Temple, Jesus' life was spent among sinners. The One who reminded us that the sick have need of a physician simply cannot be pleased with the P.B.D. church that seldom ventures out of its church building to know or minister among the winebibbers and sinners. The reason this condition exists is that there are no Specialists in the church who are specifically hired to develop a "program" to minister to those who are poor, blind, imprisoned, and downcast — the specific tasks Jesus listed as His own job description. If the body of Christ is to be doing the tasks of Christ, the P.B.D. structure can be seen as not only inefficient, but downright defective!

Indeed, the "stranger evangelism" practiced by the P.B.D. church does more harm than good. The Monday night forays by the church into the community to invite people to return with them to attend church and accept Christ are devoid of even the desire to develop true friendships with those strangers visited. The 15 minutes spent with those visited is often little more than an encouragement to attend the next public service.

The term used for the event is "Prospect Visitation." The term clearly reveals the value system of the P.B.D. church: people are viewed through the windows of the programs: "they are a prospect for our Sunday school class; he is a good prospect for our church — I happen to know he tithes." What is more demeaning or dehumanizing than turning a person into a prospect? When the living stones are turned into programs, the vocabulary also becomes demeaning.

Worst of all, life in the P.B.D. church does not provide the all-important *koinonia*, or "fellowship," needed to create true community, lifestyles where people build up one another. I recall a visit Ruth and I made to a small church in southern Indiana. I insisted on our being put into the Sunday School class for our age group. There were about 15 of us in the class. The man who was serving as moderator said, "Folks, I ran into Bill Foster in the hardware store yesterday. He explained to me that he and Helen were divorcing, and he has moved out of their house. They talked it over and decided that neither one of them would feel comfortable coming back to our class under the circumstances. Each one is going to go elsewhere, and he asked me to tell you this so they wouldn't be embarrassed if either one bumped into you." After a few moments of stunned silence, one of the class said, "Why, I attended our class party in their home a month ago. I didn't know they were having problems. Did any of you know their marriage was in danger?" Everyone shook their heads "No." I asked, "How long were you folks together in this class with them?" The group had been together three to four years — never becoming close enough to sense such a deep problem! The couple floated off into oblivion, sincerely wanting to be left alone as they went through their traumas.

The P.B.D. structure provides little time and space for people to become close to one another. The programs insulate members from each other. When they meet, it's in the neutral setting of the church building. Each encounter is carefully programmed: there's choir music to be rehearsed, a Bible lesson to be studied, a budget to be prepared. Bonding together in love and commitment is not a central part of the agenda. Some create community and genuinely experience love and acceptance. But most church structures view community as an extra.

While all the preceding issues may be ignored by some, this issue of not living in true community is utterly unbiblical, totally indefensible, and tragically inexcusable! The P.B.D. removal of true community deeply grieves the Holy Spirit.

The "Parish Mentality"

Another problem with P.B.D. churches is their "parish mentality." A Baptist, Methodist, or other brand of church planter will enter a portion of a city and mark off a "church field." He recognizes the existence of "sister churches" (same brand) in neighboring districts, and considers their "church fields" out of bounds. Each "local church" sifts through its limited territory seeking for "like-us people" until most are finally drawn into the membership. Stagnation finally sets in. Recognition of the other brands (denominations) of churches also in the area is limited; such pastors barely know each other. They only cooperate when Billy Graham comes to town to hold a crusade. None of these churches pay much attention to the unchurched of the area at any time, even though it's obvious by counting noses on any given Sunday morning that 60-75% of the people in their parish areas are not attending anywhere.

The planting of new P.B.D. churches has become a serious problem. As long as churches are built upon a P.B.D., they will be forced to erect P.B.D. structures for them. You can't have one without the other! It now costs in excess of one million dollars to build a new church facility in many urban areas. As a result, many new subdivisions are devoid of churches.

This conviction isn't true of all cell group churches. Many of them have grown so large they cannot gather the local church together for celebrations in the small facilities available to them. Frequently, it becomes cheaper to build and own than to endlessly rent.

Dion Robert slept beside the desk of his office for years because the church had no space for his family to live. He preached seven times every

Wednesday, Friday, and Sunday in a tiny, crowded room that might be used by 75 or 80 Westerners. He packed 300 Ivorians into it! With 1,950 cell groups in Abidjan, he obviously needed an auditorium to assemble his people for celebrations. In that city about 80% are unemployed, making the costliness of construction a terrible burden. Many of us helped him with his financial need, and the cell group church now has a spartan "Temple" which might seat about 2000 Westerners, but seats 6000 people "African style." The cell groups built it with their own hands. As they received the money, they bought a few more bags of cement and reinforcing bars. It went up slowly, over a period of more than seven years, and is now complete. Dion Robert will soon need to preach seven times a Sunday in the new "Temple," for his congregation is multiplying the cells four times each year.

He will soon face the problem Yonggi Cho struggles with in Seoul: a need for even more space to use when the flock needs to be taught the word of God. The 10,000 seat auditorium was enlarged to 25,000, but it was still inadequate for the members to squeeze in to seven Sunday services. Cho has solved his current problem by adding a second 25,000 seat auditorium on the opposite shore of the Han River. Including the auxiliary auditoriums built into a high rise building next to the original sanctuary, he will now preach to over 70,000 people in each service. That's what can happen when churches have no "parish limits!"

In the cell group church, the growth of the congregation comes through the ministry of the cells, not just the "celestial funnel" of scintillating music and unique preaching. Cell group members travel to locations provided to be taught the word of God.

The "Lordship Evangelism" Controversy

A great controversy has raged among P.B.D. evangelicals over "Lordship Evangelism" during the later part of the twentieth century. The premise is that we are not telling people what salvation really involves. There should be more stress on the fact that one is not a Christian until he or she confesses Christ to be Lord over all dimensions of one's life. We are told we should insist on total commitment by every person claiming to be a believer. The controversy is a reaction to the cheap "easy believism" to be found in American churches. The suggestion is that people should be told up front that they can't be lukewarm Christians!

The debate is purportedly about authentic conversion and evangelistic preaching. It totally ignores the real problem which causes this "sit and soak" variety of church members. Such wimpy believers are the direct result of a church life that builds programs, not people, on the foundation of Christ. P.B.D. structures were designed to feed mediocre members. When a preacher presides over a P.B.D. church and allows 15% of the congregation to "fill positions" in programs, he must admit that Lordship for them is simply oiling the machinery. While he comes out of his study after 40 hours of preparation to deliver his sermon, he must realize he has failed to model the life of an involved Christian who sits down by wells to talk to women who have been married five times and now live in adultery. If he is not going to pay any attention to the equipping of the saints, what can he expect to have in the congregation? When 85% of the congregation who are not enlisted to work in the programs are herded from one meeting to another, and one sermon to another, the pastor should not be surprised when there are large numbers of mediocre Christians. Until he is willing to change what he is doing how can he expect to get different results!

Dion Robert has no problem with "No Lord" church members. He actually prepares his messages from the feedback from the weekly cell servant reports. They indicate the spiritual and personal problems of people in the cells. He preaches on these subjects.

The cells meet to internalize the truths he presents. His preached word is briefly reviewed in their next meetings. If his sermon dealt with stealing, bitterness, or even adultery, the presider of the cell begins by asking each member in turn, "What is the state of your soul concerning this issue?" Each person frankly shares his or her condition. This is followed by the cell members building up one another, supporting one another, and helping one another through moments of weakness and sin. Week after week, this takes place in all the cells. "Lordship salvation" for a cell group church is not a theology to be debated by pastors and professors; *for the living stones, it's a lifestyle.*

In a cell group Ruth and I attended for months, we had a precious wife call the group to gather for a special session. As we sat around a kitchen table, she said, "I have called you together to confess my sins. I have sinned against my Lord, but that means I have also sinned against you who make up His body along with me." I shall never forget the power of Christ's presence in our midst that night! When we got into the car, I said to Ruth, "That's the closest we're ever going to get to the New Testament church. If we travelled in a time machine and went back 2000 years to go to church, it wouldn't have been much different from what we have just experienced!"

Straight ahead lies yesterday! The first century church has returned to us in a simple, straightforward format. It's composed of deeply committed people who form cell groups. For them, as for the early Christians, this is their "church," their "Basic Christian Community." They not only worship — they also minister to those who are poor, blind, imprisoned, and stepped on. They grow so fast that in the United States they can average multiplying into two groups twice a year. They are God's solution to the decaying P.B.D. church problem. *They are where we go from here.*

I return to the disturbing point that has been made before in this book and will be repeated again and again. The cell group church lifestyle is too New Testament to be blended into a P.B.D. structure. It causes endless conflicts for those who attempt it.

The P.B.D. church competes within its own membership for people to fill the program positions. It's not unusual to find a truly dedicated worker who teaches a Sunday school class, serves on the official board, sings in the choir, and works on the finance committee as well. This person is assuredly a "pillar of the church." How do you think he or she will react when the suggestion is made that the church is now going to add on cell group life? Does this person have time to attend even one more "something" each week? Can the P.B.D. exist if all such people abandon their obligations to become relational, ministering, caring persons? Of course not.

Therefore, the pastor who attempts to insert cell group life into the P.B.D. system can rightly expect the leaders of his church will not participate at all, or only passively. The leaders in the current structure will try to do cell groups according to the old P.B.D. rules, and it won't work.

If the cells get off the ground, it will be done by involving those who now "sit and soak." It's mighty hard to get clinkers to burn after the fire has gone out. They have fallen into the habit of doing nothing for so long that a major value change is required. I have prepared *Life-Basic Training* as a small group module for such people, and it is quite effective — but should not be followed in a P.B.D. setting by forming a "second church," a cell group church.

We are not without experience in such matters. If the church forms a "right wing" and a "left wing," the result is not a Bird of Paradise! Pastors who have attempted to mix P.B.D. and cell groups have found themselves among the lists of the unemployed. The old leadership, still in power and tolerating this foreign object called "The Pastor" for a season, can be brutal when the "mere nothings" of the cell group movement begin to take hold.

Nor will the Specialists endorse a pattern of church life which threatens their careers and their programs. One pastor had a longing for many years to lead his church, mainly servicing those over 50 years of age, to transition into cells. Many of his staff members had served the church longer than he had and were almost unmanageable. When I was brought in to consult with the staff about the value of cell groups, the Minister of Education took me to his office. He bluntly said, "As long as I am in this position, I will fight the pastor, you, and this idea to the end. I have too much to do already, and this would fall on my shoulders to implement. I don't care what the pastor wants. I am solidly opposed to any new responsibilities around here."

The fact that the church, with over 900 members, had only seen converts among the children of church members for four years meant nothing to him. The knowledge that a barbecue shop across the wide street from the church was a haven for crack cocaine selling didn't bother him at all. The awareness that the church was fast becoming a haven for the elderly was of no consequence to him. What did bother him was his own personal schedule and his unwillingness to win the world Christ died on the cross to redeem. He was the ultimate example of a Specialist gone to seed!

My friends in the "Fullness" and "Deeper Life" movements must, sooner or later, realize that they cannot bring the Lordship of Christ to folks who are nurtured in a Lordship of Programs structure. In this transitional period, some are convinced that we must simply create a hunger for God in individuals. *To wrench them away from the importance of living in community in cells where they will discover their spiritual gifts is a great blunder.* As my close friend Jack Taylor has stated, "There is no better place under heaven for spiritual gifts to be properly developed than in a cell group. It is there, and nowhere else, that Christians can be taught to appreciate, desire, and exercise spiritual gifts. The cell group is the channel of power. It is the gateway to enter into the supernatural, the entrance to every believer discovering the power of God to heal, to deliver, and to provide growth." No matter how wonderful a theological position may seem, the heart of changing values is not theology but the practical application of it in experience. The valid church is only peripherally experienced in a P.B.D. setting. It requires the people of God to gather themselves as God intended before the setting for the experience will allow His fullness to flow.

Back in the 1970's, a pastor visiting our cell group experiment in Houston said to me, "One thing that bothers me is what is going to happen to the members of your church when they get a taste of this lifestyle and then move to another city. Will they be content to go back into traditional churches?" I answered, "I hope not!"

The power of culture is a strong magnet which draws people back into the kingdoms of this world. The P.B.D. church is more a worldly kingdom than a part of the Kingdom of God, providing personal significance and power, social life, and contacts to its members. It doesn't do a lot to equip them for warfare in heavenly places. So, for those who don't want to accept the Lordship of Christ, the church as we have known it is a safe haven.

For those who step into cell group church life, that's not an option. Every time the cell meets each person is to be a minister or a receiver of ministry. There's really no place to hide! As an Australian friend of mine in Sydney said to me, "When I came into this lifestyle, there was nothing more important to me than being flat out for God!"

A Study In Contrasts:
The New Testament and the Traditional Church

	THE NEW TESTAMENT CHURCH	THE TRADITIONAL CHURCH
LOCATION	Moved From House To House	Meets In Church Buildings
SIZE OF GROUPS	Small, Intimate Groups	Large, Impersonal Groups
ACTIVITIES	Daily Fellowship	Weekly Worship Services
SUPPORT SYSTEM	Building Up One Another	Problem? See The Pastor
RELATIONSHIPS	Intimate; Helping One Another	Remote; Little Transparency
DISCIPLING	"Mouth To Ear;" Modeling; Personal Values Shaped	Classes, Notebooks; Little Modeling; Values Not Shaped
PRIMARY TASKS OF LEADERS	Every Believer Equipped To Do The Work Of The Ministry	Directing The "Program Base Design"
PRAYER LIFE	Hours Daily; Heavy Emphasis	Individual Choice; Limited
PASTOR'S DUTY	Model The Life Of A Believer	Preach Good Sermons
EXPECTATIONS OF MEMBERS	Ministering To Others; Total Servanthood & Stewardship	Attendance; Tithing; Work In The "Programs"
PERSPECTIVE	Cell Groups The Focal Point	Congregation The Focal Point
KEY WORDS	"Go And Make Disciples"	"Come Grow With Us"
TEACHINGS	Apply The Scriptures To Needs And Relationships	Subscribe To The Distinctive Beliefs Of This Church
SPIRITUAL GIFTS	Regularly Exercised By All Believers To Build Up Others In The Cell Group Gatherings	Either Downplayed Or Often Used As A "Crowd-Pleaser" In Public Services
COMMITMENT	To Increase The Kingdom; Unity, Body Life	To Enlarge The Institution; Uniformity
EVALUATION TEST	"How You Serve"	"What You Know"
SOURCE FOR SECURING STAFF	Servant Workers Developed Within; Tested Before They Are Set Apart For Ministry	Trained, Professional Clergy

3

A Better Cell Group

Theology breeds methodology! When methods are used without a proper theology, they become uncontrolled headaches. There must be a biblically based foundation behind cell groups. For those launching a cell group church, this is vitally important.

In the P.B.D. church, all sorts of cells have been tried. Prayer cells, Bible study cells, navel-gazing cells, closed cells (so we can "go deeper"), therapy cells — all kinds of cells have been started without little thought to the theology behind them. Most of them have been ineffective, and some now think the "fad" of the cell group is passing away. Not so! We are simply seeing the self-destruction of small groups which have been built upon the sand instead of the Rock.

Robert Banks of Fuller Seminary described some cells which are conceived and birthed with serious problems:

The Cell of Self-Centeredness

"What's in this group for ME?"

The first of these is a cell which is not "owned" by anyone, let alone by the entire group. It is attended with a spirit of self-centeredness by its constituents: "I come to this group to be enriched by it. I don't have any commitment to it, or to the other people in it. Furthermore, when the group no longer meets my needs, I'll leave it. My only reason for attending it is for what

I get out of it." The purpose of such a group might be for Bible study, for losing weight, or to get through a personal crisis. While it might continue for some time, the average attender will drop out after a few weeks or months. This cell lacks a basic spirit of servanthood, so necessary for true Christian community to exist.

The Cell for Personal Enrichment

In this group, there is a sincere desire by the members to create a climate where personal growth can take place. They want to "peel off layers" to become totally transparent persons with each other, believing that in this openness they will come to new levels of spirituality and self-awareness. They mistakenly feel the only way to accomplish this is to create a closed group. Thus, they become alienated from all but themselves. In so doing, they limit the resources God might use to create new life in them.

"Us four NO MORE!"

Such a group eventually ossifies. Whether it meets for "deep Bible study," for personal sharing, as a prayer group, or for some other reason, the seeds of demise are planted by the very way it has been structured.

This type of group also can be created unknowingly by a church that limits the membership of a cell to the formal membership of the church. Such a decision gives total license to the congregation to ignore the unbelievers around them, becoming closed to all but themselves. It has been tried over and over — and it has never, ever worked!

I recall a church that did this very thing a few years ago, changing their Wednesday prayer meeting in the sanctuary into groups meeting in homes. It was popular for a little while, but then boredom and ossification set in. The leadership eventually had to disband the groups entirely. Such a congregation will resist using any type of small group for a long, long time!

Theologically, this cell violates the basic New Testament teaching that maturity does not develop in a vacuum. To really have a growth group, the Christian community must be in touch with its environment, penetrating it like salt and yeast within dough. Quite often the insertion of just one new person into a group brings fresh insights to those already in it. Jesus warned us against becoming like the Pharisees, who kept to themselves and even refused to allow their garments to be touched by outsiders. Living things don't live very long in a vacuum. Thus, those who have experimented with this type of cell have had little success.

The Cell for Strengthening the "Witnesses"

Of all the models we have considered thus far, this one is most to be respected. It is composed of a group of Christians who sincerely desire to witness as a normal lifestyle. They see the office or the shop as a mission field. They are constantly sharing their faith with those who work around them. They face rejection and scorn, and often don't know what to do next in their ministry to unbelievers. These dear folks form a group to gain new strength for their battles. When they meet together, they bind wounds, praying for each other and for those they are seeking to bring to Christ.

Alas! Their theology has bred their methodology. They have not been helped to see that such a witnessing lifestyle does not work best. Does a hand, a foot, or an arm function apart from the other parts of the body? Can one person have all the spiritual gifts necessary to reach the lost?

Ours is a generation of "Lone Ranger Christians." It was not so in Jesus' generation. He never sent his disciples out one by one, but two by two. (We shall discover later why this is so important.)

Of a certainty, the members of this group are sharing their faith in a most valid manner. In the same way every root penetrates the soil around it, we must touch the people around us who need salvation. That's not the problem. The theological flaw is that these Christians meet together alone, and then go to witness alone. *How wonderful it would be if they included each other in the relationships they establish with unbelievers, and included unbelievers in their group life as well.* This group is close to reality, but still limited in its goal of winning the lost by not taking full advantage of the witness of God's people building up one another in a cell.

The "Football Team" Cell

This type of group has existed for years, often not even recognized as being a cell. It includes some of God's finest children! These may be teams of men who meet every Sunday afternoon and go to the jails to hold services for the inmates. Or, it may be a group of women who visit a home for the aged and brighten the lives of those who are shut-ins. Teens may "blitz" a football game, passing out tracts and witnessing to those in the stands. College students may descend on the beaches of a city during their Easter break, seeking to share their faith with beer-guzzling crowds who have come to find fun, not Christ. There are many times when the family of God may see the need to go as a team to share their faith.

US

THEM

While there are valid reasons to do this, the deficiency of this cell group's life is that there is no way to share the reality of "body life" with those being contacted. The evangelism used presents a message, but it does not offer a community of love.

And . . . saddest of all, we begin with the suggestion that the best we have to offer "them" will not be realized until we are dead. True . . . the "blessed hope" of the Christian is that we are absent from the body, present with the Lord. But, what about the interim? Why do we not offer them the joy of entering Christ's community now? More important, why do we remain apart from them except for our forays into their territories on specially promoted occasions?

Thus, the body of Christ exhibits itself once again as being separated from the world around it. Like a football team that goes to the huddle to work out a strategy, and then faces the other team on the scrimmage line, we come to "scrimmage" on special occasions with the crowds of unbelievers.

In Hong Kong, I participated in an evangelistic witness in front of an ancient Buddhist temple. The park was filled with men, mostly retired or drifting through life. A group from Australia joined us for the evening. They had come from their church to help win the Chinese. *The first thing the leadership did was to create a space for the Christians, separating them from the unbelievers.* This was done by stretching a yellow ribbon around chairs set far apart. The "Us-Them" philosophy was painfully evident.

To be sure, the crowd was so heavy that without some barrier there would have been no room for the street service to take place. I'm not criticizing the yellow ribbon as much as what happened next.

The Christians from "Down Under" had a great relationship with each other. They sang, clapped, prayed, and entered in with gusto — but they never blended with the men. Their inability to speak Cantonese must be taken into account, but the main problem was that they were so connected to each other there wasn't a deep interest in being connected to the crowd. Most stayed inside the yellow ribbon.

Sam, the man who led the service, was a part of those men. He had formerly slept on the streets, a heavy heroin user. Yellow ribbons meant nothing to him. He reached out with his heart, his voice, and God's power as he shared. When he began to speak words of knowledge that exactly pinpointed sin in the lives of some of the men, we literally saw a few run away in fear of God's power.

I'm not trying to be critical of the Australians; bless their hearts, they were doing all they knew to do! That's the problem with most of us: we don't know any other way to serve the Lord apart from what we have observed.

One church solved a part of this "Us-Them" problem by planting a ministry in the midst of a low income Spanish community, creating bedrooms as a "half-way house" for men coming out of prison. These team members didn't just go out. They also brought in — and the communities of the poor and imprisoned had opportunity to share daily in the lifestyle of the family of God as they were joined to their cells.

Costly? Yes! It's a Sunday afternoon picnic to go to the jail service and then return alone to the church building for the evening service. It's costly to say, "Convict, come and live among us."

Have you heard of Jean Vanier? A graduate of the Royal Naval College with a Ph.D. in philosophy, he seemed to be a candidate for a university professor's position. In 1964, he founded l'Arche at Trosly-Breuil in the suburban area of Paris. They are now spread over the world.

The Arche communities gather up people who are mentally handicapped. With fellow Christians — all of them highly educated — the deliberate choice of these Christians is to live in small groups with society's castoffs. In *Community and Growth*, Vanier writes,

> Certainly we want to help them grow and reach the greatest independence possible. But before 'doing for them,' we want to 'be with them.' The particular suffering of the person who is mentally handicapped, as of all marginal people, is a feeling of being excluded, worthless and unloved. It is through everyday life in community and the love which must be incarnate in this, that handicapped people can begin to discover that they have a value, that they are loved and so loveable.[1]

Something within us shrinks from the cross, from the faith that demands all, from the call to total commitment. In the cell group church, such issues must be settled by each incoming person. *We must not use the body of Christ selfishly simply to get our needs met, nor can we abuse its witness by offering a limited ministry in Christ's name.* The radical theology of the New Testament would say to those in the "Football Team" cells, "How can you serve the prisoner, the aged, the teen in the football stands, the beer-guzzling students at the beach, and do so in a way which will cause you to live with them, and for them to live with you?"

Obviously, God does not call all Christians to open a community for retarded persons. But He does call us all to open our groups and to be constantly involved with those who don't understand that we have more than a cognitive message to transmit; *we also have a lifestyle for them to receive!*

Here's a strong word, spoken with great conviction: the only type of small group which should limit its membership is a clinical one designed for therapy, supervised by professionals.

The "Bible Worm" Groups

Over the years of talking with Christian workers about cell groups, my concern about this type meets with the most resistance. I would first like to state for the reader that I am strongly committed to the "inerrantist" position, and have literally worn out at least a dozen Bibles in my lifetime. Don't consider what follows to be a downgrading of that precious book which God breathed into existence through men who wrote as the Spirit gave them utterance!

Let's attend a typical Bible study group. It will probably be one of two types: a true Bible study cell, or a pseudo Bible study cell.

In the first type, the group sits in a circle. The leader (there must be a leader!) follows an outline. Perhaps the church has purchased some of the slickly printed small group material that is so popular just now. Or, perhaps the outline has been typed or mimeographed by one of the church staff. A section of Scripture or a topic is to be covered. A commentary may be used to throw light on the passages. The group then discusses the material, being cautioned by the leader not to "chase rabbits."

There are two problems with what is taking place. Too often, the group will "pool its mutual ignorance" about the passage. The leader may say, "Jim, read the next two verses." (Jim reads them.) "Who has an insight to share about these verses?" Since no one in the group has the gifts of teaching or putting deepest knowledge into words, speculative comments are often made. The evening is ended with prayer. Little light has been shed on the Scripture by this method. Even worse, true community has not developed. All the participants have been insulated from each other by the Bible study itself. They go away strangers to one another.

I attended a group like this in Australia. The hostess sat to my left, obviously ill at ease. She requested the group to speak softly so her children would not be awakened. Her participation in the group was minimal. No one else seemed to sense she had a personal problem. Through the evening, I tried to draw her into the discussion, without much success. The time for prayer finally came, and I said, "I sense that you have a special need tonight. Can you share it with us?" Her eyes brimmed with tears: "I wrenched my back today. I have been sitting in this chair gritting my teeth because I am in pain. I just want to get this over with, so I can go to bed!" The formal Bible study format had so limited our true relationships with one another that we were oblivious to her plight. In a cell group, the most important ingredient should be the people in the circle . . . not study materials. Thus, one drawback of this first type of Bible study group is the way it insulates the members from each other.

The second problem occurs when there is a person in the group who is gifted to teach. The dynamics will now be those of a large group rather than a small group. Therefore, it is usually profitable to revise this cell to make it a large gathering, and let the teacher's gift be used with more people.

The most effective "Bible study" groups I have observed are the pseudo-Bible study cells. These don't really focus on the Bible; they use their group as an excuse to get together and share deeply. Usually these groups will begin with the reading of Scripture, but the evening is spent in sharing. Those who attend such groups find them most meaningful and will speak with great conviction about the worth of their "Bible study" group — not knowing it is actually a fellowship group. There is, however, a missing ingredient to both of these types.

Why Did God Give Us the Bible To Study?

The answer is found in Scriptures like these:

> All Scripture is inspired by God and profitable for teaching, for reproof, for correction, for training in righteousness; that the man of God may be adequate, equipped for every good work.
> • 2 Timothy 3:16-17

The goal of all Bible study is to equip the Christian to serve! This verse tells us we are to be "made adequate," a Greek word (*artios*) which describes becoming suitable, adapted for activity. This same word also appears within *katartismon*, "building up," used in Ephesians 4:12, to describe the Body of Christ as becoming effective ministers.

In James 1:22-25, we are solemnly warned against coming to the Bible without a readiness to become "an effectual doer" of what we discover in its pages. Thus, Bible study groups which study the Bible for the sake of studying the Bible should be declared unbiblical. Unfortunately, few Bible study groups (or Sunday School classes) ever project themselves beyond their study into active servant ministries. This is why I have called these "Bible Worm" Groups.

> Husbands, love your wives, just as Christ also loved the church and gave Himself up for her; that He might sanctify her, having cleansed her by the washing of water with the word, that He might present to Himself the church in all her glory, having no spot or wrinkle or any such thing; but that she should be holy and blameless. • Ephesians 5:25-27

This lovely passage describes our Lord Jesus Christ in the act of bathing His beloved. Through His death on the cross, He has created His Bride. These are to become one, His "body." He will dwell within her, performing His redemptive ministry through her activity. Christ takes the cleansing "soap" of the Scripture, adds His flowing, living waters, and cleanses her of all spots and wrinkles. The Bride of Christ is made glorious, holy, blameless!

The cleansing Scripture is applied by Christ to the church. His motive is not to have a clean body to display, but to use. He is not willing for a single child of Adam to perish. His activity is to touch the poor, the captives, the blind, the downtrodden. It will be through His body this mission will be accomplished.

When we gather around the Scripture, it should always be done expecting Christ to use it to cleanse and equip us for His work. Therefore, Bible study should focus far more on the confirmation of the Bride's life and task than on information.

Unfortunately, the study of the Bible seldom penetrates our value systems. It remains cognitive, focusing on knowledge and on a few "principles for living" we glean from it. Only when we meet with a deep sense of our life together as His Bride will we know how it makes us "one flesh," gloriously empowered to do His work in our world. *The proper use of the Scripture will always be in its application to ministry.*

After 30 years of intimate participation in small groups within P.B.D. church life, I have come to the conviction that the all-important teaching of the Scripture should be done by those who are gifted to do so. When the small group assembles, they should have already been taught the Scriptures. Groups are for developing relationships and sharing experiences, not for cognitive input! The best cell group experiences I have ever had were when, after the teaching had taken place, a time of sharing from the depths of our spirits occurred. The application of the Scripture, cutting like a two-edged sword, must be mingled with the flow of the *charismata*, the "grace gifts," provided by Christ for us to build up one another.

I know it's a long, long journey to what I am describing. But we must abandon the use of groups in Jesus' name on the level of the intellect and the emotions and move on to the level of the spiritual. At that level, the people of God discover and develop their gifts, making real all the theory they have absorbed in years of Bible study which did little to impact their value systems.

Again . . . "Theology Breeds Methodology"

In the following chapters, careful attention will be given to the importance of establishing each cell on solid principles, as well as on the foundation of Christ. When this is done, there is a radical departure in the understanding of cell group life from the models we have been examining.

One of the greatest struggles of those wishing to make the transition from P.B.D. church life to cell church life involves this shift in thinking: *the cell is the church, and the church is the cell.* It is the basic building block of the larger community called "local church." There must be no competition with it — none at all! Everything in the city-wide structure must exist for the cells, be operated by the cells, and must strengthen the life of the cells. *As in the human body, the life of the church is in the cells.*

Are people to be reached for Christ? It is done through cells. Are people to be built up in Him? It is to be done through cells. Are children to be nurtured? They are to be exposed from the start to the cell as normal church life. There are no Specialists and there are no programs in the cell group church. When Bible teachers share, they have in their heart that all listeners are ministers, and the word of God is spoken to equip them for their service. When praise music is sung, its purpose is to join the body to the Head in holy worship.

When prayer is used, it is not the intonation of a "holy man," but the mutual sharing of all present. For this reason, the Korean church has universally prayed aloud in unison for years. (It seems "strange" to Westerners for such a prayer pattern to be used, even though they see nothing "odd" about singing "A Mighty Fortress Is Our God" at the top of their lungs.) Half nights of prayer are common among cell group churches. On occasion, the cell itself may engage in this practice, or may join in with sister cells in the district for the activity.

Cell groups usually come to a time when they must multiply to remain viable. Six or seven people can become 14 or 15 in a short time. When that happens, it is mandatory for the cell to become two communities. Except for the most resistant cultures, this will happen in less than a year — often within six months.

When conducting a seminar on this topic, I am always asked: "How can you say that the work of the cell group is the building up of one another, and then add that they must multiply in six months?" This is a question asked by those who have not spent any time in the cell church! Those of us who have experience know that edification does not require a special set of people, but a special work of the Holy Spirit within the people.

There comes a time in the life of every group when each person "rewinds his tapes" and begins to replay them. For this reason, groups who remain together for long periods of time stagnate and ossify. My usual reply to the question is, "Those who insist that the quality of their group life is dependent upon the people in it are thinking carnally. In so thinking, we are not 'discerning the Body.' The richness of a cell group church is discovered when the group multiplies and the power of the Spirit's flow remains constant. We soon discover that while the faces have changed, God's power is still present to invade all the strongholds in people's lives and set them free."

It takes about three generations of cell group multiplication before the true life of the church is established. The "relearning curve" from a P.B.D. mind set is not easy. The pastor must resign his "Holy Man" lifestyle and learn to make tents, as did Paul. He must mix with the publicans and the sinners and learn how to bring God's power among their messed-up lives. The totally involved lay volunteer must get far enough away in time from the P.B.D. structure to no longer desire its leeks and garlic. When the transition has been made, there will be no desire to return to the old way.

Of course, none of this is a problem to those who have not been trapped inside the P.B.D. churches. The world is full of men and women who have experienced them and have withdrawn from them. Many of them are looking for transparency to go along with their faith, and are open to the cell group church.

From years of personal experiences, I can assure the reader that there are untold thousands in addition who have never had a contact with organized religion, and are sincerely searching for answers to why they were born. That's why the New Age movement has made such headway. People who will believe the lie Shirley MacLaine and others have peddled about reincarnation and the occult must be desperate!

The tragedy is that the New Agers are stealing the unreached who rightly belong to Christ, simply because we who are His children are fighting a shadow war inside our church buildings instead of storming the gates of hell.

The Lost Sheep and the Confused Shepherds

The P.B.D. church has not only spawned cell groups with problems, it has also generated amazing monstrosities when it comes to administering them. This was brought to my attention by someone, somewhere in the past as we sat in a restaurant late one night. I have no idea who first described the models set forth in this section, but I have seen all of them in operation! You will nod your head and smile as you review the possibilities of those who begin to use cells as gimmicks, knowing not what they do.

The Ivory Tower Model (Pray and Hope)

Those who seek to administer groups in this manner are usually preoccupied with other interests but desire the growth they have heard small groups can bring. The senior pastor of a large church often adopts this pattern. He turns the work of the cells over to a subordinate and never looks back. The poor staff member seeks to develop a deep commitment to a lifestyle the pastor shuns.

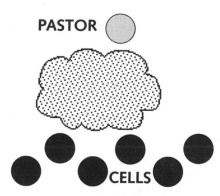

PASTOR

CELLS

**IVORY TOWER
(PRAY and HOPE)**

No amount of smiling endorsement of the cells by this pastor will compensate by his tacit "Don't do as I do . . . do as I say!"

Yonggi Cho is adamant in his insistence that if a cell group is going to be effective, the leadership of the church must be participants. In all churches which have had effective cells, every single staff person — including the secretaries and the janitors — were involved.

Praying and hoping is not enough. The members of the congregation must be assured this is not another one of the projects which may pass away overnight. The Minister of Music and the choir must be involved, along with all others who serve on committees, etc. It's better not to begin at all if this is not possible.

The Umbrella Model
(Compete for Best Study Materials)

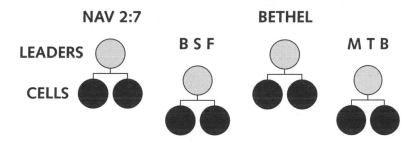

This model occurs when the vision of a church is foggy and its goals unknown. Different curriculums are introduced by staff or members who have become enamored by this or that discipleship or Bible study group pattern. Usually a desire to be polite to one another squashes any comments that this pattern will not be profitable. Thus, the congregation is split into varied interests, none of which create community. Groups which meet on a cognitive level for such courses will forfeit "body study," that powerful life in which the agenda is focused on the members and their ability to edify one another through the expression of their spiritual gifts.

A word of tribute must be included here for the ministry of Bible Study Fellowship. It has steadfastly refused to be under the mantle of any church structure and has quietly created cells that are extremely effective in providing community for Christians who are trapped in the P.B.D. structures. Only heaven will reveal the good this ministry has done in our day. It's a pity that American churches have not scrapped their entire structure to adopt the simple plan of BSF. I know of one Methodist woman who nearly dried up in her church. It was in BSF she met Christ, and through her the entire family became believers. I had the privilege of leading her husband to Christ over a spinach salad at his country club. This auto dealer became one of my closest friends.

The Smorgasbord Model
(Shopping Cart Plan: offer everything except direction)

One completely sincere pastor I know decided he would let the umbrella model expand even further. He created a large cafeteria line of groups for his people: prayer groups, Bible study groups, discipleship groups, videotape groups, etc. *It kept people busy, but failed to create community or to reach people.* Such "busy work" can kill a church!

The Terrorist Model
(Shoot down the Authority Figures)

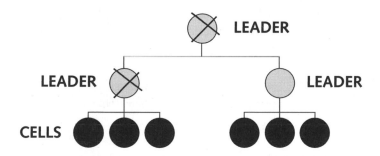

This little nightmare is the reason many pastors are dead set against any and all cell groups. Unless the small group happens to be a Sunday School class which meets on campus, they will not be allowed by him.

This model only develops when there is not a proper spirit between leadership and laity. In all the years I pastored a cell group church there was never a single time when a rebellious group set out to become independent and assault the leadership. It rarely happens, and then only when communication patterns are poor.

The Junta Model
(Leadership Dissipated Among Equal Elders; no one "in charge")

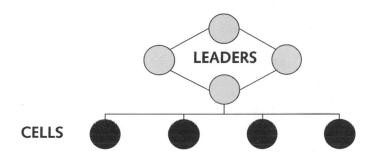

Junta models suffer badly from the weakest link in a chain of equal elders. All it takes is one stubborn individual who will hold out against everyone else to stalemate the church indefinitely. It sounds spiritual for all the leadership to be equal in vote and for the group to wait until there is total agreement, but the carnality residing in the best of us can create impossible situations! There must be one chair "where the buck stops."

The Skunkworks Model
(Each Group Designs Its Own Model)

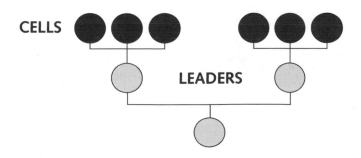

In this inverted pyramid pattern, the pastor and other church leaders encourage each group to create its own lifestyles. From the "holy huddles" come the various activities which the groups will execute. Invariably, two or three strong personalities in each group make decisions for the rest. Thus, the "calling" of the group is not universal. As the weeks go by, the enthusiasm for the group task wanes. Those who were not really committed drop out first, often with scoldings from the more "spiritual." After a generation of this model, small groups may never be resurrected again.

The Jungle Model
(No Clear Lines of Assistance)

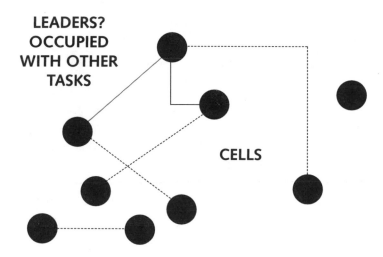

Quite often this model develops slowly as groups grow and multiply. Instead of providing capable leadership to each group, the matter is ignored. Without clear guidance available, groups begin to cast about for help with their problems and questions. Soon leadership by default has been created. It is then impossible to create clear lines of assistance. Such glaring errors are a sign that the leadership of the Body did not plan for growth and was incapable of handling it when it came. Growth will be hindered and some will become frustrated and drop out of the groups.

The Revised Utopian Plan Model
(Out with the old, in with the new;
"Hmmm . . . leadership is starting over . . . again!")

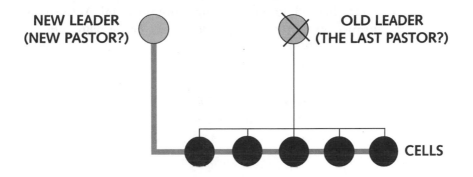

This takes place when a traditional church calls a new pastor or staff member. His egotism demands that what the previous leader did be discarded, and his "better plan" installed.

It is important to know that any attempt to develop a cell group church will require at least two to three years to take root. Actually, the explosive growth does not take place until the second or third generation of converts has matured enough to enter leadership positions. Churches who keep their pastors for long periods fare better than those who are constantly turning them over.

The Pyramid Plan
(Spend your time recruiting, not serving . . .)

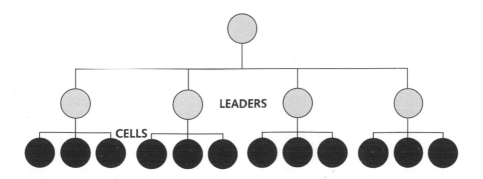

Those who are responsible for the cell groups must be involved in their ministries, not just their training. As cells develop, it is necessary for seasoned workers to become equippers of new cell group servants. These people must not be personally responsible for the life of a single group. It will be necessary for them to revolve among the cells they serve. If they do not faithfully do this, they will become "absentee landlords" of their groups. The first sign something is wrong may be when they dissolve!

A Better Way
(Led by the vision of the Senior Pastor:
Cells, Congregations, Celebrations)

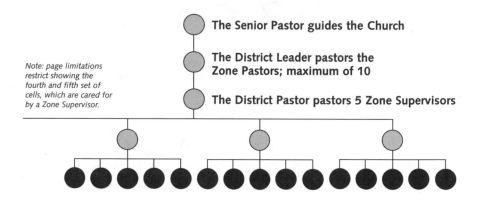

The Senior Pastor guides the Church

The District Leader pastors the Zone Pastors; maximum of 10

Note: page limitations restrict showing the fourth and fifth set of cells, which are cared for by a Zone Supervisor.

The District Pastor pastors 5 Zone Supervisors

This is the pattern followed by virtually all cell group churches. The interesting thing is that many of their pastors have never met, never compared notes. Each situation may vary with culture, the skill of the pastor to organize, and the spiritual strength of the congregation to reach out and invade Satan's territory.

The clear direction set for the church by the pastor is a mandate for the congregation to focus on one thing alone. As one cell group pastor said to me, "This one thing we do!"

With a clear focus about the people to be reached and the plan to accomplish it, the church moves ahead in harmony and with commitment.

Pastor David Yonggi Cho goes to Prayer Mountain once a year to fast and pray, seeking God's mandate for the church's life for the next 12 months. When he returns from that time with the Lord, the goals which are given to him are printed and framed. These framed statements are then hung on every wall of every church worker on the staff. All is in perfect focus, and everything done by every person is directed toward meeting that objective.

The basic difference between the first nine models and this final one is simply a clearly defined set of goals! As one Chinese pastor in Singapore said when the missionaries asked him what suggestions he had for their work: "Have a goal, and help us to understand what it is!" He then expressed the frustration of working with leaders who had never decided where they would end when they started out.

Cells, or "small groups," in the P.B.D. church are always tacked onto the existing structures. Thus, they are ineffective and poorly managed. Let's move on to view a better concept!

4

My Journey into the Cell Church

I want to share my own pilgrimage into the cell group church. Occasionally, I'll deliberately chase a rabbit in this chapter to help you understand things to follow. I'm praying as I write that the truth of the journey may motivate you to do something about your own . . .

For me, the journey started in 1965 as I turned 36 years of age. I had spent all my life living in parsonages: first my father's, then our own. I had preached in dozens of congregations during my education in Christian colleges and seminaries and years spent serving the ministry of Billy Graham. When I turned 36 I was absolutely, completely disgusted with traditional church structures that catered to self-needs and ignored the unchurched.

I could not understand why American churches universally suffered from stunted growth. Only a few dozen have been able to grow beyond 5,000 members, and only a couple of dozen have Sunday schools that are larger than 2,000. In the light of the population explosion, that seemed ridiculous. In the light of the book of Acts, it seemed intolerable!

What those statistics revealed was that America's churches stagnate and cease to reach the unreached people who exist all around them. I asked myself, "Why do churches quit growing? Why are half or more of their members inactive? What in the world is wrong?"

By then, I had already planted over a score of brand new churches in the Northeast. Ruthie, the boys, and I moved four times in five years, and I preached as many as six times every Sunday. In each new town, we started churches in the homes of a few believers. We grew rapidly as long as we met in that way. Everyone pitched in; everyone shared his excitement with friends over the newly forming church. Folks got converted regularly.

We would grow each church large enough to call a pastor and erect a "starter building." It puzzled me that, along with lovely new buildings and seminary graduates in the pulpits, nearly every one of those churches stagnated within a few years.

It is now 25 years later. Most of them have not added another 150 members since they were constituted! Only a few I know about have added to the original "starter buildings."

Next, I spent five years flying all over Texas as an evangelism consultant for the Texas Baptist Convention. I conducted endless evangelistic meetings foolishly advertised as "Revival Meetings," which unchurched folks boycotted en masse.

I preached to those I thought were the problem: "dead" church members who didn't care that the world was going to hell in a handbasket. We had altars full of folks weeping and asking the Lord to send a mighty harvest. The love offerings were great — but the harvesting profitability of these meetings was poor. Four months after each meeting, every church plodded along as it had done before, barely reflecting any fruit from our efforts.

Of the 4,500 churches our Division of Evangelism worked with, only a handful baptized as many as 100 people a year. Hundreds of them baptized absolutely no one, and repeated the awful statistic year after year! I asked myself, "How can this be?" It revealed that hundreds of preachers in the pulpits of those congregations never personally won a soul to Christ. Could that be possible?

I had hit upon my first real answer to one reason traditional church structures stagnate in America. As mentioned in Chapter Two, a majority of church workers don't have a single friend who might be described as a genuine unbeliever. They spend all their time insulated from the unchurched, working among church members. Their so-called "personal evangelism" consists of little more than sharing a well-memorized plan of salvation with total strangers on a visitation night, or preaching evangelistic sermons from behind insulated pulpits. Many of them only did the latter. Few of them had earned the sordid reputation of our Lord, who was criticized for being "a friend of winebibbers and sinners."

I deliberately broke with the pattern and began spending the so-called "happy hours" in the Sportsman's Lounge near the Baptist Building in Dallas, talking to the beer-drinking unchurched. To my amazement, I discovered most of them had quit going to church years ago. They still believed in God, but they no longer believed in the traditional church. And they had no intention of going back!

They were quite vocal about the matter. Universally, they viewed the church as a set of programs which required buildings, meetings, and money. They resented this depersonalized church, where people never really got down to earth and opened up to each other, where they had to attend every activity or have a guilt trip laid on them in a sermon, and where the church collected money for its own projects but spent little helping hurting people within the community. Most of all, they resented the lavish buildings which were often used only a few hours a week. One said to me, "That church over there just spent millions for an auditorium which will be used no more than five hours a week. They also built a health club. It's paid for with tithed money from its membership, but they are now charging a monthly fee equal to what a profit-making health club charges! How can you justify that? How do they represent a Christ who deliberately lived simply? I believe in God, but I will never, never set foot in that church!"

Of course, his comment in a bar never reached the ears of the hundreds and hundreds of people who pack that auditorium on Sundays or the massive staff that keeps the machinery oiled. The lack of communication between those who won't come and those who do come to that facility is a great part of the problem.

So, here was the chasm. Christians were working their heads off inside insulated church buildings, believing they were doing "the work of the Lord." The people who needed their love never saw them at all. How could we be so blind? Was it not obvious the church was dying for lack of relationships with the unchurched?

The God of Abraham said to him, "I want you to let me guide you to a new location so we can become closer to one another." *Abraham was about to get a huge jolt!*

Jehovah didn't lead the patriarch to a tranquil garden where they might fellowship together in peace. He led him into the big middle of the vilest, most licentious, infant-sacrificing, Baal worshipping tribe in the Middle East and said, "Abraham, this is where I want you to live as you fellowship with me!"

How odd of God! No — how typical of the God who is "not willing that any should perish." He planted His worshiper among the captives, the hell-raisers who lived without anyone to witness of His love. While he didn't know it at the time, Abraham had just become a foreign missionary! He could have been the first mortal to capture the heartbeat of God and write the words later made famous by C. T. Studd:

> "I do not wish to live
> 'Neath sound of church or chapel bell;
> I want to run a rescue shop
> Within a yard of hell!"

Certainly, our Lord Jesus Christ might also have penned that couplet. His life was dedicated to seeking and saving those who were lost.

The typical traditional church fails the test! It endlessly preoccupies itself with its own routines. What it needs is to move its location from its buildings to the uncircumcised Philistine tribes a block or more away. It needs to so encounter God that it will have its name changed, as did Abram, who lived in the covenant relationship as Abraham, the man who received the very name of God into his own.

I was taught by my denomination that the Sunday School was our "Knight in Shining Armor," by which traditional churches would win America to Christ. Yet, when I examined the ten largest Sunday Schools in Texas — all with over 2,000 enrolled — I was stunned to discover they averaged fewer than eight adult unbelievers in actual attendance! Who was kidding whom?

Where did we come up with the idea that unconverted people are burning with desire to get all dressed up on Sunday morning instead of sleeping in, bursting with enthusiasm to drive to a church facility, and filled with an insatiable thirst for Bible study? After attending Sunday School for my adult age group in over a hundred churches, I was even more disgusted. The quality of the teaching in most classes was wretched.

I came to a conclusion. I now knew why churches didn't grow. Traditional churches were insulated islands of Christians, who didn't try to relate to the totally unchurched in the community. I discovered larger churches had actually hired one or more workers to go visit the visitors because the church members could not be persuaded to do so. Many pastors required their entire church staff to visit new people weekly since the lack of enthusiasm among the congregation to do so left few other options.

I did some serious statistical research next, using the annual reports in our state building and interviewing 300 pastors. Less than 1% of the salaried "pillars of the church" were investing one hour a week developing personal relationships with the huge masses of totally unchurched.

What about the memberships in the churches? Were they not in the marketplace all week long? Did they take advantage of the opportunities to share their faith? Let me share what I found out about them . . .

Tom Wolf, former pastor of The Church on Brady in Los Angeles, showed me something I had never seen. The Greek word *oikos*, translated "household," refers to people we relate to on a regular basis. We may know a hundred or more individuals, but we spend quality time (one hour a week of direct conversation, for example) with a limited number. When I took surveys among hundreds of church members who attended my seminars, I uncovered a shocking fact: the "world" of a typical Christian seldom contains more than eight or nine *oikos* people! Only a few had a personal friendship and spent quality time with hard-core unbelievers. Most of the time, these unbelievers were relatives who had become impervious to further discussion about Jesus' claim of Lordship over them.

The depressing conclusion was this: *the typical church-goer relates to only five to eight people for at least one full hour per week per person, and half of those Christians cannot name a single unbeliever among their close friends.* Many of them have not even made a new acquaintance in the past 12 months. They live in little personal bubbles, having no interest in people who live and work close to them. When church members have no "root system" to make contact with unbelievers, they are powerless to be used to win others.

Even sadder, the rhetoric from the pulpit about the need to reach the lost for Christ falls on deaf ears. A proper theology breeds motivation for ministry. One pastor had a real gut-level discussion with his deacons about why not one of them had led a soul to Christ in the past year. He called me, shattered with their totally honest comments: to a man, their personal beliefs were that God would somehow take in the unbelievers even if they did not come to Him by way of the cross. He had a deacon board composed of universalists, although they publicly nodded their heads when he preached on eternity without Christ or the tragedy of living without hope. If churchgoers don't believe people need to meet Christ, their motivation to reach unbelievers is a minus zero.

Perhaps you are thinking, "Hey! Wait a minute! My church is really alive! We aren't like that. We're reaching others!" Of course, you'll think that way. If you didn't, you couldn't exist within the traditional church. Perhaps your church is "The Great Exception." But, where does your harvest come from? How many unchurched are represented in it? Is your growth your worst enemy, blinding you to the yet unreached all around you? Are you blind to the reality of those ignored?

I recall scores of conversations with pastors and education directors which went something like this:

> Me: "You are showing significant growth. Have you evaluated the source of your growth?"
>
> He: "We have so many visitors on Sundays we can't keep up with the load. As long as they keep coming and we keep visiting, that's all we have time to do!"
>
> Me: "But what about the nearly 70% in this city who never go to church? What are you doing to reach out to them?"
>
> He: "Well, we have a jail ministry on Sunday afternoons."
>
> Me: "How many do you have in your church family from that ministry?"
>
> He: "I don't really know. Perhaps none."

Years later, after I had developed and proved a workable strategy to reach the unchurched, an Arkansas pastor spent hours with me discussing the need for a "root system" to penetrate the unchurched college students next to his university church. I shared with him the simple strategy of using cells. I suggested he develop them as contact points in the dorms. He went home with much excitement. A few weeks later, he called to say, "Ralph, I've aborted the idea. We can't seat all the people attending our two morning worship services. If we launch an aggressive outreach like cell groups, it would only compound our seating problem. I have decided not to proceed."

Amazingly, He had limited the ministry of his church to the seating of his auditorium!

I concluded that traditional church growth came mainly through the baptism of the member's children, transfers from other churches, or by a sickly and minimal evangelism harvest among people who actually visit worship services. Traditional churches, I discovered, have absolutely no strategy for touching the unchurched. I made up my mind to do something about it.

I began to spend sleepless nights in our Dallas home. The dead churches who had no flood of visitors ran a maintenance organization. The growing churches, usually located in newer housing areas, simply "visited the visitors." In both cases, the unchurched were unreached. There was no sign of this ever changing in the traditional church!

The sleepless nights were then filled with writing a strategy for an experimental church, a church which would find solutions to these problems. Soon, the document was 68-pages long. One day, Ruth and the boys sat me down and said, "Look! You've got to do more than walk the floor. If we need to, we'll all go to work to support the family needs. Let's go and do it!" That was all I needed. We began to pray about the location for the test, and God opened a door for us.

In 1969, a non-traditional church in Houston was formed with 38 courageous pioneers. We called ourselves *The People Who Care,* and became a "Parable Church." Without knowing what we were doing, we stumbled into the patterns which were being used by other cell group churches we didn't know existed. We had no idea that a patched tent in a slum area of Seoul was housing another group that was also stumbling into the new patterns. Their pastor was sleeping behind the pulpit. They would become the largest local church in Christian history, now numbering over 800,000 members.

We would be used in a different way by the Holy Spirit. In 12 years' time, *The People Who Care* (West Memorial Baptist Church) ministered to thousands of people. We would send over a score of couples to seminaries or to work with other Christian groups. Dozens more would go to strengthen weaker churches in the city around us. We touched a nation, and then a world, with our lifestyle and our books which shared our way of living and loving and reaching the lost. Hundreds of believers came to learn from us, and we interned up to 15 workers during each of the summer months.

Without spending millions on fancy buildings, *The People Who Care* found themselves with a baptism ratio of one convert for every 4.5 church members from the very first year of their new lifestyle. Year after year, the ratio stayed the same. Traditional churches around us required up to 42 members to produce one baptism. At best, the traditional church ratio was twenty to one.

"Surely," we thought, "if we explain this strategy to reach the unchurched, traditional churches will adopt it!" As our congregation grew and grew, so did our vision of renewing traditional churches.

We formed home cell groups, where our unchurched friends were made to feel welcome. They loved these get-togethers! We made the rounds of all the taverns in our area and met unreached men and women. We held barbecues in our back yards and met unmet neighbors. Our wives joined bridge clubs as a contact point with women in the area. My eldest high school son hung out where teenagers bought drugs, and we started small groups with them. We even opened "The Giant Step," a ministry for prostitutes and pimps who were heroin addicts. Forty of us stayed with them by shifts, around the clock, in an old rented house, putting wet towels on their foreheads as they vomited their way through withdrawal. Later, we took them into our homes to show them how Christian families lived.

It was in 1971 that I recognized another serious flaw in traditional evangelistic methods. They set too high a platform for evangelizing unbelievers. That platform was Bible study. If the unbeliever didn't want to study the Bible, they were ignored! That one single attitude of the church has deprived millions of people from receiving the Gospel.

Scripture teaches us a different pattern. In Athens, Paul gave us a model: for those who would not begin with Bible study, he quoted their pagan poets. He had the sense to know we must "become all things to all men, that by all means we might win some." He eventually brought some Athenians to the Scriptures, but he did not start with them. He worked up to the Scriptures. Cell group churches recognize there is a way to reach the unchurched who refuse to enter into Bible study. It is by serving them at the point of their deepest need.

We discovered scores of folks who would not be caught dead in a Bible study but who were delighted to spend an evening talking with us. Slowly, we reached the people we called "The Outsiders." We brought them into our cells of love, to eventually face the power of the written Word and finally to declare Christ as Lord.

We stumbled on "Target Group Evangelism" and formed the first evangelistic cells we had ever seen. Cal Wheeler, a local garage shop owner, started a group for kids with motorcycles, and Cal Thomas used his television contacts to start a breakfast group for politicians and business men. Bill and Betty Lottman formed a group for parents of retarded children. Soon there were over 20 target groups, each creating a root system to penetrate the unchurched people around us. We grew and grew, learning all the while, sharing our failures and our victories as God gave them to us.

When we baptized, each convert represented months of patient servanthood. In two years, we were 600. A large number had been unchurched persons before being touched by our cells.

The Associated Press covered our ministry. So did several magazines. In 1973, Francis Schaeffer joined us for our first National Conference on the cell group church, where we explained our lifestyle to scores of pastors. What a rich time that was for us all!

In 1974, the church allowed me to go to Singapore and work on developing cell group churches there. While waiting for our visa, we took a temporary assignment in Saigon — just in time to see the nation fall to the swarming Viet Cong. Our time in Singapore was stormy. The mission there wasn't ready for innovation, and our presence as a "Change Agent" was resented from the first. In spite of their lack of cooperation, we were able to see 18 house churches planted by our Chinese brothers. It was my first taste of pure cell group life, and I carefully developed the equipping materials to make it work.

In our absence, a traditional pastor sought to restore old patterns to the Houston church. It fell apart; members scattered to the winds. When we left in June of 1973, there were over 600 people. When we returned to resume the pastorate in July of 1977, there were only 77 people left in the Sunday school. By 1980, we required two worship services, had a staff of 13, and once again had "Target Groups" up and running.

In 1979, the denomination asked us to test our pattern in 80 traditional churches. It flopped. The P.B.D. churches were not ready for change. I resigned my pulpit once again, determined to devote full time to discover what more could be done to help traditional churches get out of their shells. A precious friend loaned us $100,000 for the venture. We spent two more years revising our materials to make them more palatable to the denomination. Negotiations were renewed with its leadership to use the cell group evangelism strategy, and we came within days of signing a contract for me to work for them.

When the word leaked out about the new project, some denominational leaders were terribly threatened. In a stormy meeting, one executive said to me, "I won't allow another evangelism strategy to be offered to our churches. The one I have is all they need!"

In 1982, the hammer fell. The pressure was too great from the opposition. The denomination opted to sever all relations with TOUCH Ministries. My denomination slammed its doors to revision of the P.B.D., which might have opened its doors to the burgeoning mass of unreached persons in our society. After 20 years of seeking to bring "renewal" to the traditional church, our journey had come to a dead end.

Thus, when our work was done, the Holy Spirit gently ended the life of our parable church and years of my ministry, both committed to bringing renewal to our sister P.B.D. congregations.

After my resignation in 1980, the church again floundered. Pastors who followed didn't understand our motives for abandoning the traditional "large church" mold to become a "cell church." Members once again fell away.

Finally, West Memorial Baptist Church totally lost its original identity. It was dissolved on December 31, 1988. Both its constitution and incorporation were dissolved by a new pastor and a new membership that knew nothing about our original vision. The successor church, with a new name, a new theology, and some P.B.D. type cells, invested the massive profits from the sale of our property and developed its new "large church" lifestyle, complete with many programs, in another location. The dear pastor and his people are doing a fine work, using quite traditional concepts.

The original members are now scattered into dozens of ministries and scores of groups, and the original vision now exists only in our memories. We "old timers" still network, often talking on the telephone, visiting or writing, sharing what God is now doing because of what He did in the past. As one former staffer said to me, *"We had no way of knowing it at the time, but we were living in Camelot!"*

Afterglow: What's Left?

Much of what we learned pastoring in Houston and Singapore is readily applied to the new cell church structures. We developed a 20-week training program for cell group churches, giving them tools to reach the unchurched. We originally called it *Touch Basic Training*, and it now has been rewritten into the *Opening Hearts Trilogy*. It's a part of an entire equipping structure which will be explained in later chapters of this book. It's the main thing that has come from those years of trying, learning, and preparing.

My purpose for sharing all these details with you is for you to understand why people migrate from the traditional church to the cell group church. It's not a movement of sick neurotics; it is the migration of thirsty hearts. And it's not to imply that everyone is called to be a part of the migration. Most of those who have life investments in the traditional church probably will not do so. It's certainly not necessary to join a cell group church to be in the Lord's will. Christ is among all His churches, not just some of them. In Revelation, He stood among the Laodiceans and the Thyatirans, and He is among all the problemed churches today as well. But He is also developing a younger Bride that is far more beautiful. There's a definite movement to report . . . a movement which will be significant as we begin this next century.

In the chapters which follow, I am going to tell you about the world I live in at the present time. It's a world where cell group churches see from 20% to 100% growth every single year. Where do you go from here? Don't settle for less than the Holy Spirit will give!

If you are still thinking, "Where did you get the idea that 'bigger is better?' Those cell group megachurches are too large for any true Christian lifestyle to be lived out. Seas of people are not healthy."

My friend, that's not true! Anything that is living is growing. The cell group churches may contain thousands of members, but the only thing a person can "join" is a cell group that numbers no more than 15 persons. The building block of all living organisms is a cell. Anyway, cells don't grow; they multiply into more cells. Thus, the growth is composed of tiny "mini-churches," where there is a potential for more intimacy and transparency than one can ever find in a traditional church.

Is There Hope for the P.B.D. Church?

By 1990, we had spent 15 years holding dozens of seminars to show P.B.D. pastors how to begin home cell groups to reach unchurched persons. Over $190,000 went into creating the printed and videotaped training materials for use in the TOUCH strategy.

However, most pastors faced such resistance to a new relational evangelism strategy by their church leadership that they never got it off the ground. I consulted with 200 churches who tried to install the ministry of cells to reach the unchurched. Approximately 75 churches actually formed cell groups. By 1985, 21 of the 75 pastors who developed evangelistic groups were fired or were forced to resign by lay leaders who were totally threatened by the pastor's new outreach strategy. Their dismissals were directly related only to their attempts to revise the P.B.D. structures and their challenges to the memberships to get off the church campus and become involved in long-term faith sharing with their pagan neighbors.

In four of those situations, I flew in at my own expense to plead with church leaders to understand their pastor's motives. In every case, I was simply stunned by their feelings of fear toward accepting a new concept!

Two seemingly insurmountable problems face the transition of a traditional church into a cell group church. The first is a pastor who reigns over a churchly kingdom. In this situation, the clergyman is unwilling to assume his role as an equipper, unable to say, "Let them increase, even if I decrease!" Such a man will never release the laity to take over the priestly duties God has reserved for them.

The other problem is the church member who balks at the idea of becoming a responsible, ministering person. In many cases, personal significance and power is provided by holding an office in the church or a teaching task in the Sunday school. Impure motives for service have built many "power bases" for carnal people within church life. These church workers have no intention of entering into true servanthood. Those who "hire a holy man" to do the work of the church feel they have done their part when they drop their tithe into the offering plate.

The conflict can work either way: a pastor tries to move a congregation that is unmovable and gets his head chopped off. Or, some inside a congregation press the pastor to let the laity begin to minister off the campus, and they get their heads chopped off.

In 1985, I concluded that it was impossible to change the P.B.D. church. I determined that once a church has structured itself along certain patterns, it is virtually impossible to make any significant changes. Even something as simple as changing an order of service is liable to create strife.

When that twenty-first pastor called me from California to tell me his three-year long struggle to develop relational church structures had ended in his forced resignation, I began to ask myself a serious question: can new wine be put into old skins? I concluded then that the answer is "No!"

But the tide has changed the last ten years. I have seen God creating new wineskins out of old churches. He is not only renewing the Spirit in many places; He is also reforming their structures. The cell church had now come into its time. Now it has risen as a powerful force in the worldwide church. He is renewing and reshaping His church from the Southern Baptist to the non-denominational charismatic, from the Presbyterian to the Church of God, from the Vineyard to the Evangelical Free. Are you ready to join in?

Theology Breeds
Methodology

Part 2

5

Community:
The Reason for Cells

Since theology breeds methodology, it will be valuable for us to shape a biblical view of the cell group church. We must begin by recognizing that the primary assignment in a cell group church is to develop "Basic Christian Communities." When we understand this, we become dissatisfied with groups that serve as a "gimmick," an optional feature, or a "quick fix" for sagging attendance.

Because community can occur most completely only in small groups, a cell group, numbering less than 15 people, is all important. Essential elements of community include interpersonal commitments and a sense of belonging. Community takes place when there is a shared life, allowing common goals and commitments to develop between all of its members.

In *The Different Drum*, M. Scott Peck writes:

If we are to use the word [community] meaningfully, we must restrict it to a group of individuals who have learned how to communicate honestly with each other, whose relationships go deeper than their masks of composure, and who have developed some significant commitment to "rejoice together, mourn together," and to "delight in each other, make others' conditions our own."[1]

In the "kingdoms of this world" shaped by Satan, Christian community cannot exist. Only in the "Kingdom of God" can it be truly discovered. When Jesus went about announcing the "Gospel of the Kingdom," He was inviting fragmented humanity to enter into something it could not experience elsewhere.

As the extended family is the *oikos*[2] of society, so the cell group is the extended family, the basic building block, of the people of God. A large-group gathering of Christians (more than 15 persons) cannot provide the essential ingredients required for community. Nor will community develop if a small group meets fortnightly or monthly, or even just once a week. While the typical cell group will have a special time to be together weekly, there is a strong bond between the members who often spend time with one another between meetings. Couples may share an evening, ladies may go shopping, children may spend a night at the home of one of the other children in the group. They are family.

It is not possible to define community to someone who has never experienced it. Like falling head over heels in love, it must be experienced to be understood. Those who have been fortunate to enter into Kingdom relationships can never again be content with the shallowness of institutional church life.

Some years ago, I entered into a small group relationship with two other men. Hans was from Switzerland, working temporarily in Dallas. Erwin was a graphic artist. We began to meet together on Fridays for lunch. It was not long before I found myself looking forward to our times together, not really understanding why our weekly hour and a half meant so much to me. With these men I shared the deepest feelings of my soul, my longings to find a more authentic Christian lifestyle. I didn't know it at the time, but we had formed a community. There were frequent telephone calls between our luncheons, and we edified one another with Scripture verses, insights, and thoughts that came to us during our personal prayer times.

27 years later, I have had many experiences with the power of community. Yet, I shall never forget the power of God that flowed between us back then. Hans has long ago returned to Zurich. Erwin went on to produce the *Benjie* movies. Because of their affirmations, I left the security of denominational ladder-climbing to enter a journey to find renewal for the church. God was good to me: I had actually found all there was to discover in that simple community with those two men.

Have you also discovered that the Gospel of the Kingdom is "among us?" Then, you will relish the thoughts that follow.

The Highest Life Form in the Universe

Why is God a Trinity? Most of us get bogged down just trying to understand it! The Athanasian Creed is our best source to grasp it: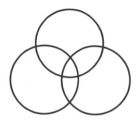

> . . . we worship one God in Trinity, and Trinity in Unity; Neither confounding the Persons: nor dividing the Substance [Essence]. For there is one Person of the Father: another of the Son: and another of the Holy Ghost. But the Godhead of the Father, of the Son, and of the Holy Ghost, is all one: the Glory equal, the Majesty coeternal. Such as the Father is: such is the Son: and such is the Holy Ghost . . .

Whew!

Even after we grasp this, the key question still remains: Why is God a Trinity?

The Koran insists He is one! It is heresy, the Islamic firmly believes, to teach otherwise. Every time he genuflects in prayer, he rises with one finger raised: "He is one!"

Why is God not a duality? We are told that "God is love." Only two persons are required to give and receive love. Would two persons in the Godhead not have been enough? Obviously the answer is "No," for God is a Trinity. A powerful truth emerges from this fact. Where there are three, there is — for the first time — community. There must be at least three before community can exist. God, by His very nature, has always lived in the richness which exists only in community.

John Samaan meditated upon this in a *Servants Among The Poor* newsletter:

> . . . within God's very nature is a divine "rhythm" or pattern of continuous giving and receiving — not only love, but also glory, honor, life . . . each in its fullness. Think about it for a minute. God the Father loves and delights in the Son (Matt. 3:17), Jesus receives that love and pleases his Father as an obedient and loving Son (Jn. 8:29), and honors the Spirit (Matt. 12:31), while the Spirit glorifies both the Father and the Son (Jn 16:14). Each

person in the Trinity loves, honors and glorifies the other and receives love and honor back from the others, because He is worthy. There is never any lack.[3]

It must be said with reverential awe: *He who is Eternal has always existed in the lifestyle of community* — with only one break in this continuity. That single exception occurred at Calvary. As Christ took the ugliness of our sin into Himself, He cried out, "My God! My God! Why have You forsaken Me?" The vileness of our sin, received into His sinless body, severed the eternal community of the Godhead! (The worst part about sin is that it always destroys community.)

What was it like for our Lord to experience separation from the Godhead? To know what Jesus experienced, we would have to enter into the perfect community of the Godhead. Unfortunately, our humanness precludes that for us.

Man Created for Community

In Genesis 1:26 God said, "Let Us make man in Our image, according to Our likeness . . ." An essential characteristic of love is its desire to enlarge community. Eden was not paradise because of its beauty but because it was the place of unbroken relationships. It was the place of giving and receiving, the continuous actions that take place wherever there is true community.

God knew the risks in carrying out His decision to create Adam with the freedom of choice. This freedom permitted Adam to enter into fellowship with the Triune One, but it also allowed him liberty to choose hate instead of love, disobedience instead of loyalty, selfishness rather than servanthood. Knowing the end from the beginning — and knowing what Adam would choose — God *still* made His decision. We begin to realize how much God treasures community as we consider His perilous commitment to allow man the liberty to decide things for himself. Community must always be a voluntary matter. We are never forced into it; it is something we desire.

Then, from Adam's side, God took a bride. Adam gave a rib and received a help mate. She was "bone of his bone, flesh of his flesh." Like him, she was formed to live in community. Their capacities were significantly different. Someone has said that God put a part of His nature in man, and another part in woman, so they would not be complete without one another.

With Adam, Eve could bring forth new life to share their intimacy in family relationships. No child could ever be born apart from physical union: there would be, for each baby, a father and a mother — and baby would make community. In God's plan, unbroken relationships were always to exist.

The Great Destroyer of Community

Community was precisely what Satan attacked and hated. He succeeded in destroying all the potential relationships which might exist in Eden. God to man, man to wife, brother to brother — all were smashed to pieces!

Life after Eden quickly became a tragedy. Man's first knowledge of violent death became the ripened fruit of the ugly jealousy of a brother against a brother. Community among men was replaced by loneliness, fragmentation, and a tragic, needless grave.

In Genesis 4:16-24, we trace the line of the "God Rejecters." The genealogy cynically tells us how this family tree sought to gain personal significance. Enoch built a city; Jabal was a cattle rancher; Jubal was the first musician; Tubal-cain became an industrialist. We end with a crazed man shaking in fear, confessing he is a double murderer! Totally missing is any mention of community between these men and God, or with one another.

Satan's tactic was obvious. In each case, these men gained their significance from their personal achievements. At the same time, man discovered his deficiencies could be devastating to his self-image!

Then Came Generations of Men Who Lived in Community

In Genesis 4:25-5:24, we trace a parallel genealogy which also begins with Adam. Significant differences mark these generations from the one just presented, introduced by the comment in verse 26: "Then men began to call upon the name of the Lord."

Not one mention of personal achievement is recorded as these new men are described! The only thing we are told about them is that they chose to live in community with Jehovah. In contrast to the accomplishments of the previous family, only the life spans of these men are carefully recorded. For those who live to gain personal significance, the length of their earthly life is of no consequence to God; for those whose life is spent in communion with Him, every day is precious.

Contrasted to his insane cousin Lamech, Genesis 5:24 reports that "Enoch walked with God; and he was not, for God took him." What a difference! Enoch's significance was not in what he did or did not do, but in his entering into communal fellowship with his heavenly Father. The lesson of the two genealogies sets a theme for the rest of Scripture: the only "accomplishment" that makes man's earthly life worthwhile, or that will outlive him, is his fellowship with God.

Community in the Old Testament

Throughout the Old Testament, the theme of God and man entering into community is recurrent. With Abraham, with Moses, with Israel, with David, God offered intimacy as an alternative to estrangement.

Ruth's words become symbolic for those who cherish community:

> . . . for where you go, I will go, and where you lodge, I will lodge.
> Your people shall be my people, and your God, my God.

Is it surprising that she is found in the genealogy of Jesus Christ?

As the self-centeredness of Israel reaches a crescendo, in Hosea 11:8 God weeps over their lack of communion with Him, as a parent agonizes over a child with bad values: "How can I surrender you, O Israel? . . . My heart is turned over within Me . . ."

Will Jehovah abandon the desire to live in community with His created ones? No! One after another, His prophets are given ecstatic visions of the future. Isaiah foresees a community where lions sleep with lambs and swords are beaten into plowshares. Jeremiah is promised that Israel will be restored to the land. Ezekiel envisions a glorious Temple in a kingdom of righteousness yet to come. In turn, prophets saw the end times when God and man will live together in intimacy and love.

Community in the New Testament

Then God comes — to actually dwell among men! During the act of impregnating a virgin, God the Father declares His intention of penetrating the human race with His love. Unlike His presence among Israel as a cloud of smoke or fire, He will now become visible through His Son, drawing all men unto Him. Christ confronts Satan, even as did the first Adam — not in a garden, but in a desolate wilderness.

The activity of Satan through the centuries is designed to create prison cells which separate men from one another. The father of lies gave them the alluring name "Kingdoms of This World." He brashly offered them to Jesus, who flatly rejected them. Instead, Christ would establish a kingdom not of this world! It would be a kingdom which unites men.

The Lord's "job description," provided by the Holy Spirit 742 years earlier in Isaiah's scroll, was an assignment to repair the horrid breaches in community caused by man's selfishness. To the poor, to the spit-upon, to the prisoners, to the blind, Christ would bring hope and salvation.

He created community for His followers. From men who would normally never even speak to one another, Jesus shaped 12 disciples. A commando-like patriot rubbed shoulders with a quisling tax collector. Fishermen related to men who tilled land. What unlikely combinations!

He lived with them for three years, modeling a lifestyle of love and acceptance. These 12 men discovered that community can be a difficult place to mask limitations, egotism, ignorance, and jealousies. Try as hard as they could, they were unable to hide the selfishness within themselves. They manipulated Jesus to gain preeminence over one another, striving for significant positions in the "pecking order" of the little community. He saw through every one of their manipulations and kept loving them. In true community, men look past warts and pimples to see the potential within one other.

Slowly, very slowly, these men recognized they must abandon their competitive lifestyles. The greatest among them would be the one who would become the servant of all. They discovered the essence of community is a sense of belonging: their true worth is not their reputation, but their readiness to give themselves unsparingly to the rest.

By living with 12 men, God in human flesh had made a clear statement of the way community develops. While thousands pressed him from every side, He chose to be with one cell of life. Indeed, existence lived apart from that cell had no value. He did not simply gather them once a week for a "discipleship class." He lived with them. They took trips, went fishing, visited Jerusalem, had cookouts by the sea. They camped in the mountains. They shared a common purse.

Of greatest importance, they had a purpose. If community is created without specific goals, there will soon be conflicts and the whole thing will collapse. In *Home for the Heart*, Bruno Bettleheim writes,

> I am convinced community can flourish only if it exists for an aim outside itself. Community is viable if it is the outgrowth of a deep involvement in a purpose which is other than, or above, that of being a community.[4]

Jesus was preparing them for His work. He did it without a great amount of teaching, choosing instead to let them watch as He modeled before them. Indeed, to the modern purveyor of discipleship materials, His pattern is perplexing! He barely *discussed* how to pray; instead, He took them to all-night seasons of prayer. Finally, some of the disciples said, "Jesus, don't you think it would be important for you to teach us how to pray? After all, John has taught his disciples about this subject."

Glancing over at them, He said, "Fine. Pray like this —" He gave them what we call "The Lord's Prayer," which took about one minute to recite. He might as well have concluded with a comment like, "Any questions?"

What a contrast this was to the hours and hours of praying He had modeled for them in the hills! Had they been wiser, they would have realized prayer is not taught — it's caught.

He delayed another important lesson about praying until they had returned from their first assignment. Jesus had sent them into Galilee to minister. After they returned, a man approached him with his son, explaining that the disciples who had come to his village failed to set the boy free from epilepsy. After Jesus healed the lad, the disciples asked: "Why couldn't we do that, Lord?"

Why had He not told them about that *before* they went out to minister? The reason is significant: when living in community, there are "teachable moments" which cannot be anticipated. Value systems are created in the context of *living, not studying*. This is one of the reasons values are always shaped faster in cell groups than in more formal church structures. When one faces a crisis or wrestles with a sin, the group can respond immediately, rather than having to wait for an official program or lesson or a pastor's sermon to touch on the problem.

Jesus' Body on Earth

Christ first dwelled within the body shaped by the Father in the womb of Mary. His ministry then continued through the new Body, which replaced the first one. That new Body would have all the faculties and resources of a human body, plus all the eternal power and reality of the Godhead. Christ's indwelling spirit in the new Body would assure this would happen.

Matthew mentioned in 12:18 the prophesy of Isaiah,

Behold, My Servant whom I have chosen; My Beloved in whom My soul is well-pleased; I will put My Spirit upon Him, and He shall proclaim justice to the Gentiles.

The beginning of that ministry to the Gentiles was launched in a region where they were a distinct minority. The completion of His ministry would require Jesus to dwell in all the world throughout all generations, in every "kingdom" Satan would establish on the continents of the earth. He accomplished His task by creating His own Body from human bodies specially selected for this purpose. How simple was this task for the One who had spoken all things into existence by His Word!

Jesus personally named His new Body. He called it "the church" (*ecclesia*), meaning "the called-out ones." These special treasures would be indwelled by Him. Through their bodies He would perform His ministry. All the supernatural power of the Godhead would flow into and through them, even as rivers of water spring up from an artesian well.

He referred to the "called out ones" three times before His death. On the first occasion, He described them as a building under construction. He would be both the Foundation under it and the Builder of it:

. . . Jesus . . . asked his disciples, "Who do people say the Son of Man is?" They replied, "Some say John the Baptist; others say Elijah; and still others, Jeremiah or one of the prophets." "But what about you?" he asked. "Who do you say I am?" Simon Peter answered, "You are the Christ, the Son of the living God." Jesus replied, "Blessed are you, Simon son of Jonah, for this was not revealed to you by man, but by my Father in heaven. And I tell you that you are Peter, and on this rock I will build my church, and the gates of Hades will not overcome it. I will give you the keys of the kingdom of heaven; whatever you bind on earth will be bound in heaven, and whatever you loose on earth will be loosed in heaven."[5]

His other two references clearly point to the church as an intimate *community* of people. He anticipates the friction which could only exist in settings where people are living together in close relationships:

If your brother sins against you, go and show him his fault, just between the two of you. If he listens to you, you have won your brother over. But if he will not listen, take one or two others along, so that 'every matter may be established by the testimony of two or three witnesses.' If he refuses to listen to them, tell it to the church; and if he refuses to listen even to the church, treat him as you would a pagan or a tax collector. I tell you the truth, whatever you bind on earth will be bound in heaven, and whatever you loose on earth will be loosed in heaven. Again, I tell you that if two of you on earth agree about anything you ask for, it will be done for you by my Father in heaven. For where two or three come together in my name, there am I with them.[6]

For the *second* time, He has referred to the flow of power between heaven and earth through the activity of the church. Is it conceivable that He will not demonstrate the same eternal power in His new Body that He demonstrated in His first one? Of course not! He will continue to transform the poor, the captives, the blind, and the downtrodden. Thus, *every* member of His new Body will participate in the divine power required for ministry.

Notice carefully: in this Scripture, Jesus saw the church existing in communities as small as "two or three." Ponder the intimacy of personal relationships and the covenant commitments described by the procedures for handling conflict in this passage.[7]

Read the passage again: does it not verify the cell group concept of church life? M. Scott Peck rightly says,

Currently the Church is not only not the Body of Christ, it is not even a body, a community. It must become a community before it can serve as the Body of Christ.[8]

One may well be justified in wondering whether our Lord saw the church as anything, ever, larger than a cell group capable of experiencing true community. He Himself could have created large group structures: He never did. It was enough to address 5000; He chose to live with 12. He did not ignore the crowds, but he focused his energy on developing a small group. The basic building block of the Body, which would be inhabited by Jesus, would be composed of cells, not masses of people who do not experience community.

The Birth of the Church

When was the church born? The common teaching is that it was birthed at Pentecost by the Holy Spirit's action. Not so! The discussion of the birth of His new Body must have occupied a large portion of His dialogue on the Mount of Transfiguration with Moses and Elijah. The full meaning of His death would involve giving birth to His new Body. From the side of the first Adam had come his bride; even so, the second Adam's bride would come from His riven side.

A woman delivering a child would never endure birth pains as extreme as our Lord's suffering to birth the church. His Body became a battleground between the forces of heaven and hell. The only available link between a holy God and sinful men, He endured all which could be hurled against Him as Satan attempted to forever sever this connection. Jesus demonstrated for the church that "the gates of Hades will not overcome it." Satan became a defeated foe; Christ led captivity captive. When He cried, "It is finished!", the devil became a whimpering puppy, chained to the victory chariot of the King of Kings.

We must not detract from the crucifixion event by teaching His bride was birthed painlessly by the Holy Spirit in an upper room at the Feast of Pentecost. The whole point of Calvary is that filthy goblets cannot receive pure water until they have been cleansed. Jesus died to justify sinful men through His act of propitiation on the cross, to make them pure. The breaking of His body and the outpouring of His blood made peace with God possible for mankind, and it also made it possible for Him to indwell a pure, new Body. *He became the Head of His Body at the cross.*

The Beauty of the Lord's Supper

This is the very reason the Lord's Supper became precious to the cell groups from their very first gatherings. It was a constant reminder of the place and the cost of their birth and their life.

Well-meaning believers have often turned this ordinance into a trite, emotionless ritual of church life. In the method of intinction, people kneel in rows at an altar. There is no awareness of community as people come and go from seats to the kneeling pads. In the congregational method, the closest thing to intimacy among participants is impersonally passing a tray down the row to the person on your right. God intended it to be more.

This ordinance was instituted in the upper room of a house with 13 persons who had lived in community together. It was not meant to become a sacrament. It was not intended to be cut off from its meaning. It is the activity of a community, which means the activity of a cell group. Where is there any scriptural justification for its use in large clumps of Christians?

It was meant for use in *small groups* where there is community, where there is a sense of Christ as the Head. It takes the church back to its beginnings, reminding it over and over of the place and the costliness of its birth. It was, indeed, a unique "birthday party" as the early church shared it with one another.

In the early church it was a part of the Agape Feast held by the cells. In *Paul's Idea Of Community*, Robert Banks explains that each time a cell gathered, the common meal would begin with the breaking of the bread and close with the passing of the cup, a Passover tradition which had been carried on for centuries.[9] Thus, the "love feast" began and ended with a reminder that the life of this *ecclesia* began at the cross.

The Body Is a Battleground

If, in Christ's first body He suffered all that we suffer, it must be obvious that His new Body will also know suffering. The new Body, the church, is to be a battleground. The struggle between the forces of Christ and Satan will take place in it. "Onward, Christian Soldiers" sounded this note in earlier years. In contemporary praise music, the theme has been picked up in "God's got an army, marching through the land." We cannot recognize the validity of a church which insulates itself against conflict:

> Beloved, do not be surprised at the fiery ordeal among you, which comes upon you for your testing, as though some strange thing were happening to you; but to the degree that you share the sufferings of Christ, keep on rejoicing, so that also at the revelation of His glory, you may rejoice with exultation.[10]

The conflict is with Satan, who is determined to devour the Bride. One does not penetrate the kingdoms of this world without facing conflict. The good news we bring is that the greatest among us is the one who serves. Every world system teaches that's a lie, that the greatest is the one who sits at the head of the table. That conflicts! In fact, our good news "turns the world upside down!"

When the church fails to enter the conflict, battles rage within the lives of individuals who are captives of Beelzebub. When the church does not storm the gates of hell to release captives, their misery is our responsibility. One example of this is the way the church treats the "problem" of homosexuals by speaking hatefully of them from the pulpit, snubbing them if they attend services and freezing them out if they try to become active participants in the life of the church after conversion.

It is the task of the church to enter into conflict. That's done by cell groups in far greater depth than possible in large groups.

This was graphically illustrated in Abidjan, Cote d' Ivoire, at an Easter harvest retreat held by the massive cell group church, the Yopougon Baptist Church and Mission. Tens of thousands attended the retreat, among them more than 15,000 who would be converted. That West African culture is strongly dominated by witch doctors and the worship of demons. Thousands of women sacrifice a goat to a demon when desiring to become pregnant, pledging to dedicate the child to the evil spirit when it is born. Youngsters are taught to worship demons from their earliest childhood.

We were introduced to 100 teams who were prepared to minister to persons who might manifest demonic activity during the services. As we began to praise, unbelievers in the audience began to scream and writhe on the ground, overcome by the conflict between the demons living within them and the power of the Holy Spirit around them. The teams ran into the crowd and carried the demon-possessed to an area reserved for ministry activity.

I observed those precious Christians as they worked with those possessed. Eighty percent of them had themselves been delivered. The tormented would roll back their eyeballs until only the whites could be seen. They would scream most tragically as demons within resisted the attempt to expel them.

How precious was the release experienced by those who had been screaming just hours before! As I saw these same people the next day, "clothed and in their right minds," I longed for the church worldwide to become engaged in the spiritual warfare that can heal adulterous lives and restore stormy marriages, heal diseases, and generally set people free!

As I recall those experiences, I realize that only small groups can deal with the problems in those lives. It took all five members of the group to assist the burdened person. These deliverance cells have become for me a symbol of what Christ wants His Body to be doing. The setting free of prisoners, the declaration of the Good News to the poor, the recovery of sight by the blind is a team effort.

Preparation for the Coming of the Body

After His resurrection, He breathed on the disciples, telling them to receive the Holy Spirit:

> Again Jesus said, "Peace be with you! As the Father has sent me, I am sending you." And with that he breathed on them and said, "Receive the Holy Spirit. If you forgive anyone his sins, they are forgiven; if you do not forgive them, they are not forgiven."[11]

The word "As" in this passage is an essential connection between Jesus' mission on earth and their continuation of it. The disciples did not ask for the Spirit to be given to them; the act was Jesus' decision! He put His own life's breath into their bodies. They were thus linked to Him as the new Body He was to enter. Note that His focus in this Scripture is related to the *mission, not personal sanctification*. Jesus had prayed in John 17 that they, along with all believers, should not be taken out of the world, but be protected from the evil one. He now directly connects their receiving of the Spirit to the harvesting of unforgiven sinners. The word "breathed" used here is not used in any other place in the New Testament and is identical to the word used in the Greek Septuagint in Genesis 2:7:

> Even as God breathed into Adam's nostrils the breath of human life, so Christ breathed into them the life of His Spirit.

When Jesus ascended to glory, He removed the human body He had inhabited since his birth in Bethlehem. He instructed 120 of his followers, including the 11 disciples, to await the baptism with the Holy Spirit. He would soon minister in the world through His new Body! He told them it would happen "in a few days."

Community in the Body of Christ

Why did they have to wait? Could not the Holy Spirit have come upon them right away? No. Something had to happen first: they had to become bonded into a community. Meanwhile, God's Spirit was patiently poised in the heavenlies, ready to give life to Christ's new Body.

These men and women shared their lives together for ten days in the upper room of a wealthy man's home. They didn't listen to sermons, nor did they organize Bible studies. There was no formal agenda. They had each other; their fellowship with one another was the essential ingredient of their time together. Their ten days of sharing together was God's way of helping acquaintances become a *family*. There could not be church until there was *community*.

We may surmise they would naturally form themselves into small groups during those ten days. That's what naturally happens when 120 people gather, without formal structures, in one room. People must have moved from group to group as the days passed. They developed intimacy with all of the others as they spent those days together, sharing information about their lives, their families, and their contacts with Jesus. They also shared their pain, their heartaches, their problems. As they did so, they moved closer and closer to the goal Christ had for them: they were "in one accord."

I can imagine the disciples over in one corner, trying to piece together the truths Jesus had taught them. As new insights came to them, they probably summoned the whole group to hear what they were discovering.

Perhaps Peter jumped to his feet shouting, "That's it! That's what He meant! How could we have been so blind?" The room would be silenced by his sudden outbreak, and he would excitedly tell them what the disciples had just realized. Things of the Spirit blended into things of the Body and the soul as they ate, shared, and prayed together. A Sabbath would come and go as they were together. Some would go out to bring food back; others briefly ran necessary errands or perhaps cared for family needs. The focus in the room always remained on their life together. (Was it in this setting that the first Agape Feasts took place, as they followed Jesus' instructions to "do this in remembrance of me"?)

Day by day, an extended family was being shaped from diverse backgrounds. Their lifestyle, which would suddenly proliferate into 300 or more cell groups, was being learned in the same way Jesus had taught His disciples: by living together.

Power for Ministry

Then, it happened! As hundreds, even thousands, filled the streets for the Day of Pentecost, the clear sky resounded with the noise of a violent wind. How those on the outside responded to that noise we shall never know. Inside the upper room, we know exactly what took place. The same *Shekinah* Glory, which burned within a bush before Moses, now became tongues of fire which rested upon each person's head. The Glory entered their lives, and their spirits and words were under His control. Power for ministry had come to the Body of Christ.

John forecast this event by saying,

> I baptize you with water. But one more powerful than I will come, the thongs of whose sandals I am not worthy to untie. He will baptize you with the Holy Spirit and with fire.[12]

They had waited as instructed, and they had literally received power when the Holy Spirit came on them. Clearly, the empowering was in connection with their mission: "you will be my witnesses in Jerusalem, and in all Judea and Samaria, and to the ends of the earth."

They knew immediately the identity of the One who had entered into them. They knew — in the same way a sleeping husband knows the familiar footsteps of his wife in the darkness of the night. They had walked, talked, eaten and spoken with Christ, and they knew He had come back to live within them. They were the first to be able to say,

> And we, who with unveiled faces all reflect the Lord's glory, are being transformed into his likeness with ever-increasing glory, which comes from the Lord, who is the Spirit.[13]

As they mingled with the crowd, speaking with a power which translated their words into the languages of the hearers, they were the first to declare,

> God has chosen to make known among the Gentiles the glorious riches of this mystery, which is Christ in you, the hope of glory.[14]

As Peter explained, the Feast of Pentecost has not yet completed its fulfillment: it merely began to be fulfilled at that time. The pouring out of the Spirit triggered 3,000 conversions in a few hours. Not yet a day old, the church had grown to 25 times its original size. It was learning quickly that the Bride could not set goals to be met. Rather, it would become the agent of supernatural activity as Christ continued to perform His ministry.

Peter's proclamation called for a response to the manifestation of the spiritual power they had observed. He simply said, "This is that . . ." The first "evangelistic sermon" was little more than an explanation of God-sent power.

The Bride's Lifestyle

Without delay, the life of the Bride became structured as cell church life. No one had to organize it, write a handbook, or even create a system. The pattern was adopted by all, and within 24 hours it was in full bloom. There was no need to elect anyone, select anyone, or ordain anyone:

> Those who accepted his message were baptized, and about three thousand were added to their number that day. They devoted themselves to the apostles' teaching and to the fellowship, to the breaking of bread and to prayer. Everyone was filled with awe, and many wonders and miraculous signs were done by the

apostles. All the believers were together and had everything in common. Selling their possessions and goods, they gave to anyone as he had need. Every day they continued to meet together in the temple courts. They broke bread in their homes and ate together with glad and sincere hearts, praising God and enjoying the favor of all the people. And the Lord added to their number daily those who were being saved.[15]

Salvation was definitely not a personal affair. Their priorities were to hear the apostles teach in the temple courts, and to fellowship, break bread (the Agape Feast), and pray, moving from house to house (Acts 5:42). They never stopped proclaiming Jesus as the Christ, and their meetings were always open to seekers and converts. Their love for each other was intense. Barnabas, from Crete, ordered a parcel of land he owned back home to be sold, giving the funds to aid other believers.

A common concern for the needy caused the distribution of possessions and money to be channeled through the Apostles. This policy was intended to avoid the embarrassment of directly giving or receiving assistance from other members of the cell. At the same time, they learned that the Spirit would focus on the fact that though their Lord "was rich, yet for their sakes he became poor, so that they through His poverty might become rich." They gave out of love, not obligation. We can only imagine the impact this witness had upon unbelievers!

The pooling of funds before distribution also caused one of the first problems: the Greek widows complained that they were not getting a fair share of food. The apostles rightly delegated the problem to a group of seven men with Greek names. Gradually, as needed, structures were created.

Most important, body life was composed of communities of cells, while miraculous acts continued to verify they had become the body in which Jesus lived. They lived in and out of each other's homes, and became true families of faith. The division between the natural and the supernatural did not exist for them — nor was there a separation between the secular and the sacred. Theirs was not a weekly meeting to be attended; it was the life of a spiritual family, and involved them in each other's lives on a day to day basis.

Conclusion

In Acts, the gospel has to break out of hindering traditions. Its last verse says of Paul: "Boldly and without hindrance he preached the kingdom of God and taught about the Lord Jesus Christ." Nonscriptural traditions have always been the enemy of the church. Hindrances to the development of community today must also be rejected.

Some will argue that their traditional church experiences community. I do not doubt that a degree of community exists. But God has much more in store. Cell groups are the best way true community can be experienced by all Christians.

It is not a "purist's dream" to suggest the church should re-structure itself around this truth. Rather, it is a return to a lifestyle which has been bastardized by centuries of unbiblical, crusted traditions that have kept people from encountering one another. The cell group is not just a portion of church life, to included among with a dozen other organizations. It is church life; it is the place of family and connection; and when it properly exists, all other competing structures are neither needed nor valid.

> A community should not be primarily a grouping of shocktroops, commandoes or heroes, but a gathering of people who want to be a sign that it is possible for men to live together, love each other, celebrate and work [together] . . . A community is a sign that love is possible in a materialistic world where people so often either ignore or fight each other.
>
> Christian communities cannot be outside society. They are not bolt-holes for the emotions, offering spiritual drugs to stave off the sadness of everyday life. They are not places where people can go to salve their consciences and retreat from reality into a world of dreams. They are places of resource, which are there to help people grow towards freedom, so that they can love as Jesus loves them. 'There is no greater love than to give one's life for one's friends.'
>
> • Jean Vanier

6

About Oikos . . .

To fully understand the importance of the cell group church, we must consider the word *oikos*, a Greek term that describes the basic building block of society. It appears throughout the New Testament and refers to the *personal community*, which exists for us all. It is translated into English as house or household. For example, in Acts 16: 31, Paul and Silas used it when they said, "Believe in the Lord Jesus, and you will be saved — you and your household."

Oikos: The World's Way of Forming Cell Groups for All

The *oikoses* each of us lives within are not large. We may know several dozen, even several hundred, people, but quality time spent with others is extremely limited — and only those to whom we devote quality time can be said to be a part of our *oikos*, our personal community.

Each of us has a primary group that includes some of our relatives and some of our friends who relate to us through work, recreation, hobbies, and neighbors. These are the people we talk to, relate to, and share with for at least a total of one hour per week.

It is most unusual to find a person who has as many as 20 people in his or her *oikos*. For many years, I have surveyed the sizes of the *oikoses* of those attending my seminars and classes. Christians usually average nine people, and a large percentage of them had not developed a single new *oikos* relationship in the past six months!

Life is made up of endless chains of *oikos* connections. Every person is already entwined in these relationships. If people are accepted into an *oikos*, they feel a security that does not exist when meeting a stranger.

In every culture of the world, the intimacy of *oikos* connections is considered to be sacred. The Chinese have a special word for close friendships, and such bonds are considered to be a sacred thing. In Argentina, I was shown a gourd and a metal tube with holes on one end of it for the drinking of *maté* tea. A most intimate *oikos* custom in their culture is sharing the *maté* by drinking from the same tube. Usually, the ceremony is limited to family members. The Argentine who explained this to me said, "Recently, I went to visit a friend who was sharing a gourd of *maté* with his wife and children. He paid me the highest honor by inviting me to participate."

Oikoses Vary With Emotional Strength

In *Pastor and Parish — A Systems Approach*, E. Mansell Pattison has examined this basic structure of human life in depth. He has sought to describe contemporary *oikos* relationships in psychological and sociological terms:

> I have found that the normal person has about twenty to thirty people in his or her psychosocial system. . . . There are typically about five or six people in each subgroup of family, relatives, friends, and work-recreation-church associates. About 60 percent of the people in this normal system interact with each other.

> In contrast, neurotics have only ten to twelve people in their psychosocial systems. Their systems include people who may be dead or live far away. . . . Only about 30 percent of the system is interconnected. It is as if the neurotic, having a variety of individual relationships, is like the hub of a wheel having spokes that radiate outward but are not connected by a rim. Thus the neurotic has an impoverished psychosocial system.

> For psychotics we get a third pattern. Here there are only four to five people in the system. The interpersonal relations are ambivalent and nonreciprocal. The system is 90 to 100 percent

interconnected. The psychotic is caught in an exclusive nonpermeable small system that is binding, constructive, and destructive.[1]

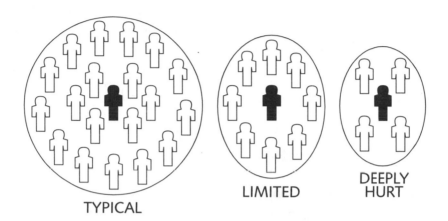

TYPICAL   LIMITED   DEEPLY HURT

Since the world began, men have always lived in *oikoses*. Every single culture, without exception, has them. The security of the individual is in the affirmation received by those who are significant in the *oikos*. In the earliest hours of childhood, the mother is the one who provides affirmation by her presence and her attention. As the child develops, this affirmation is received, or not received, by the other household members. Then the school teacher becomes a part of the *oikos*, and later it becomes the adolescent's *oikos* group which must approve him. In the workplace, affirmation is tied to promotions and raises in salary.

Each *oikos* becomes a part of a larger social structure, as we shall see in the next chapter. The important thing for us to grasp here is that every human being lives in a special, tiny world, often being forced to relate to people who are forced upon him or her by *oikos* structures. Today, the hurts of being thrust into a home where the mother is an alcoholic or the father is a daughter molester composes a significant ministry for cell group churches.

As you read this, consider the implications of this in your own life. Take a moment to write down the names of all the people you spend one full hour each week sharing with in a direct, person-to-person manner. (This hour can be accumulated a few minutes at a time, scattered over seven days, but it must be regular — and it must be face to face.)

Studies of American family life indicate that the typical father spends only seven minutes a day in direct communication with each of his children — a total of 49 minutes per week. That's not enough time to honestly include them in his *oikos*.

The overpowering impact of a limited few upon each of our lives must be considered. For example: who are the significant others in your own life, whose approval or disapproval is important to you? (I have counseled with those who are still trying to please a disapproving father, who has been dead for years.) Who do you fear may reject you, and who do you look to for affirmation? Meditating upon one's own *oikos* can bring great insights!

Christian Workers Have Oikoses Lacking Unbelievers

My own survey of this subject among Christian workers has revealed amazing facts. I have polled over 5,000 pastors, pastor's wives, church staff members, and missionaries in at least 30 countries. It is a rare thing to find those who are in "full-time Christian work" who have unbelievers in their primary *oikos*.

Unless she is employed in the secular world, the wife of a Christian worker is least likely to have a single contact with the unchurched. Her *oikos* is filled only with church people. On one occasion, an educational director of a large Fort Worth church put his head in his hands and wept with embarrassment as he realized he had spent his entire career within the confines of church work. He could not remember having an *oikos* with an unbeliever in it since he graduated from a secular college.

Consider the unbeliever with a well-established set of *oikos* connections, and the stranger from a local church knocking on his door to offer Christianity! Throughout this book, we shall return to that issue. It is critical to the matter of evangelism strategy. In a world of strangers, we ply our "soul winning" with little understanding of the nature of life for those we seek to reach.

Jesus Constantly Invaded Pagan Oikoses

While the church pulls people out of their *oikoses* and gives them membership in an organization which swallows them up, the New Testament reveals a different approach to people relationships. Jesus constantly did His work by invading *oikos* groups. He knew there was no other way to share the gospel except to penetrate these small clusters of people. It is obvious that each *oikos* is based in a house, not an institutional building. Thus, the Lord spent his time going from one house to another.

In Luke 19:2-5, we see Jesus making contact with Zacchaeus. He says to him, "Zacchaeus, . . . I must stay at your house today." In Luke 7:36-38, we find Him in the *oikos* of a Pharisee who has invited Him to have dinner with him. While He reclines at the table, a prostitute comes and pours perfume on His feet. What amazing examples of *oikos* penetration!

In Matthew 8:14, He enters Peter's house and heals one of the *oikos* members living there. In Matthew 9:10, He eats dinner with His disciples and many tax collectors and sinners at Matthew's house. Again, he penetrates an *oikos*; in Matthew 9:23 as He enters the ruler's house and sees the flute players and the noisy crowd. In Matthew 17:25, Peter finds Him in a Capernaum house, where Jesus speaks to him about paying taxes. We read in Mark 3:20 that Jesus entered a house, and a crowd gathered, "so that he and his disciples were not even able to eat." In Mark 7:17, He enters a house where His disciples quiz Him about a parable. In Mark 7:24, He enters a house to be alone, only to be swamped by a crowd who learned where He was staying. In Mark 9:33, He is in a Capernaum house when He asks the disciples, "What were you arguing about on the road?"

The Early Church Penetrated Oikoses, Too!

In Acts 5:42 we read that the early church went from house to house. In Acts 8:3, when Saul wanted to destroy the church, he knew where to find the people of God. We are told, "Going from house to house, he dragged off men and women and put them in prison."

It is interesting to see in Acts 10 how the Holy Spirit arranged for Peter to get from the house of Simon the Tanner to the residence of Cornelius, where his conversion took place. The penetration of *oikoses* is the pattern for ministry in the first century.

Conversions are frequently recorded as sweeping an entire *oikos* into the Kingdom. In Acts 16, both Lydia and the jailer are converted along with the members of their *oikos*. The first act of Lydia after her conversion was to invite Paul to stay at her house.

Rejection by One's Oikos for Becoming a Christian Is Painful

Jesus reminded us in Matthew 10:36 that following Him can be a costly decision: "a man's enemies will be the members of his own *oikos* . . ." Making a decision to follow Him can cause mayhem in relationships with primary people. This is why He said in Matthew 10:35, "For I have come to turn a man against his father, a daughter against her mother, a daughter-in-law against her mother-in-law . . ." In verse 37, he calls for a decision between the *oikos* and the Kingdom: "Anyone who loves his father or mother more than me is not worthy of me; anyone who loves his son or daughter more than me is not worthy of me . . ."

In Singapore, there is a Zone Pastor from a Hindu home. After his commitment was made to follow Christ, the *oikos* descended on him with wrath. His uncle waited until he was present to say to his father, "Why do you allow your son to disgrace us all like this?" Another example in contemporary Southeast Asia is a young physician who followed the Lord at the price of his Muslim family declaring him dead and buried. *Oikoses* can be ruthless when one chooses another path for life.

Our Lord's Body Is Called an "Oikos"

However, there is a very special *oikos* for those who have faced the ultimate rejection. Hebrews 3:6 says, "But Christ is faithful as a son over God's *oikos*. And we are his *oikos*, if we hold on to our courage and the hope of which we boast." Consider additional Scriptures that speak of this truth found in 1 Peter 4:17, 1 Timothy 3:15, Ephesians 2:19, and 1 Peter 2:5:

> For it is time for judgment to begin with the *oikos* of God; and if it begins with us, what will the outcome be for those who do not obey the gospel of God?

> . . . if I am delayed, you will know how people ought to conduct themselves in God's *oikos*, which is the church of the living God, the pillar and foundation of the truth.

Consequently, you are no longer foreigners and aliens, but fellow citizens with God's people and members of God's *oikos* . . .

. . . you also, like living stones, are being built into a spiritual *oikos* to be a holy priesthood, offering spiritual sacrifices acceptable to God through Jesus Christ.

The concept of *oikos* describing the church should make us recognize the significance of the cell as the Basic Christian Community. Scripture refers to the early Christians as members of this spiritual *oikos* by speaking of those who have come to faith by family units, rather than just by personal commitments:

Crispus, the synagogue ruler, and his entire oikos believed in the Lord. . . . Greet also the church that meets at their house. . . . Greet those who belong to the *oikos* of Aristobulus. . . . Greet those in the *oikos* of Narcissus who are in the Lord. . . . some from Chloe's *oikos* have informed me that there are quarrels among you. . . . Yes, I also baptized the *oikos* of Stephanas. . . . You know that the *oikos* of Stephanas were the first converts in Achaia. . . . Aquila and Priscilla greet you warmly in the Lord, and so does the church that meets at their *oikos*. . . . the saints send you greetings, especially those who belong to Caesar's *oikos*. . . . Give my greetings to . . . Nympha and the church in her *oikos*. . . . May the Lord show mercy to the *oikos* of Onesiphorus. . . . Greet Priscilla and Aquila and the *oikos* of Onesiphorus.[2]

Truly, the early church thought about the chains of *oikoses* to be won while they simultaneously rejoiced that God had formed them into Basic Christian Communities. For the church to live at *oikos* level was certainly God's plan, and assuredly the pattern which was followed until men's carnality got in the way.

Two Members of the Oikos Family

Two concepts are shared in the Scriptures which directly tie to our consideration of the church as *oikos*. The first of these words is *oikonomos*.

This word appears in an *oikos* context in a comment made by Jesus in Matthew 24:45:

> Who then is the faithful and wise *oikonomos* [servant], whom the master has put in charge of the servants in his household to give them their food at the proper time?

The *oikonomos* was the servant in an *oikos* who was assigned the oversight of physical needs within the household. He had direct access to his master's funds and was responsible for providing physical necessities "at the proper time." In the early church, the *oikonomos* spirit invaded the cell groups, who shared their possessions as physical needs became known. The concept of "stewardship" as we know it today goes far astray from the spirit of the *oikonomos* in the house churches. (See my chapter in *The Shepherd's Guidebook*, entitled "Too Much Month At The End Of The Money.")

The second word is *oikodomeo*, discussed heavily in other parts of this guidebook. It shares similarities with its first cousin, *oikonomos*. Both are words directly related to the *oikos*, and both have a stewardship in mind in which God provides what His people need. However, *oikodomeo* does not deal with physical needs: it zeros in on spiritual necessities. Thus, the flow of spiritual gifts is emphasized in connection with its application.

In both cases, the heart of the Christian life is not related to a word for "Temple," or "Synagogue," or "Church Building." As the basic fabric of human life is embedded in the *oikos*, even so the life of the Body of Christ is to be *oikos* based.

In a later chapter, we shall consider the assignment of Jesus to penetrate unreached people through using the *oikos* principle. Let's move now to a consideration of the "kingdoms of this world" which embrace the *oikoses*.

Putting Cells
in the Kingdoms

While developing an urban strategy in Brussels a few years ago, I discovered *A Gospel for the Cities* by Benjamin Tonna.[1] This Catholic scholar opened my eyes to the areas of *social systems* and *social structures* as he applied the concepts to church life. I took his chapters back to the Scriptures and found a new awareness of why God is creating cell group church structures in today's urbanizing world.

In Matthew 4, Jesus is being tempted by Satan in the wilderness. In verses 8-9, the two are standing on a very high mountain, and Jesus is shown "all the kingdoms of the world and their splendor." Satan is proud of his kingdoms, and assumes they will also appeal to Jesus. He offers them all to Jesus if He will only bow down and worship him. (Imagine the importance Satan placed upon the Son of God bowing down before him! *He was willing to surrender all the kingdoms in exchange for being worshiped by Jesus.*)

Jesus didn't share Satan's value system. He knew something Satan didn't: the Kingdom of God was about to be established. He had come to invade the kingdoms of this world and to release their captives. He flatly refused the offer.

As we reflect on this encounter, we begin to realize that Satan intentionally created kingdoms for men which promise "splendor" as the carrot-on-a-stick, suspended one inch in front of their noses, tantalizing them to grasp it. Grandeur and magnificence was Beelzebub's great desire; why should not all men want it as much as he did?

Appealing to this basic desire within men to become significant, the evil one placed them in cells — *prison cells* called "kingdoms." It's the task of the church to set these captives free. There's a radical difference between the kingdoms created by Satan and the one Jesus came to plant among men. Grasping this difference helps us understand why a new lifestyle for the church is necessary to impact the urban world.

How Satan Created the "Kingdoms of this World"

Satan launched each of his kingdoms by urging clans to understand the reasons for their existence and what the world around them signified. He then craftily manipulated their conclusions, their "worldviews," defined by Kraft as the "culturally structured assumptions, values, and commitments underlying a people's perception of REALITY."[2] (We may also refer to worldview as their basic belief system.)

> WORLDVIEW

Within every kingdom, people next built a value system on the foundation of their worldview. These enmeshed values encompassed all the events of life: conception, birth, puberty, marriage, work ethic, wealth, power, death, and scores of other areas. These values permeated their daily life. With each thread woven into their values, the way to attain "splendor" was further spelled out. Without exception, "sitting at the head of the table" became a common goal in every separate kingdom.

> VALUE SYSTEM

Exactly what was considered valuable varied from kingdom to kingdom. The discrepancies between these value systems kept kingdoms from merging, or even making it possible for people to easily transfer from one kingdom to another. Geography and language also separated people. Satan wanted to divide his blinded subjects forever, because, above all else, *he is the archenemy of community.*

When Kingdoms Clash

Malaysia is a classic example of what can happen when two kingdoms try to live together with different value systems. Malays are an easygoing, friendly, communal kingdom of people. They live in *kampongs* and wear *sarongs* made from a simple tube of cloth. Fish from the nearby sea, bananas, coconuts, and spices, along with noodle or rice based foods, make up their diet. Working day and night to store up gold is patently absurd to them. Having time to relax, be at home with family and visit friends is considered to have great worth. They are a simple people, worshipping Allah and praying five times a day.

Enter now a kingdom of Chinese immigrants. These people have a different value system, and they place great worth in gaining personal wealth. They are not too interested in relaxing or visiting with others. They want to have expensively tailored clothes, fine homes, and many servants. They worship the ancestors, Buddha, and the scores of idols they brought with them from the "middle kingdom." In a relatively short period of time, they developed huge tin mines, amassed great wealth, and began to control the economic base of the nation.

Conflict was inevitable! The Malay's abhorrence of idols, the differences in values of all types, finally caused political crises. *Bumiputra* was passed by the Malay-dominated government to force the Chinese industrialists to surrender their power to Malays. The two cultures live today with deep cleavages between them. The kingdoms of this world do not possess the potential for developing community.

Satan is a devouring lion, a liar, and a thief. The deception with which he brainwashed the kingdom-founders totally eliminated their awareness of the living God. They chose to worship snakes, animals,

> RELIGIOUS
> STRUCTURES

even chunks of carved wood or rock. They believed all kinds of spirits surrounded them. They "exchanged the truth of God for a lie." Not a single worldview in any of the kingdoms of this world left a place for Jehovah among their deities.[3]

Westerners are ignorant of the permeating power of world religions and the way they fill their adherents with fear. In an unforgettable historical novel about life in a Calcutta slum called *City of Joy*, Dominique Lapierre explains:

> . . . these people lived in a state of osmosis with their deities. [Remember] the role these gods played in everyday life. Any intervention of fortune, good or bad: work, rain, hunger, a birth, a death — in fact everything was ascribed to the gods. . . . No other people honours its gods and its prophets as fervently as does the population of Calcutta — despite the fact that the heavens often seem to have completely abandoned the city to its

tragic destiny. Every day, or almost every day, the slum and other areas of the city resounded with the noise of some procession bearing witness to the mystical marriage of a people and its creator.[4]

Are the Western kingdoms any different? Only in the way the entrapped people act out their religious customs. Many church members in America and Britain also seek to manipulate their deity, cajoling God to heal or provide success in their business ventures, or to protect their family. They have used the God of the Christian religion to get what they want, often promising Him large tithes if He will make them successful and rich.

Distinct in the more developed nations is the worship of abstract things rather than carved idols. Many people bow at the shrines of their employer, their greed, or power to control wealth. They are just as pagan as Calcutta's idol worshippers, no matter how well they dress or how often they attend church. "Splendor" is always, in all cultures, the carrot-on-the-stick!

Each person entering a kingdom by birth must be taught how to properly act out the values. Teaching the behavior expected in the kingdom is important in child-raising. Parents make comments to their children

ALL MUST "ACT" RIGHT

like, "We don't act like that in this family!" Discipline and the withholding of affirmation enforces the training of youngsters to act by the code of the kingdom.

Those entering kingdoms through marriage, adoption of a new religion, or both, must also be carefully tutored on how they should "act." They may be suspect for years to come by those who were born into the kingdom: "Is that person really one of us?"

Affirmation is a reward, and separation is a punishment for not "acting right." This destructive behavior is found in all cultures. *Satan's great lie is that your significance depends solely on your performance.*[5]

REWARD & PUNISHMENT

The gnawing fear of rejection — not only by the family unit but by the kingdom — creates prison bars far more powerful than steel! Satan has kept his subjects in his control by instilling them with *fear*.

While walking the beaches in Thailand, I came across a youth hostel run by the Catholic church. I sought to visit with an Irish nun and was quickly frozen out by her attitude. Finally I said, "Sister, in our lifetime can two people like us ever be friends?" She said to me, "In my lifetime, this is the first time I have ever talked face to face with a Protestant!"

Ours is a world where people live in prisons. Reaching others must be done with an understanding of what Satan has done to stop it from happening. I have often probed those who have converted to Christ from another faith. In many of these interviews, I discovered they were expulsions from their normal kingdom, searching for another kingdom where they might find significance. While this is certainly not true of all, it is a definite factor in studying the source of conversions.

Take the teenager, for example, who is drawn into drugs. She is gradually rejected by her parents and all others in her *oikos*. In limbo, she has two choices: live with other addicts, or find someone to take her in. She may marry to escape (thousands do), or she may search for the true significance for living. Christ is her answer, and we should rejoice to draw in the lost sheep. It's an important task for the people of God to find and affirm such persons — *but there are many, many more we will reach through the mighty power of God using the kingdom power and Jesus' strategy for the cell group church.*

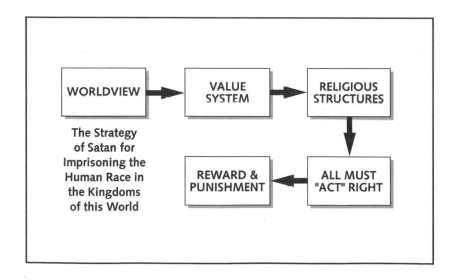

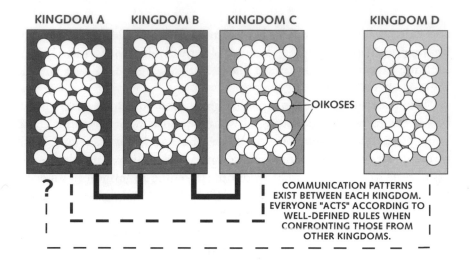

Life in Rural Kingdoms

The diagram above shows people living in kingdoms in a small town. Life here is essentially rural and unsophisticated, providing few diversions for inhabitants. Note that each Kingdom contains many *oikos* groups of approximately 15 people.

In the diagram above, Kingdom A contains immigrants from Poland. They have brought their culture, their tastes for foods, and their religion with them. They moved near the small steel mill on the west side of town. All the Polish men work together there.

Kingdom B is a collection of Irish immigrants. They migrated in a stream from their homeland when starvation forced them to do so. They are farming in the area, raising corn and other vegetables. They share only their religion with the Polish but have created a new parish with a priest imported from Dublin.

Kingdom C is made up of Dutch settlers, sharing neither culture, food, nor religion with A or B. They are dairy farmers. The manure from their cattle wafts from the east side of town on some days, making their presence known to those living in the other kingdoms. They are staunch Reformed Church people, faithfully attending the church they erected near the town square.

These groups all send their children to the public school. The second generation from each kingdom has been drilled by the parents about the way Polish or Irish or Dutch people act (there's that word again!) when meeting people from another kingdom. Each child dutifully follows the communication pattern taught at home, choosing close friends from the "right crowd" at school.

Events like a high school football game draw people from all three kingdoms, and while they do sit in kingdom groups in the bleachers, they shout for the home team and backslap each other when their sons have won a game. Peace and tranquillity reigns, except when a Polish girl is courted by a Dutch boy. Both of them are roundly censured until they end their innocent affair. It's not "acting right" for a Reformed boy to go out with a Catholic girl!

A new factory comes to town. It's going to provide specialized engineering for the automobile industry. A subdivision is erected to house the nearly 300 families who move in from many parts of the nation. Catholics in the new group find a warmer welcome in the Irish parish than the Polish and gradually assimilate into the church.

Many in the new subdivision are evangelical Christians. They erect a spartan building for worship in the middle of the subdivision. They form kingdom D. They are very active in their church life, and many quickly gain significance through elected positions. Many special Bible teachers come to visit them. Between work, family, and church, they have no time to meet neighbors.

When Pastor Brown pressed the new congregation to take a special "soul winning course," nearly everyone attended. They were shown how to use a small booklet to explain the "plan of salvation," and everyone memorized a brief presentation of how to accept Christ. At the end of the course, they went out two by two to knock on doors and "win the lost." Some were assigned to each of the three kingdoms. They used maps to find the streets.

Their visits were coolly received. Not much was known about this new Evangelical church by the Polish, the Irish, or the Dutch. Mrs. Zwilski listened attentively; but when pushed to pray, she thought, "What would my Polish friends think of me if I left our parish? I'm loved and respected there. I barely know these people. Would they even accept me as one of them?" Slam! The prison bars closed tightly around her, and the visitors left saddened by her lack of interest in the state of her soul.

After making three visits each, the hardy group of evangelists returned to report their results. A team that had visited their next door neighbors found a woman who was almost in tears. The adjustment to the new town and her husband's heavy work schedule had made her very lonely. Although she had been raised in a family that never attended church, she had been considering visiting one. She was most receptive and made a commitment to receive Christ. All rejoiced at the success of their training course.

The Evangelical congregation concluded that those in Kingdoms A, B, and C were not "under conviction" and that they would find their "prospects" in their own area.

What Happens when a Kingdom "E" Person Appears?

The problem of how to "act" when meeting someone from a strange new kingdom can be a serious one. If no clear guidelines have been set, one of three possibilities will be selected. The kingdom person can *avoid, attack, or adapt.*

My Houston banker and I had a conflict over the Vietnamese that suddenly migrated into our area. Having lived and ministered among them in Saigon, I knew they were impeccable about meeting financial obligations; yet the banker refused to extend them credit. When he met the first one, his mind computed: "small, dark skinned, broken English, poorly dressed — like the Mexican illegals who walk in here asking for car loans." It took heavy pressure from our church before he agreed to make loans to our Vietnamese members. After a few months, he took me out for lunch in appreciation for changing his mind. Not a single loan made to these immigrants had defaulted. He just didn't know how to "act" when meeting people from a strange kingdom.

When pastoring "P.B.D. style," I often visited unbelievers on visitation night. All too often, as I went through Scriptures to explain how they might become Christians, they would interrupt to say something absurd like, "You know, my mother's grandfather was a Methodist minister." *It irked me!* I was talking to them about eternal life, and they wanted to talk about their family tree. I would mumble, "How interesting!" and return to the gospel presentation.

I didn't understand what was going on in the other person's mind: "Have I ever known anyone like this guy? None of my kingdom friends 'act' like him. Here he sits with his Bible open, preaching to me. *Strange!* Wait a minute — my mother used to tell me about her grandfather, and how he used to read the Bible to her. Wow! I didn't think I had any sort of link to this guy — but I do!" In his excitement over his discovery, he interrupted me, certain I would be delighted to know that one of his ancestors had lived in my kingdom. I was too foolish to realize what was going on and offended him by not caring about his discovery!

Can a Church Become a "Kingdom of this World?"

In the illustration about the new evangelical church that came to town, that's exactly what happened. It became a human kingdom, isolating its people from the other kingdoms. With an evangelical worldview and value system, the pastor and members taught their children and incoming people how to act. The rewards for "acting right" included being elected to the distinguished position of Deacon, or head of the Sunday school. Those who truly loved their Lord also loved the affirmation and significance they were given in Kingdom D. They lived insulated from the other kingdoms, all the time "doing the work of the Lord," blissfully unaware they were not doing His work at all.

Their foray into the other three kingdoms to evangelize didn't take their own kingdom life into account. Inviting those in other kingdoms to make a decision to accept the Lord involves converts facing the displeasure of their own *oikos*, and those in contiguous *oikoses*, and potential expulsion from their kingdom. Few converts will be made when people are required to change from one kingdom to another.

It's a brutal but true fact: *most churches have become just one more of the kingdoms of this world.* We shall not deny they have a proper theology, but their ecclesiology violates the clear teachings of our Lord, and Satan gleefully imprisons them in their own kingdom structure.

Kingdoms in the Urbanized World

Before we fully discuss that last statement, we must learn about a recent development in the history of man: the impact of *urbanization* on the kingdoms of this world. Let's imagine Mary has left the small town previously described. She's going to go to work in the city, 300 miles away. She has contacts with two other girls from her high school class who have found her a secretary's job. They have invited her to share their apartment. Being Polish, Mary feels a bit insecure about moving in with a Dutch and an Irish girl. That was only the beginning: in the office, one of the other secretaries is Jordanian and another is a black from Harlem. She quickly discovers her boss is a hard-swearing atheist. She is the only Catholic in the business.

Suddenly, all kingdom boxes have been mixed together for her! In her confusion, she decides to attend the local parish church. She gets up on Sunday morning (her roommates quit attending church long ago) and goes to mass. The priest seems to be unconcerned about personally knowing her, and the sanctuary has only a few dozen people in it. She goes away deeply disappointed, deciding not to return. Without her family to monitor her churchgoing, there's really no reason for her to do anything she dislikes doing.

She wanders through the quiet city streets, enjoying the sun and the sabbath lack of traffic. She crosses a boulevard — and suddenly everything has changed! She has entered an area that is no longer "middle class" like the district where she lives. She's in an elite section. Expensive cars are parked at the curbs, and apartments have uniformed doormen. She reads the names on the door plates of town houses: the Zwinkowskis live next to the Fields, and next to them are the O'Haras and the Al-Aqbars. Feeling she doesn't "belong" in this area, she retraces her steps. It was the last time she ever ventured into that district.

Like all city dwellers, she carves out a portion of the city that provides for her needs. Within a few months, a few blocks of the area where she lives and works becomes her habitat. The shopping mall, the theater, the local tavern where her age group congregates until midnight, and a few other locations have become the entire "city" for her.

She dates a young man who works in the shipping department where she works. She discovers he has used drugs to find the "ultimate reason" for living. She refuses his offer to "take a trip" with him. Another man comes into her life: after the third date, she discovers he's not really divorced. He still has a wife and three kids. She is disgusted by the news.

The city is making her suspicious of people. She withdraws more and more into a *restricted community* of people she feels she can trust. Loneliness becomes a large problem for her.

One of the other secretaries encourages her to "try astrology." She is also told about the Koran and the Book of Mormon. She investigates them all. Slowly, slowly, she begins to create her own private religion. It contains fragments of her Catholic faith, but also includes Eastern mysticism and concepts from the cults and the television preachers who talk to her about "prosperity truths" in their programs.

Wanting to expand her skills and earn more money, she decides to attend a community college and take computer courses. She meets a number of other young people who are also interested in computers, and she quickly forms friendships with them. After-class gatherings at a nearby lounge encase her in a group of eight people who enjoy serious conversations but also party a great deal. She finally moves in with one of them, a Jewish boy who offers her free rent if she will share his utilities and their food.

When he asks her to marry him, she struggles with what her family will say — but elopes anyway. She shrugs off the hostility she feels when she takes him to her town to visit: after all, she doesn't have to put up with her Polish relatives for very long before returning to the big city.

Urban Roles Are Acquired; Rural Roles Are Assigned

She had received her kingdom prison cell as a child from her parents. Her new prison cell was one she slowly developed in the context of the impersonal city. That is the important difference between rural and urban structures.

In her home town, relatives and other members of her Polish kingdom monitored her movements and urged her to live by the agreed-upon values. In the city, no one cared if she used drugs, stayed out all night, joined a Protestant church, or switched jobs. Emotional isolation and living without primary relationships are commonplace among city dwellers.[6]

How, then, do people in the city find relationships that are meaningful? They often find others with common interests or performing similar functions. Christians should understand this and take advantage of their opportunity to penetrate *oikoses* by targeting interests, needs, and responsive groups. Such persons exist in every sector of a major city.

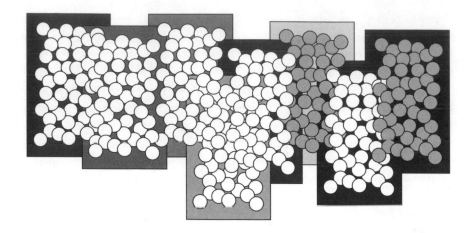

The Kaleidoscope of "Kingdoms" in the Urban Setting

In this illustration we see the urban culture. The boundary lines between kingdoms are confused. There may be an Italian section or a Mexican section, but the blur of people with different religions, foods, and values is unmistakable.

Old and new values swarm around urbanites. Every vice known to man has advocates. Subcultures for deviant groups produce disciples which must be tolerated. Homosexuals may live next door. One cannot trust neighbors who have never even been met. Thefts of homes and cars cause residents to live in fear behind locked doors and burglar alarms. Personal privacy is their only way to handle the chaos of an unharmonized society. "Privatized religion," as well as the rest of life, becomes a normal lifestyle. One's religious views are seldom revealed to others. They may have absurd logical contradictions, but they are never scrutinized for validity.

My urban strategy study of Brussels caused me to see the loss of respect for the church which exists in the city. Of all the institutions of the community, the religious ones had the least impact. Since Catholicism claimed 95% of the population, I interviewed a delightful bishop who spoke frankly to me. He shared how Cardinal Suenin had come to direct the parishes of the city, distressed because only 2% of Catholics ever darkened the door of a church except for the "four seasons" of their lives: christenings, first communions, marriages, and burials. (At the time, there were only 300 Belgians attending Evangelical churches in the city!) Their survey of the population revealed a "couldn't care less" attitude among Catholics. Citizens were filled with stories about corruption among the priests, and they bitterly resented the pressure to pay, pay, pay into church coffers. The institutional church was prehistoric, out of touch.

Realizing the people's cynicism could not be overcome by building-centered activities, Cardinal Suenin encouraged "Basic Christian Communities" to form in home settings. He urged the laity to develop and lead these cells, assigning priests to guide the lay leadership. For the first time in a century, Catholics in Brussels began to be directly involved in some form of church life. The bishop who shared all this with me had a special light in his eyes as he spoke of that "golden age" of the church when, in a city of 1,000,000 people, up to 5% of the parishioners became active.

For the first time, the people of Brussels had found community in their religion, and they flocked to it. In the estrangement of a European city where isolation was rampant, they had found something in religion that met their deepest need. To be sure, the attendance at formal services in the church buildings was only slightly impacted by these home meetings, but something important was finally happening in the church.

Sad to say, tradition won again! Suenin was replaced by a new cardinal, who set about to switch the direction of the cells away from Bible study, prayer, and sharing. He required all of the cells to get involved in projects related to social justice — and the groups died away.

Evangelicals in the city never did understand this resurgence in the formal church. If they had, they could have gleaned a large number of people who had once again been disappointed by the religion of their forefathers. To this day, Brussels remains one of the neediest mission fields in the world.

What Is the Place of the P.B.D. Church in the City?

How do church structures, shaped in the small town or rural area, fare in the city? *Very poorly.* They are out of step with this complex culture, often pastored by a man who himself has lived his life in a small town. He may have received limited orientation for his urban assignment. He is frustrated by the lack of effectiveness of his work. Programs, which were so adequate in his town pastorates, don't attract city dwellers.

While some metropolitan churches have tried to solve their problem by becoming "sanctuaries of safety" within the city, the problem of ministering in a diverse society of many languages, cultures, and value systems, is a serious one.

The P.B.D. church, which flourished so well in the simple structure of the small town, is in trouble. If it locates in an ethnic area, it might survive as in a village, servicing a special group. If, however, people of all languages and races mingle in the community around the church structure, the problems are immense. In a World Class City as many as 93 languages are spoken. As ethnics migrate into new areas, churches caught in their path lose their existing congregations and seem impotent to reach the new settlers. Churches dry up and blow away in these circumstances.

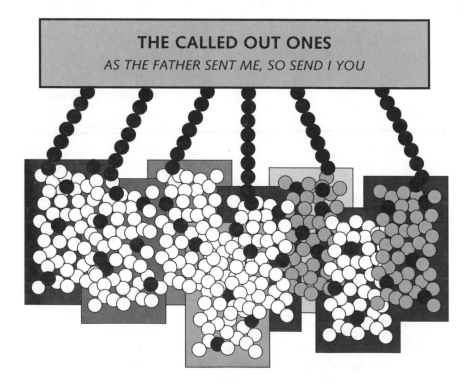

THE CALLED OUT ONES
AS THE FATHER SENT ME, SO SEND I YOU

The Cell Group Church Is a Viable Urban Model

In many parts of the earth today, cities are being penetrated effectively by "Basic Christian Communities," the cell groups of churches which bury themselves within the kingdoms of this world. This is precisely what Jesus meant when He said,

> The kingdom of heaven is like yeast that a woman took and mixed into a large amount of flour until it worked all through the dough.[7]

Over and over again, scores and scores of times, I have observed and participated in the penetration of all the social structures of urban society through cell groups. In Dallas, Ruth and I chaperoned an Arab lad and a Jewess who had both found Christ in a cell group and who had fallen in love. In Houston, we saw homosexuals and an atheist school teacher face their need for Christ through a Share Group determined to penetrate the unchurched. Cells with physicians, cells with politicians, cells with pimps, were all experienced by *The People Who Care*. Dion Robert in Abidjan, Ivory Coast, has networked firemen to firemen, policemen to policemen, and slum dwellers to slum dwellers through his cell groups.

Unreached People Are Imprisoned in Tiny Oikoses

I want to extend a quote that appears on page 134. It presents extremely significant data. E. Mansell Pattison helps us understand why it is so crucial for cell group churches to be formed. They are the only possible way to penetrate the lives of unreached people:

> I have found that the normal person has about twenty to thirty people in his or her psychosocial system *[oikos]*. . . . About 60 percent of the people in this normal system interact with each other. . . . In contrast, neurotics have only ten to twelve people in their psychosocial systems. Their systems include people who may be dead or live far away. . . . Only 30 percent of the system is interconnected. It is as if the neurotic, having a variety of individual relationships, is like the hub of a wheel having spokes

that radiate outward but are not connected by a rim. Thus the neurotic has an impoverished psychosocial system.

For psychotics we get a third pattern. Here there are only four to five people in the system. The interpersonal relationships are ambivalent and nonreciprocal. The system is 90 to 100 percent interconnected. The psychotic is caught in an exclusive nonpermeable small system that is binding, constructive, and destructive.[8]

Think of it! The more a person is hurting, the more he or she needs Christ, the less possibility there is that the people of God will make contact!

Could anyone not believe Satan is the archenemy of community after knowing these things? He imprisons people in the small towns with one sort of kingdom prison and uses a far more deadly one in the cities. The more societies he can infest with isolation, the greater are his chances of losing people to the power of Christ. His isolation has made it extremely difficult to gain access to those who need salvation. Worst of all, his diabolical plot in isolating churches from their environments is working extremely well at the present time.

In the light of Pattison's comments, consider again our ministry as Christ's body: He is to be in us, preaching good news through us to the poor, proclaiming freedom for the prisoners and recovery of the sight for the blind, and releasing the oppressed. Every one of these hurting groups are so bound they cannot come to us. In every single case mentioned in Luke 4:18, people helplessly wait for us to come to them. There is no other way for them to be reached apart from our penetrating *oikoses* that are not "normal," where fragmentation of the social group has happened, and where hopelessness and loneliness reign in the kingdom.

In Singapore, we created Share Groups to minister to those trapped in their isolation in the huge housing developments. We advertised groups for "Lonely People." We were surprised by the number who responded to our invitations, dropped in letter boxes. The first meeting of the first group took place in Toa Payoh housing estate on a Tuesday night. The fledgling Christian workers were overwhelmed by the instant, honest sharing of those who attended. On Thursday night, one of those who had come went to the top of her 20 story block of flats, removed her shoes (a Chinese custom when entering a house or committing suicide) and threw herself over the parapet. The following Sunday afternoon when I went to train this team, I found them weeping. One of them said, "Oh, pastor Ralph! We came too late! We came too late!"

If the church is ever going to touch the very ones referred to in Luke 4:18, it must be done through cell groups! Not only can cells of Christians penetrate more deeply into neighborhoods, but the ministry which then follows requires the "surrogate family" atmosphere of the cell group.

Satan has done his cruelest work by shaping his kingdoms with the lie that splendor will be awarded to those who are loyal to him. Along with the search for significance comes alienation from others. Whether the pressure leads to drugs, alcohol, depression, or becoming a workaholic, lack of intimacy is always the result. We, who have been called from darkness into light, are their only hope. The church must penetrate these kingdoms by developing cells that will touch these unreached ones.

Grace Gifts in Cell Group Life

The Life of the Flesh Is in the Blood

Cell group churches, the "body of Christ," are living organisms of the highest level. As such, we may consider the circulatory system which nourishes the human body.

Blood brings life-giving substances to all cells and excretes noxious wastes from them. It transports oxygen, protein, salts, and other chemical substances to various body parts, keeping them healthy. The adult male body holds about five liters of blood. Some loss may take place without ill effects, but if too much is lost, death quickly follows. Cells cannot survive without the nourishment provided by blood.[1]

Blood is transported by a complex circulatory system of tubes which carries it to the cells, where it interchanges materials with them according to their needs.[2] For many years anatomists believed the arteries contained air, since after death the arteries are always found empty.[3] Only when there is life in the body does the blood constantly flow under pressure from the heart, doing its important work.

Gifts: The Spiritual Blood in Christ's Body

The God who created the human body has also made the body of Christ to survive through the work of "spiritual blood." This life-giving substance is called in 1 Corinthians 12:1 "the gifts of the Spirit." In the Greek, the term is "the spirituals." That term describes specific capacities flowing into the body cells through the channel — the artery — of the Holy Spirit.

The gifts of the Holy Spirit are not given because one has become a super-spiritual person or because one has gained great biblical knowledge. Gifts are not rewards! As the human body cannot live without fresh blood, so the believer and the cells made up of believers cannot exist for even a *second* without a constant flow of spiritual gifts. They are given to all at the moment of conversion, necessary for spiritual life to function. Thus, every new believer must be helped to understand and utilize spiritual gifts.

For those who insist that any one gift is universally poured out for all believers, it is important to know that Paul repeatedly expressed that the various spiritual gifts are distributed to the church. There is no scriptural validation for pressing a spiritual gift upon any Christian.

"The spirituals" are provided in order that the body of Christ may be used by Him to perform His work. The cell group church must become completely dependent on the Holy Spirit for all its service. *Its life is in its special blood.* Spiritual gifts transport the power required to perform a task and export from the cell noxious wastes. As in the human body, if the blood pressure gets too low the body becomes tired, passive, and powerless. The cells of Christ must never be viewed as social gatherings or cognitive groups which simply share emotional needs with some form of Bible study. They must function on the level of the Spirit, and that means *they must operate through the activity of spiritual gifts.*

The Service Gifts

Since all gifts are given to complete the work of Christ as He flows through us, the ones specifically mentioned in the Scriptures should be understood. Among the eleven service gifts mentioned in Scripture are:

The Foundation Gifts
These two very basic gifts reveal the Christian's readiness to obey the Master and to enter into ministry:

1. The Gift of Service[4]
2. The Gift of Giving[5]

Serving has to do with using one's life to meet the needs of another person. The word is literally "table waiting." In the Greek, the word is *diakonia* the source of the English word "deacon." In 1 Corinthians 16:15, the entire Stephanas family is described as having "laid themselves out to serve God's people."

Giving involves using one's possessions to meet the needs of someone else. The word describes a person quite deliberately parting with something in his possession, so that a change of ownership is produced. There is a note of abandonment in the act, like the Heave Offering in the Old Testament.

The Ministry Gifts

These three gifts are given in differing strengths to various members of the body and make it possible for us to function together to fulfill His calling:

3. The Gift of Helping Others in Distress[6]
4. The Gift of Faith[7]
5. The Gift of Discerning True Spirits from False[8]

Helping Others in Distress is a word meaning "to feel sympathy with the misery of another, especially such sympathy as manifests itself in act, less frequently in word." The use of this gift communicates — nonverbally — that God is on the throne! Cheerfully helping others in distress is a powerful spiritual gift!

Faith is a gift, according to Romans 12:3, which is given in varying measures to believers. Some are given a greater measure than others. We might call this gift the "spiritual eyes of the body." The retinas of the eyes of faith can discern heavenly realities before they become a part of earth's activity. There's foreknowledge in the use of this gift. As the late Manley Beasley used to say, it's "Believing something is so, when it isn't so, because you know God will make it so."

Distinguishing True Spirits from False provides the protection of the Holy Spirit for the body, sensing and isolating the source of a foreign invasion by foreign spirits. It's a capacity that involves guarding others, protecting them in their naivete from the attacks of the evil one. It may be a demonic attack which is involved, or it may be the discernment of a human spirit who is not under the Lordship of Christ and who can do irreparable harm to the unity of the cell. Jude warned in verse 12 about men who are "hidden reefs in your love feasts when they feast with you without fear, caring for themselves." Mature believers will have this discriminating gift for use in the family of God.

The Equipping Gifts
Five of these are built upon the Gift of Leadership, an undergirding endowment for their use.

6. The Gift of Leadership[9]
7. The Gift of Prophecy[10]
8. The Gift of Teaching[11]
9. The Gift of Wise Speech[12]
10. The Gift of Putting Deepest Knowledge into Words[13]
11. The Gift of the Counselor[14]

The Gift of Leadership is not an office — it's a spiritual gift. Those who are anointed by God to provide direction do so with an unction that is unmistakable. This is not a talent. It's a divine flow from Christ, selecting those He has ordained for guiding others. In the Old Testament, the example of David being anointed with oil for the work of serving as Israel's king is a lovely illustration of how God sets apart special people to flow with this gift. Hopefully, every cell leader will possess a double portion of this "spiritual!"

The Gift of Prophecy is highly recommended by Paul in his discussion of the *charismata*. "Inspired utterance" is one translation for the Greek word *propheteia*, "prediction." It is to be used "for some useful purpose." When we were in Vietnam as missionaries, there was a short-term worker who was causing a great deal of misery to all who were working with her. One of the women missionaries received a word from the Lord which revealed the worker was a lesbian. When confronted, the girl was shattered by the accuracy of the prophecy. It led to repentance and a search for help.

The Gift of Teaching requires a person to be constantly taught in turn by the Holy Spirit. Back in Numbers 3:1, the sons of Aaron are also referred to as the sons of Moses. The reason for this had to do with the importance of their teacher. Moses, their teacher, was considered to have given them birth through introducing them to the Law. So it is with the gifted one who imparts the revealed will of God and instructions which order the relationships between Christ and His body members.

The Gift of Wise Speech and the *Gift of Putting Deepest Knowledge Into Words* are very close to one another. Those who share deep truths and those with Spirit-given wisdom combine to provide guidance for younger believers. One provides truths, the other insights into how they apply to life situations.

The Gift of the Counselor is also called the "Gift of the Paraclete" — the "one called alongside to help." It uses the same root word used for the Holy Spirit. More than a psychological evaluator, this person is one who understands the deepest agonies in the life of another, suffers with others, and prays to the Lord about each problem.

All These Gifts Are For The Body To Exercise

All these gifts should be used in cell group life. The Foundation Gifts can be utilized by the new Christian almost from the day of conversion. Their use will lead to the maturity of Ministry Gifts. In turn, their use will develop believers to exercise the Equipping Gifts.

It cannot be emphasized too frequently that spiritual maturity is required for some gifts to be useful, but all Christians have gifts which can be used to build up others in the life of the body. It's very important that a great deal of emphasis be placed on the new Christian understanding and using spiritual gifts. If too much time erodes this process, the gifts will not be manifested and the work of Christ will not be done. Paul insisted that all spiritual gifts are simply an indication of the presence of Christ in the midst of His body.

The Sign Gifts

There are four *sign gifts* which may be useful in ministry:

1. Tongues[15]
2. Interpretation of Tongues[16]
3. Healings[17]
4. Miracles[18]

Tongues are divided by Paul in 1 Corinthians 14 into two categories.[19] First, the use of tongues with interpretation is a *public sign* which expresses Christ's attitude. It can be a negative sign of judgment for unbelievers who are present in the body life meeting, or it can bring a positive sign for the believers.[20] Second, it can be a *private prayer language.*[21]

Paul discouraged the use of public tongues as an activity which does not build up the body as strongly as does prophecy. At the same time, he indicated that he spoke in tongues more than anyone in the church in Corinth. His use was obviously in his private prayer, not in public.

Is this a contradiction in our premise that the gifts are primarily provided for the edification of others? Rather than a contradiction, it may be seen as the exception. For a full treatment of this entire subject, there is no better exposition than *Showing the Spirit* by Dr. D. A. Carson of Trinity Evangelical Divinity School.[22]

Interpretation of Tongues is to accompany every instance of the public use of tongues. As Carson writes,

> . . . the tongues-speaker, in consequence of edifying the church and the concomitant need for intelligible utterance in the church, should pray for another gift — the gift of interpretation.[23]

How the interpreter is to be identified in advance of the message in tongues is not specified in Scripture. The comment in 1 Corinthians 14:27, "let one interpret," does not necessarily mean there will be one who interprets all tongues messages, although some hold to that view.

The public use of all gifts remains constant: to build up the body. For a Christian community to receive valid prophecies or tongues with interpretation, as with any other gift manifestation, *they must be relevant to the needs of the people present.*

Healings and Miracles are God's special moments when He shows His grace and His power to bless us. There are special prerequisites for healings which are set forth in James 5:14-16 which involve the elders as participants. In other instances, the prayer for healing may be a ministry of a cell or of an individual.

To repeat for emphasis, the primary use of these gifts remains *the building up of the body of Christ!* They are also used to demonstrate the reality of our Lord's body to unbelievers.

The Purpose of Gifts

As discussed on page 60, spiritual gifts exist for ministry, not for personal enjoyment. Paul makes it clear in 1 Corinthians 14 that one can misuse and abuse gifts, turning them from their purpose to childish toys. The clearly stated purpose for the gifts is this:

> What then shall we say, brothers? When you come together, everyone has a hymn, or a word of instruction, a revelation, a tongue or an interpretation. All of these must be done for the strengthening of the church.[24]

Studying all Paul says about gifts in Romans 12, 1 Corinthians 12-14, and other scattered passages should make it clear that Christ intended for gifts to be the blood in the circulatory system of the body, flowing to cells for empowering and cleansing. From the very moment of conversion, every single believer is to be a channel of grace gifts to the body's members. Whether a convert's age is 15 or 75, spiritual gifts are given for the building up of the rest of the body of Christ and for ministry to a broken world. They must be taken from a Bible study topic to being literally applied in the cells.

The Cell Group Must Operate On the Level of the Gifts

Not Just the Intellect

e.g., Bible Studies
"How does this apply to us?"

Not Just the Emotions

e.g., Begin With Our Needs
"How can we advise one another?"

The Gifts of the Spirit

Life-giving power received; removal of noxious waste
*"He who has an ear, let him hear what the **Spirit** says to the churches."*

9

Gifts Belong in Cell Groups

DEAR PAUL,

In 1 Corinthians 12:1 you wrote, "Now about spiritual gifts, brothers, I do not want you to be ignorant." Oh, Paul! If you were among us today you would be broken hearted by the ignorance of our generation about the proper use of spiritual gifts. If you were to journey through the churches you would discover believers have fallen into two ditches.

The ditch on one side contains those who play down the gifts, discouraging their use as "experience-centered." They're totally ignorant of their own special relationship to spiritual gifts — *including the elders!* They downplay everything except Bible study. They teach that any display of the power of God mentioned in the Bible is off limits for this age.

In the ditch on the other side are those who have become totally enamored with the "sign gifts." They exhibit certain gifts in public meetings, seldom or never exercising them for the purpose of building up the body. They ignore your warning that "if the whole church comes together and everyone speaks in tongues, and some who do not understand or some unbelievers come in, will they not say that you are out of your mind?"[1]

Those in both ditches have not yet grasped the importance of body life or the use of all the gifts in their proper setting. Sad to say, they are mortal enemies. Unity is impossible between them; sometimes merely being civil to each other is difficult.

Paul, neither group believes you were serious when you said, "Since you are eager to have spiritual gifts, try to excel in gifts that build up the church."[2] You see, our generation has made the church into a big blob of protoplasm that no longer has hands, feet, and inward parts. It just has a "membership list." I know you won't believe it, but they are actually divided about equally into "active" and "inactive" members. Worst of all, neither group pays much attention to the need for cells with true community. Therefore, they are puzzled by your comment that:

> When you come together, everyone has a hymn, or a word of instruction, a revelation, a tongue or an interpretation. All of these must be done for the strengthening of the church"[3]

They just can't figure out how everyone can participate as you have directed because their "coming together" takes place in large numbers of people who sit in rows, not in circles, and they barely communicate with one another. It should be obvious to them that their idea of "church" is erroneous, but it isn't clear at all.

Paul, take heart! The Spirit has been at work, and more and more cell group churches are emerging from the ashes of the first Reformation. Things are going to get better!

The stranglehold of a new style of church life called "Program Base Design" is a new method now being used. It bottles people up inside special buildings we now call "churches," and they are removed from ministries to the unchurched. Since most Christians know little about "body life" or being equipped for ministry, they have ignored the gifts and their use. Remember us, Paul. We wish you were here to help us in this generation! If it were not for the letters you wrote, we wouldn't even know the mess we're in. Thank you for impacting us through them.

YOUR FAITHFUL SERVANT,
EPAPHRODITUS CCXXVII

How Can a True Church Exist and Ignore Spiritual Gifts?

A seminary professor I highly respect for the wonderful books he has written says flatly to his students, "Don't place emphasis on spiritual gifts in your teaching. You just stir up problems." His Evangelical orientation has made him wary of anything related to the subject. *Why do we fear what Scripture clearly endorses?* How can we discharge the power of the written word while downgrading its teaching because we resent contemporaries who abuse gifts? This is what a friend calls "throwing out the baby with the bath water."

Charles Kraft has expressed my own feelings in his book *Christianity With Power:*

> I want all that God has for us in this area, but in a balanced, reasonable way. The extremes in power ministry still bother me greatly. I have no desire to move toward these extremes. As I attempt to analyze my own experience, I see genuine growth in an area of legitimate Christian experience that I had previously not explored. "Why," I ask, "should this area be the exclusive preserve of Pentecostals and charismatics?" If — as I believe God has been showing me over the last seven years — spiritual power is the birthright of all Christians, why are we Evangelicals not appropriating this part of our inheritance?[4]

In my book *This Gift Is Mine,* I took a hard line against those gifts that didn't fit my Evangelical background. I am delighted that the book is out of print because I no longer hold to the views I expressed in 1974. During these years I have lived in the cell group church, I now have no question that God provides any gift that people need to be built up or cleansed. But I have a problem! Let me tell you what it is . . .

Faking Gifts Isn't Necessary — Unless You're a Fake!

My heart is heavy as I pen these words, for I am thinking of the routines that have developed around the abuse of spiritual gifts in P.B.D. charismatic circles. A high percentage of these churches have no cell groups. Without cells, the display of spiritual gifts must take place in their public services. Frequently, these become a sideshow of gifts being displayed without true ministry.

These large impersonal settings cause the gifts to be displayed as a part of scheduled events. Well-established worship patterns, duplicated over and over in these charismatic services, are routine. They are just another version of the Evangelical "hymn, hymn, announcements, offering, choir, sermon, benediction" pattern. Ritual is ritual, whether done with raised hands or with robes and candles, with overhead projectors or Baptist Hymnals. Spiritual gifts aren't designed to be ritualized.

In Brisbane, I visited the worship service of the largest church in town. They had developed a form of cell group life, and I wanted to study them. I was disappointed to discover they used the charismatic worship pattern.

There came a prayer lull in the praise song time. Someone had to speak in tongues in the service; it was expected in every meeting. A woman near the front did so. After a brief moment of waiting for the interpretation to be given, the pastor went to the microphone and delivered a flowery translation, mostly quoting clearly recognized fragments from the Psalms and the prophets. An Australian friend whispered to me: "Every time I visit here, he's the only one who interprets tongues."

Soon after, I was chatting with another charismatic pastor. I asked him, "Why is it that most of the time the pastor is the one who interprets tongues in your public services? Are there no other gifted people who can do it?" He smiled sheepishly and said, "To be honest with you, I do the same thing in my church. You never know when some nut may embarrass you!" Such manipulation of spiritual gifts is unconscionable. When they are used out of context, Christian leadership often feels compelled to perpetrate a hoax that must deeply grieve the Holy Spirit.

The first time I was in a large group meeting where someone had a "word of prophecy," I was impressed by the story of a ship which had sails but no wind. A mighty wind arose, and the ship moved faster and faster toward its port. The wind was the Holy Spirit; the ship was the church; and a mighty movement was about to start. *I have heard the identical, or near-identical story spoken in a public meeting several times.* Who said it first? Who's copying someone else? Why?

I mentioned this matter to Viv Grigg, one of the most devout brothers I know, who currently ministers to the poor by living in a squalid Calcutta slum. We were eating together in Auckland at the time. He grimaced and said, "The men I know in New Zealand who are truly prophetic would never think of speaking out in a public meeting."

It's one thing to be in a small group where God is working and where people know each other so well they can't get away with faking their gifts, and another thing to be in these large meetings where "gifts" are manifested routinely to fit the program at just the right time. This perfunctory abuse of gifts is not right!

My deep respect for Yonggi Cho includes the way he conducts his multiple Sunday worship services. It's just about as formal as a Presbyterian church. While they recite the Apostle's Creed, no one manifests any spiritual gifts. Yet he is a leader among those who believe in their full use.

This is not to discredit in any way the work of the Holy Spirit in large assemblies. God can do anything He desires, regardless of the size of the group. It's the *faking* of the true manifestation of gifts that I point to in these remarks. At Faith Community Baptist Church in Singapore, the presence of God has been so powerful that people entering the auditorium have been swept to their knees in prayer before the meeting began. Many have been healed or have received other blessings because of the work of the Spirit in the Sunday celebrations. Authentic manifestations are most certainly taking place all over the world when the people of God truly worship. I rejoice over them! It's the counterfeit that bothers me a lot, and it bothers a lot of others as well.

Focusing on a Few of the Gifts Isn't Good Enough

Among the charismatics there is excessive stress on a few of the spiritual gifts, including those which supposedly validate the recipient having attained a higher level of walking in the Spirit. Sadly, most of these folks ignore their need for manifesting the "service gifts" that God has given to the body. We shall never know until we get to glory whether Dorcas spoke in tongues, but we do know her use of the *gifts of helping others in distress* so endeared her to her body that our Lord raised her from the dead. There must be a balanced focus on all the gifts being used in edification.

The Cell: The Proper Setting for Using Spiritual Gifts

Every one of us arrives in the Kingdom "crippled inside." Living apart from God for years creates inner brokenness which must be mended. In addition, simply living in a fallen world of fallen men continues to damage us as we seek to live under His Lordship. The cell group exists as a community where the healing power of God is to be manifested.

Sharon (not her real name) had read about *The People Who Care* in Houston in a syndicated news article. She immediately packed her few belongings in a small trailer, hooked it up to her Volkswagen bug, and drove to Houston. Our family was eating dinner when she rang our bell. "Hi," she said. "I was up in Denver, and I read about your church. I decided to come down and be a part of it." We invited her to share our meal and found her a place to stay.

This attractive young woman had arrived in a lot of emotional and spiritual pain, and she required a lot of healing. We often found ourselves at the end of all our formal training and experience as we sought to help her. Again and again Ruth and I would agonize in prayer over her. God had sent her for a special purpose. Without her severe need, we would not have moved so quickly beyond our resources to discover the power of Christ flowing through us, ministering to her in a way we could never accomplish.

She impacted our lives as much as we impacted hers. Her life story would have made a granite statue weep! Seeing her slowly healed and delivered was one blessing, but it was accompanied by a second one. At the same time we were caring for her, she was building up others in our group, learning how to use her spiritual gifts. It was high drama!

She had become a part of the reciprocal ministry that takes place when cell group members build up each other through exercising spiritual gifts. We were learning to receive grace through others as we learned to be channels of grace. This is the power of the church as cells. The healers are those who are also healed.

When we begin a life together in which all are equipped for ministry, the most effective growth always takes place in an environment where we are called upon to give as well as to receive, to heal as well as to be healed.

How does Christ desire for us to be healed? Are we to find our healing independently, going to Him all alone? While that happens, it's not His primary plan for us. Instead, He gives gifts of healings to His body. Spiritual gifts are related to the body and its needs.

Christ Touches Me through You

Our Lord could have chosen to minister to each one of us apart from others, but He chose one or more persons to become agents of gifts that would minister to us. This requires participants in the cell group church to use spiritual gifts in all phases of ministry to build up one another.

Are we to live as mutual cripples who cling to one another? No! As discussed in chapter two, we are to build up one another — *oikodomeo* — through the divine flow of spiritual gifts. As we do so, growth takes place both in the life of the giver and the life of the receiver. There is one form of growth we experience as the agent of charismata and another form as we benefit from them. In all cases, the flow of spiritual gifts is required.

My strong objection to turning cell group gatherings into Bible studies is that they replace the time when a reciprocal relationship in the Christian community should take place with another cognitive activity. When the cells meet it should be for edification, not teaching.

Of course, there must be strong biblical teaching before the cells meet. *The cells must operate under the authority of Scripture previously received, but the gatherings must be for edification.* Those who gather under the shadow of Scripture will be guided by what they have previously learned. They now meet with the intention that "Nobody should seek his own good, but the good of others."[5] Instead of another cognitive-based session, the gifts must flow between body members.

Gifts Don't Come from Inner Storage Batteries

There are different kinds of gifts, but the same Spirit.
There are different kinds of service, but the same Lord.
There are different kinds of working, but the same God works
all of them in all men.[6]

How are spiritual gifts discovered by the believer? Has God latently stored up supernatural power within us as a flashlight battery stores up electric energy? No! Spiritual gifts are not stored up, ready for a special occasion to be taken out and utilized. Instead, they are like an electric current that must flow from a source to a need. If the believer is not attached to both Christ, the source, and another person with a need, there's little likelihood the gift will be manifested. Spiritual gifts are the "energizings" that service the work of God where a need exists. Thus, in the cell group each need of a body member is a valid reason for the gifts to flow.

As a result, the needs in the life of a person will call forth the spiritual gifts that are necessary for Christ to meet the problem area. In references to gifts throughout the New Testament, *the emphasis is on their activity, not the gifts themselves.*

To isolate spiritual gifts from their tasks is to create a serious problem. This was the problem in the Corinthian church. They had lost a sense of community, and as a result their participation in the agape feasts was a farce and a disgrace. At the same time the gifts were no longer being used for building up one another. They became privately used toys practiced by individuals for personal edification. 1 Corinthians 11 to 14 is a continuous discussion of the misuse of the gifts. We may outline the section as follows:

1. You have lost any sense of community, and you have no love for one another: 11:17-22.
2. Your observation of the Lord's supper is done in an unworthy manner because you do not recognize the importance of body life: 11:23-34.
3. Your use of spiritual gifts does not recognize the importance of honoring other body members: 12:1-31.
4. Love is the heart and soul of body life, causing the gifts to flow in the proper context: 13:1-13.
5. Spiritual gifts have one primary use: the edification of the other body members, and all are to focus on their ministry to others through the use of the charismata: 14:1-40.

What could be clearer? Spiritual gifts, wrenched from the place of the cell group — the only form of church life which makes it possible for every person to participate — are usually used in an inappropriate manner. Yet, even in the popular small group movements of today this fact is missed. *Away with the study booklets, the discipleship leaflets, the Bible study guides! Let the church be the church at its best, doing its work of edification through the manifestation of spiritual gifts.*

False Motives for Receiving Spiritual Gifts

What are the proper motives for a believer to receive spiritual gifts? If it is to attract affirmation or receive rewards, the motives are not proper and the gifts will not flow.

One who is close to me was taken to a meeting and pressured to "loosen his spirit" and receive a particular spiritual gift considered necessary for all believers. As the group gathered around him to pray he would receive the gift, he felt most uncomfortable. He decided he would receive anything the Lord had for him, but he wouldn't fake anything! He didn't "get the gift." The group ended their time with him shaking their heads and muttering, "He just isn't ready to go all the way with the Holy Spirit."

Thousands of people have "received their gift" because of such group pressure and a desire to be accepted as a fully endorsed member of their charismatic peer group. Since gifts can be counterfeited, this motive propels many people to have an experience which validates them as "authentic" before their friends. At the same time, they are cheated from knowing the glorious reality of Christ's power flowing through them for the building up of others. *This is evil!*

Those who pressure others to receive a gift are forgetting some important Scriptures. Let's consider some of them: "We have different gifts, according to the grace given us."[7] One term for gifts in the Greek is *charisma*, which comes from a verb *charizomai*, "to grant as a favor, gratuitously pardon; rescue." This word is used by Paul, clearly set in the context of being used to build up the body:

Just as each of us has one body with many members, and these members do not all have the same function, so in Christ we who are many form one body, and each member belongs to all the others. We have different gifts, according to the grace given us.[8]

While this can be interpreted to mean "each person has a gift different from all the other members of the body," it is could also refer to one person displaying different gifts, according to the *charismata* needed for the occasion.

In 1 Corinthians 12:4-6, the emphasis is again on the differences in the gifts. In this passage, we see the gifts automatically leading the recipient to be appropriate to the occasion:

There are different kinds of gifts, but the same Spirit.
There are different kinds of service, but the same Lord.
There are different kinds of working, but the same God works
all of them in all men.[9]

The place of the gifts must be seen in the context of their use: "All these are the work of one and the same Spirit, and he gives them to each one, just as he determines."[10]

The emphasis is on the action, not the receiving of the gift. Peter wrote pointedly about the use of gifts:

Each one should use whatever gift he has received to serve others, faithfully administering God's grace in its various forms.[11]

Once again, the emphasis is on the *action*. In addition, there is not a definite article with the word "gift" in this verse: "each as he has received gift" is the literal rendering. Thus, when spiritual gifts are seen in the context of their use in the cell group for the building up of the body, their manifestation will always be related to the *situation*.

Once Again, With Feeling: Gifts and Usage Are Inseparable!

Now to each one the manifestation of the Spirit is given for the common good. To one there is given through the Spirit the message of wisdom, to another the message of knowledge by means of the same Spirit, to another faith by the same Spirit, to another gifts of healing by that one Spirit, to another miraculous powers, to another prophecy, to another distinguishing between spirits, to another speaking in different kinds of tongues, and to still another the interpretation of tongues.[12]

Is it not obvious that God is flowing into the cell group all the spiritual gifts required for carrying out the ministry of edification? Paul points out they are a part of body life:

And in the church God has appointed . . . those having gifts of healing, those able to help others, those with gifts of administration, and those speaking in different kinds of tongues.[13]

He then points out that not all will have the same gifts: "Do all have gifts of healing? Do all speak in tongues? Do all interpret?"[14] The answer is an obvious "No." Not all have these gifts — only those who have been selected by the Spirit to be a channel of grace through their use.

Then he adds: ". . . eagerly desire spiritual gifts, especially the gift of prophecy."[15] The "eager desire" for a gift, in this case the gift of prophecy, is a manifestation of a desire to have what will build up a brother or sister in the group. It speaks of a readiness to be a servant. There is no reason at all to think Paul is suggesting we get a gift for the sake of having it. Such a thought flies in the face of the close connection between the *gift* and the *need*. As with all other gifts, prophecy is a *working gift*.

The writer of Hebrews confirms that the gifts of the Holy Spirit are distributed according to the will of God.[16] We are free to express our willingness to be used, but the Spirit decides when and where we are to serve Christ. In this context, we may remember that we may dedicate our lives for His use, but our Lord alone consecrates, sets us apart, for the work. Good news: He turns none away except those who are full of themselves.

The Motive for the Use of Our Gifts Is Love

Paul paused in the middle of his discussion of spiritual gifts in 1 Corinthians 12 and 14 to discourse at length about the motive for them: love. If Christians seek the manifestation of gifts for any other reason, they will fall into error.

In a prayer time in Indiana, a black brother in a wheelchair asked for prayer for his healing. His was a heartbreaking story. He was born deaf. A smart aleck behind the wheel of a racing automobile saw this man walking toward the road. He said to his companion, "Let's scare that guy!" Sounding a horn which was not heard, he started to sideswipe him, expecting he would leap out of the way. Instead, he hit him and severed his spine.

Deaf and paraplegic, our brother in Christ requested we pray for his healing — no small task! As we knelt and prayed, one young man cried out in agony, "Oh, God! He's my brother!" The pure love which was manifested in the group was overwhelming. It should always be so when gifts are manifested.

Over and over, the writers of the New Testament focus on the activity of the body as flowing from love. Desiring the best for another person in all situations is easier talked about than performed — particularly when you are locked into a small group where that person's eccentric behavior is obnoxious to all concerned.

D. A Carson comments on 1 Corinthians 13:1:

This value judgment is meant to be shocking. Part of its power is that Paul does not merely say that under this condition . . . it is not the gift of tongues that is only a resounding gong or a clanging cymbal, but I, myself . . . . as if my action of speaking in tongues without love has left a permanent effect on me that has diminished my value and transformed me into something I should not be.[17]

In referring to 1 Corinthians 13:2, he says,

Again, however, Paul's conclusion is even more shattering: not only are the spiritual gifts exercised without love of no value, but, says Paul, "I am nothing spiritually a cipher."[18]

Ponder the cell group implications of these verses:

Instead, speaking the truth in love, we will in all things grow up into him who is the Head, that is, Christ. From him the whole body, joined and held together by every supporting ligament, grows and builds itself up in love, as each part does its work.[19]

Follow the way of *love* and eagerly desire spiritual gifts . . . [20]

Above all, *love* each other deeply, because *love* covers over a multitude of sins.[21]

And let us consider how we may spur one another on toward *love* and good deeds.[22]

May the Lord make your *love* increase and overflow for each other and for everyone else, just as ours does for you.[23]

We ought always to thank God for you, brothers, and rightly so, because your faith is growing more and more, and the *love* every one of you has for each other is increasing.[24]

Do everything in *love*.[25]

Since you are eager to have spiritual gifts, try to excel in gifts that build up the church.[26]

Susan (not her real name) was barely a teenager when she came into our group. Her slight retardation caused the public schools to promote her from one grade to the next without much concern for her future. She stayed with us in our cells for several years. Her lack of sensitivity caused her to make wisecracks when others were sharing deeply, and her laugh rattled windows.

For a few months she was passed from group to group, with a sigh of relief made by cells who no longer had to put up with her. She then entered a cell with some believers who felt God had a special plan for her in spite of her handicap. For the first time in her life, she was frankly confronted with her unacceptable areas of behavior. The group loved her. The meetings began to manifest helping gifts toward her. One of the men said, "Susan, when you are in the group you keep your eye on me. Since you don't know when your behavior is out of line, I'm going to help you. If you see me pull on my right ear, you will know you need to stop what you are doing. You won't be embarrassed, and you'll learn to recognize how others see you." Some of the women took her aside and talked frankly to her as well about personal matters, but always in great love.

Susan's social adjustment developed more in a few months with that group than she had been able to do in a lifetime of being passed around among unloving people. The cell group rejoiced when she was hired by a fast food restaurant. She kept that job for many years. She was a tribute to those who served her with their spiritual gifts. Love had brought her to a new awareness of what she could be, and Christ built her up through His body.

Love, Plus Gifts, Equals Church Life

Living the Christian life apart from the relationships which are built in community is a dangerous thing to do. It leaves people isolated and hurting. For 18 years I conducted a daily talk show on the radio. Hundreds of letters poured in during that time, nearly all asking for prayer, nearly all written by believers. The reason they reached out to a voice that became a part of their lives each morning was because they had no one else they felt they could talk to about their hurts. When they would call, I would ask: "Have you talked to your Sunday school teacher or your pastor about this matter?" Over and over they would say, "I can't. They barely know me. I feel I would be a bother to them."

People like this turn to the radio for help because they misunderstand what church is. For example, how would you place these things on your priority list?

• God
• Family
• Church
• Work

Dion Robert, pastor in Abidjan, Ivory Coast, points out that the biblical priority for these items is:

• Church
• Family
• Work

He explains, "God is not a separate priority. He is in all we do. He is in His Son, and the church is Christ's body. Christians who put the church behind their family make a grave mistake. *The home cannot be Christian until it is within the life of the cell.* It is only then that the family lives in a place of love, of nurture, of edification. It is when the church is supreme to all else that the family and the work situations are benefitted by the power of spiritual gifts."

Knowing the divine pattern provides access to Christ in a special way. He flows through other body members to meet my needs, and He flows through me to build up other body members. When one has experienced it, there's no desire to turn back!

10

The Holy Spirit in the Cell Group

We have already seen that the primary purpose of spiritual gifts is the building up, or edifying, of believers by other believers. Each member is responsible for applying spiritual gifts to edify others. Moreover, *every single believer is to be active in this ministry.*[1] There are no exceptions.

Therefore, the work of the Holy Spirit in the life of the believer begins to take on a pattern. First, we were sealed by Him.[2] We were simultaneously baptized by Him both into Christ and also the Body of Christ.[3] He is the provider of spiritual gifts to each believer for the common good.[4] He further directs the use of these gifts when the group assembles in such a powerful way that the observing unbeliever declares "God is certainly among you."[5]

The Cell Group Is the Believer's Gateway into Gifts

The personal use of spiritual gifts in the cell is the believer's gateway into the supernatural world. In that realm, warfare occurs.[6] In that world, spiritual gifts serve as the entrance for the believer to discover how God heals, delivers, and causes growth in believers.

There is no better place for spiritual gifts to be developed than in cell groups. All necessary conditions are present for the gifts to be received and used for edification. Needs present in the lives of the believers and the small size of the group make it possible for all present to exercise gifts for building up one another in the Spirit. The modeling of the proper use of gifts can protect new believers from absurd excesses.

Members should be taught to appreciate, desire, exercise, and receive the benefits of spiritual gifts. Through using them, they can learn how to become the channels of God's power. This makes the activity of the Holy Spirit very personal to members of cells. Members must experience both the power of gifts flowing through them to edify others and the personal edification received from others who exercise them.

There is grave danger present when a cell is unplugged from the work of the Holy Spirit and the use of spiritual gifts. It has no alternative except to become a religious social club, which soon ossifies and diverts its activity to other tasks. As a result, no building up takes place in the cell. Soon, this tragic condition will occur:

> For everyone who partakes only of milk is not accustomed to the word of righteousness, for he is a babe. But solid food is for the mature, who because of practice have their senses trained to discern good and evil.[7]

How Learning to Edify Changed a Group

When an Auckland church asked me to help them prepare for cell group life, I had just been taught by the Spirit the truths about *oikodomeo*. The pastor took me to work with a small Bible study group that had been in existence for several years. We were invited by the hostess to come early and share the evening meal with her family. With much embarrassment, she apologized for the absence of her husband. She explained he owned a construction company and often worked late.

When the group arrived, I spent a few minutes teaching them about the importance of learning how to build up one another using spiritual gifts. Since they had been together for a very long time as a Bible study group, I assumed they knew each other intimately. With that knowledge, they were to ask the Holy Spirit to guide them into a ministry of edification. I asked them to pick a place to be alone and pray, to prepare themselves to edify others in the group.

As we returned to our circle, the sun was setting and the missing husband arrived. With a brief greeting to the group, he went to shower and change clothes. About 15 minutes later, he joined us.

Meanwhile, I suggested that we let the Spirit guide us into our season of edification. No one spoke a word! To get the ball rolling, I turned to the man on my left — a church leader and a strong Christian — and said, "Would you like to be the first to share?" He was petrified! He said, "I have never heard or seen anyone do this, and I'd like for someone else to begin."

One lady read us her "life verse" from the Scripture. Another read a brief passage from the Psalms. Of course, any Scripture one would read would edify — but it didn't seem to meet any special need in the lives of those in the circle.

With a sinking heart, I realized this was about to be a fiasco! I chided myself for believing that their many meetings spent intellectualizing about Scripture had caused them to know each other on a spiritual level. That was my mistake: before one can build up someone else, there must be an understanding of spiritual needs. *They neither knew how to edify, nor what needs were present.*

I turned the meeting over to the pastor, suggesting we might have a season of prayer before we dismissed. He asked, "Does anyone have a special problem we might pray for?" The hostess said, "I do. I've had a rash all over my body for months. Fever blisters are on my lips. You can see the rash on my arms and neck. My whole body is like that. I've seen dermatologists who have given me creams and pills, but nothing makes any difference. I'd like you to pray for me."

She moved her chair to the center of the room. We all gathered around her. What would happen now? Would we politely pray for her healing and move on to the next prayer request?

Then the Spirit came. A word of knowledge was given. Quietly, the pastor said, "I sense in my heart the Lord is telling me your problem is the result of great anger. Perhaps it's something you wish to share with us . . ."

She was silent for a few moments, and began to weep softly. "Yes, that could be. I am so angry at my husband! He promises us he'll be home for dinner, but night after night we eat without him. I put his food in the fridge, and usually I'm asleep before he comes home to eat it. He's broken his promises to me over and over, and I feel I am a widow as I raise our children."

There was an awareness that a special word had come from the Lord through one of the members that had surfaced a problem *that several years of small group meetings had never revealed.* Who could speak with the husband blushing red with embarrassment?

One of the men cleared his throat and spoke to the husband: "You know, I nearly lost my family doing the same thing you are doing now. In fact, my wife had packed her things to leave me. I felt I was the best husband and father possible because I worked day and night to give them nice things. The Holy Spirit had to deal severely with me. I came to realize that the very thing I was working for was about to go up in smoke. If it did, what would my past or future work be worth? It was then that Paul's writings to Timothy and Titus began to show me I would never be God's man until I managed my own household well. I had one of the most profound spiritual experiences of my life. Our marriage and our home have radically changed since the day I put my family after God and ahead of my workaholic lifestyle."

Several others then shared. Scriptures were quoted. Some spoke special words using the gift of wise speech. The Spirit of God had taken control, and oikodomeo had begun to operate.

The husband fell to his knees and wept, his face buried in his wife's lap. He prayed first — a personal prayer of confession and repentance. The group prayed along with him. The man who had shared his own personal experience laid his hand on his friend as he prayed for him.

Then our prayer time moved to his dear wife. It seemed all were now praying at once, no one desiring to "wait his turn." We all lost track of time. *The Lord had invaded His Body, and the gateway into the supernatural world had been crossed by us all.*

That's not the end of the story. The following Sunday morning, I was sitting on the front row in the church auditorium, looking over my sermon notes. Through a large plate glass window, I could see this group talking in the parking lot area. A few minutes later, they stood in a circle around me. Our cell group hostess drew back the flowing sleeves of her dress and said, "Ralph, look! No rash! No rash anywhere on my body!" Then, with deep love in her eyes, she said, "My husband wants to say something to you." He said, "Ralph, I've cut back my workday to eight hours. I took the kids to the zoo yesterday. We have a new home. I'll never be the same. God did a deep work in my heart in our cell group."

Once Caught, No Escape!

I want you to imagine the radical change which took place in the lives of those in that group from that day onwards! Once a cell group has stepped into the supernatural world, it can't ever be the same again. It's like going to school for the first time, or having your first baby: you can't ever go back and be what you were before the event. A holy boldness invades a group after it has seen the power of spiritual gifts working in its midst. They become aware that their battle is not against flesh and blood, but against principalities and powers of the air. Every experience of knowing God's mighty power, instead of just reading about it in the Scriptures, moves the group deeper into warfare and ministry.

For many years as a pastor of a P.B.D. church, I taught that Jesus' words in John 16:13 simply referred to the light the Spirit would give to the believer as he sought to study Scripture. That passage says the Spirit will guide us into all the truth. My teaching wasn't error — it just didn't go far enough. The Holy Spirit doesn't limit His guidance only to cognitive truths. *He also guides us into the application of those truths.* Without the application, what is the significance of the Scripture?

Spiritual gifts are to be used, not studied, and the Holy Spirit is the source of their use. Guiding us into their application means He must be active and present wherever, and whenever, they are used. A cell group experiencing their use will be guided into truth that cannot be discovered in any other way. Thus, the agenda for a cell group must be formed around His right to revise it at any time He chooses to do so.

Needs Precede the Use of Gifts

The work of the Spirit is always attached to needs. Jesus tied it together when He said in Luke 4:18, "The Spirit of the Lord is upon me . . ." By the Spirit the needs of the poor, the captives, the blind, and the downtrodden would be met. Thus, in a cell group it is important for the needs to surface so the gifts can be used to build up.

In Samuel Wesley's account of the religious society begun in Epworth, on the Isle of Axholm, Lincolnshire, February 1, 1701, the following statements are given:

> I. Every week at set hours, when 2, 3, or more do meet together for this Intent, First to pray to God; Secondly, to read the Holy Scriptures, and discourse upon Religious Matters for their mutual Edification; And Thirdly, to deliberate about the Edification of our neighbor, and the promoting it.

II. Those that do thus meet together, are above all things solicitous about the Salvation of their neighbor, yea they make it their business to be Christians not only in name but in deed: Least they should strive rashly to pull out the Mote from the Eies of others, not observing the Beam in their own; and lest while they preach to others themselves should become castaways.

III. For this Reason they do not admit every body promiscuously, but if any one desires to be of their Society, it must be done by the Consent of all; and therefore his Piety ought to be known to all, lest a little Leven should spoil the whole Lump. For they take it for Granted that things will then fall out well, when each of them shall be of that mind, as that it may be affirm'd upon good Grounds that This is Emanuel that dwells through Faith, of the power of God, in the Heart of every One, as in his Temple.

IIII. Nor do they allow that the number of their members should encrease too much, lest this Religious design should fall with its own weight, or at least be marr'd. Therefore when they have twelve Members they admitt no more. But if God shall stir up more, two shall desire the same Edification with them, they seperate [sic] two Members from them, to form a new Society with those that desire it, till that also grow's up to the number of Twelve, and so another new Society be form'd out of it.[8]

In our modern culture it seems legalistic, even cult-like, to enter into such a covenant relationship. Nevertheless, the focus of Wesley's group members was on becoming responsible to, and accountable for, one another. The very stress placed in this document on edification and being concerned about the beam in one's own eye gives us assurance the groups operated on principles of loving compassion, not legalism.

In *The Rules of the Band Societies Drawn Up December 25, 1738*, the following statements serve to affirm the transparency of the groups. (It should be noted that all bands were made up of one sex only. In America, we have often found much more openness when men and women meet separately.)

The design of our meeting is, to obey that command of God, "Confess your faults one to another, and pray one for another, that ye may be healed."

To this end, we intend, —

1. To meet once a week, at the least.
2. To come punctually at the hour appointed, without some extraordinary reason.
3. To begin (those of us who are present) exactly at the hour, with singing or prayer.
4. To speak each of us in order, freely and plainly, the true state of our souls, with the faults we have committed in thought, word, or deed, and the temptations we have felt, since our last meeting.
5. To end every meeting with prayer, suited to the state of each person present.
6. To desire some person among us to speak his own state first, and then to ask the rest, in order, as many searching questions as may be, concerning their state, sins, and temptations.

Some of the questions proposed to every one before he is admitted among us may be to this effect: —

1. Have you the forgiveness of your sins?
2. Have you peace with God through our Lord Jesus Christ?
3. Have you the witness of God's Spirit with your spirit, that you are a child of God?
4. Is the love of God shed abroad in your heart?
5. Has no sin, inward or outward, dominion over you?
6. Do you desire to be told of your faults?
7. Do you desire to be told of your faults, and that plain and home?
8. Do you desire that every one of us should tell you, from time to time, whatsoever is in his heart concerning you?
9. Consider! Do you desire that we should tell you whatsoever we think, whatsoever we fear, whatsoever we hear, concerning you?

10. Do you desire that, in doing this, we should come as close as possible, that we should cut to the quick, and search your heart to the bottom?
11. Is it your desire and design to be on this, and all other occasions, entirely open, so as to speak everything that is in your heart without exception, without disguise, and without reserve?

Any of the preceding questions may be asked as often as occasion offers; the [five] following at every meeting: —

1. What known sin have you committed since our last meeting?
2. What temptations have you met with?
3. How were you delivered?
4. What have you thought, said, or done, of which you doubt whether it be sin or not?[9]

The pattern of Dion Robert in Abidjan, Ivory Coast, is a valuable one to consider. From his cells he receives weekly reports about deep spiritual needs within the huge cell church membership. In each sermon he deals with the most prevalent of the spiritual needs reported. His messages are strong teachings from the Scriptures, designed to guide members to personal victory. A testimony from a cell group member may accompany his message, demonstrating how victory came from the Lord to overcome sin or doubt.

Then, the cells meet. The cell pastor reads a brief passage of Scripture, often quoting the actual text of Pastor Dion, makes three or four minutes of remarks, and then systematically asks the group members: "What is the state of your soul concerning this sin or situation?" After this first cycle there comes the opportunity for the gifts of the Spirit to flow and edification to occur. One shares who has experienced personal victory; another is trapped in the problem. Here is still another person who has never faced the problem, who listens carefully and builds strength and insights which will be a future protection from this snare of Satan. One feels constrained to pray for another; a commitment is made to "be there" for a member should the temptation be faced during the next week.

A woman, trapped in a liaison with a married man who was supporting her, was offered a place to live by another woman in her cell.

All agreed to help her as she sought to get her life back on a Godly foundation.

A child was ill; the group gathered around the sleeping baby and prayed for his healing. A person weak in her faith was encouraged, and another resisting the clear leadership of the Spirit was admonished about the danger of doing so.

Thus, the Spirit causes those in cell groups to experience His mighty work — performed through the body members.

The Holy Spirit Guides Cells into Ministry

Over the Easter season in 1988, cell groups from one London church joined hands to plant a new cell in Woolwich. This district had been the site of munitions manufacturing for generations. During the Battle of Waterloo, for example, all the men in both armies fought with identical arms manufactured in the arsenal in Woolwich. It was a prime target of the Germans during World War II; they virtually bombed it into oblivion. After the war, it became a site for low cost government housing.

Imagine the demonic powers that had controlled that district for generations without being challenged! How pleased the soldiers of Satan must have been while factories created implements of death. No Christian witness had succeeded in gaining a foothold in Woolwich. Since 1947, no church had been established among the people.

So it was that cell groups, located on either side of Greenwich, had decided to invade this domain of darkness. I attended a prayer meeting held in a Baptist church which had been "loaned" to the cell groups after being closed for many years. The refurbished, rent-free space now serves as the site for their Greenwich congregation. After prayer and training we drove a short distance to the edge of Woolwich. For the first time in my life, I learned how to sing "war songs" to the principalities of the air. We sang of our invasion with a firmness gained from our season of prayer. Never before had I been more conscious of the battle we face when taking territory from Satan. In my mind flashed the words of Abraham Kuyper, "There is no sphere of life over which Christ does not say, 'Mine!' "

On that Saturday morning, a light snow was falling as we gathered in the center of the outdoor mall. The Christians were battle-seasoned veterans; that fact became obvious as we stood in a group, singing and giving testimonies of their changed lives. I was impressed by their transparent confessions of wicked living and how Christ had brought new life. Spiritually blind residents ignored or ridiculed the hardy band, not even slowing down as they passed us.

Our orders were clearly given back at the church: as God lays a certain person on your heart, break out of the group and talk to him or her. My "tap on the shoulder" from the Spirit led me to a man standing in front of a shoe store. He was one of only a half dozen who had finally stopped to listen to the testimonies. I said, "I'm a Yank from Houston. We're about the same age. Were you in the war?" "Yes," he responded. "I fought and was wounded." He opened his overcoat and showed me the well-worn insignia of his decoration. He openly shared his life's story. His wife had died. He had been living near many friends on the other side of London in a government housing development when a stroke put him in a hospital for several months. When he recovered, he was assigned by the housing board to live in a Woolwich flat. He was without contacts, lonely, and a bit frightened. He asked, "Could you tell from my speech I had a stroke?" "No," I said. "You speak well at present. May I ask you if anyone has ever discussed Jesus Christ's reason for dying on the cross with you?" "Haven't been to church since I was a tiny lad," he said. He quickly responded to my invitation to join me in a nearby pub, where we shared from my New Testament the story of Jesus.

Three hours later, he had prayed to receive Christ and became one of the charter members of the first cell in Woolwich. The next Sunday, seven people made professions of faith in the first Woolwich gathering! God had greatly blessed our efforts.

Ministry Involves Spiritual Warfare

The first Reformation began with a man who had no illusions about the battle zones. Martin Luther's verse from "A Mighty Fortress Is Our God" makes this plain:

> And though this world, with devils filled,
> Should threaten to undo us,
> We will not fear, for God hath willed
> His truth to triumph through us.
> The prince of darkness grim —
> We tremble not for him;

His rage we can endure,
For lo! his doom is sure,
One little word shall fell him.
That word above all earthly powers —
No thanks to them — abideth;
The Spirit and the gift are ours
Through Him who with us sideth . . .

Even so, the second Reformation is being launched with an awareness of the battlegrounds to be faced today. The rise of the occult, Satan worship, and the New Age movement has caused America and Britain to be as full of demonic activity as Africa or Asia.

John described the first level of maturity after becoming a spiritual "little children" as "young men, who have mastered the evil one."[10] It's crucial that new Christians are equipped to do battle very soon after conversion. John's comment makes it important for all believers to mature in this area, not just some of them. However, this must not be taught through feelings and fervency of emotion. That cannot create a solid foundation for warfare. Objective doctrinal truth, keyed into the teaching of inspired Scripture, must be the source for the believer's battles.

The Arrival Kit is a deliberate updating of my earlier work which focuses on the scriptural foundations for converts in a cell group church. It is necessary to help "little children" learn scriptural truth related to mastering the evil one. Particularly those who manifest the gift of Discerning True and False Spirits will be of much greater worth if they are well grounded in the Scriptures as well as in experiences with them.

Ministry: The Result of the Spirit's Control

Flowing with spiritual gifts which have been exercised to build up body members, the people of God will reach out to rescue those who perish in their lostness. Every cell group which has experienced the Holy Spirit's anointing will automatically reach out to others. It is a blight on the family of God to have a Basic Christian Community which occupies itself with itself.

One of the consuming drives of the physical body is the desire to reproduce. In the same way, the healthy body of Christ will be restless until it becomes a part of the army which invades Satan's domain. "God's got an army, marching off to war," is more than a praise song. It's a philosophy of life for a cell group!

Always, always, the measuring stick for the health of a cell should not be how much they pray or study the Bible, but how much they minister. In the case of the Abidjan church, Dion Robert's Zone Pastors do not permit more than a two week period of stagnancy before they step in and ask the Shepherd, "What's wrong in your group?" Yonggi Cho told how he does the same thing with Zone Pastors. If a zone does not show conversions for a couple of weeks, he says to the pastor in charge, "You go up to Prayer Mountain and fast and pray until God shows you your problem. Something is wrong spiritually, or the cells would be reaching out!"

With such a spirit, the cell group churches can grow at a rate which far exceeds what traditional churches can expect. Wearing the "full armor of God" is intended for soldiers, not sitters!

11

The Listening Room

I want to begin this chapter with a confession. On the last page of *The Four Loves*, C. S. Lewis wrote,

> Those like myself whose imagination far exceeds their obedience are subject to a just penalty: we easily imagine conditions far higher than any we have really reached. If we describe what we have imagined we may make others, and make ourselves, believe that we have really been there.[1]

I confess that where I am going to take you in this chapter is a model of cell church life I have never fully experienced myself. There have been times, though, when it happened without being anticipated. In those precious, unforgettable serendipities where gifts flowed and edification took place, I felt as though I were caught up, as Paul, into the heavens — not as far as the third one, but much higher than the first one! And I also confess that I feel cheated. Before I die, I want to know the full reality of body life as described in Scripture. Of this I am certain: *for those who won't settle for less, all we shall describe is possible.*

A Japanese Garden

While touring Japan, an American preacher was invited to the home of a pastor for a meal. His host showed him a beautifully manicured garden behind his house.

He had constructed a small room in the middle of the greenery, barely large enough to seat two people. It had a tatami floor, a sloped roof, and a single door. On the floor was an open Bible. Above the door, written in Japanese, was a small sign. Said the pastor, "That sign tells how I use this place. Can you guess what it says?"

The American replied, "Is this where you prepare your sermons?" "No," the pastor replied; "This is my Listening Room."

Before spiritual gifts can be properly manifested in cell groups for building up one another, believers must have a Listening Room and must know how to hear the voice of God. The physical location is not as significant as the event. The believer must not only talk to the Lord Jesus in prayer, but also hear from Him in the process. *Christ must provide edification before the believer can use it.* Otherwise, the "building up" in the cell meeting is nothing more than the activity of the flesh.

The point is crucial: one must hear God before speaking for Him. Strengthening, encouraging, and comforting one another in the cell group is to be done as each person becomes a direct agent of Christ's grace. The Holy Spirit's ministry in every participant is the source of the gifts we bring to one another.

When believers hear God, *a revelation is given.* While some evangelicals vociferously object to there being any further revelation beyond the canon of Scriptures, these same people are frequently heard to say, "The Lord has showed me that . . ." or, "I feel definitely led by the Lord to . . ." In each of these instances, their words reveal that they do have a Listening Room where God speaks in a deeply personal way to their need. Like all believers, they find direction in the Scripture and also direct guidance from the Lord. If this were not true, the place of prayer and meditation would be ruled out by them as having no value.

Among other groups, things are not so cloudy. "Words of knowledge," as they are popularly called, are often manifested. (It's too bad the term has been so abused that many now recoil from any person who uses it.)

Sometimes these "words of knowledge" are so unfocused that the cynic remains genuinely skeptical. D. A. Carson tells of a pastor who called for a member of the audience named "Bill," who "had a backache," to come forward for healing. When no one responded, he became more insistent that the person identify himself. Finally, a student stood up with a backache, but said that his name was "Mike." Carson writes, "Close enough," the speaker judged, and proceeded with the "healing." Such nonsense ought to be dismissed for what it is.[2]

Once again, my own reaction to such aberrations is that the use of spiritual gifts in large crowds is radically different than when exercised in a cell group, where people know each other so well that someone would say, "Come off it, George! Who are you trying to impress?" It behooves those conducting public meetings to be absolutely certain their word from the Lord is authentic before declaring it to the audience.[3]

On other occasions, words given in the Listening Room are so powerfully correct they cannot be contested by any skeptic. When Les Scarborough was told by a godly woman in his church that he was about to enter the most difficult six months of his ministry, he listened prayerfully to her words. She shared that the Lord had given her an awareness that it would involve another church that would go through severe satanic attack. Exactly as her word of knowledge indicated, he was asked by a nearby church to advise them about a deep problem. That church was actually destroyed in the weeks that followed, and the membership disbanded. Such special guidance from the Lord cannot be scoffed at.

Such personal revelations from Christ must not be seen to challenge the finality of the Bible as the ultimate revelation of God's truth. Spirit-prompted guidance does not threaten the infallible canon of Scripture. Obviously, such direction will always be in harmony with what the Bible teaches.

The book of Acts is packed with instances of personal revelation. In Acts 10, Peter sees a vision while on a tanner's rooftop which leads to the conversion of Cornelius, who has also received direct guidance from God to send for Peter. In the life of Paul, many instances show the place of special revelation as he planted churches. In Acts 16:9, for example, he is called to Macedonia through seeing a vision of a man of Macedonia standing and begging him, "Come over to Macedonia and help us."

The Burning Question:
Is this a Normal Experience for All?

There are so many dear believers who, in a desire to be accepted by their peers, engage in the use of tongues, prophecies, and visions, that are extraordinarily trite. These fleshly counterfeits are seldom examined as directed in 1 Corinthians 14:29. (In large meetings of Christians, it is also impossible to do so!) Nevertheless, we are called back to the reality of a cell group life where a special lifestyle is carefully outlined. Let your mind imagine a house meeting in the first century, depicted by Paul in these words:

> What then shall we say, brothers? When you come together, everyone has a hymn, or a word of instruction, a revelation, a tongue or an interpretation. All of these must be done for the strengthening of the church. If anyone speaks in a tongue, two — or at the most three — should speak, one at a time, and someone must interpret. If there is no interpreter, the speaker should keep quiet in the church and speak to himself and God. Two or three prophets should speak, and the others should weigh carefully what is said. And if a revelation comes to someone who is sitting down, the first speaker should stop. For you can all prophesy in turn so that everyone may be instructed and encouraged. The spirits of prophets are subject to the control of prophets. For God is not a God of disorder but of peace.[4]

This is not a "typical" modern small group Bible study! The thrust of the passage causes us to realize the focus is on the active flow of the Holy Spirit through each person for the edification of the rest. It presupposes a deep personal knowledge of the needs of others, and time spent in the Listening Room in preparation for the gathering. It also indicates some had come prepared, while others received an unanticipated word from the Lord in the meeting. Whenever this occurred, Paul instructed the group to accept such interruptions as a special activity of the Spirit.

The concept of the Listening Room flows throughout the cell meeting. All are sensitive to what the Spirit wishes to do, and all are receptive to His message to the church.

It must be recognized that Paul stressed *the underlying motive for these gatherings was to be mutual love, and not a love for the sensational.* Those who participate are those who have learned to take up their cross daily and to live the crucified life of a servant. They do not desire to attract attention to themselves or their gifts, but rather to edify others.

Is this too "far out" for our age? Shall we relegate this Scripture passage to ancient history and see it as inappropriate for today?

No! In a very special way, those who discover the church is more than a P.B.D. structure must see the church as powerful yeast within bread or blinding light within darkness. The church is the manifestation of Kingdom of Christ which functions within the kingdoms of this world (see illustration on page 146). It should not be expected to function either on the natural plane of the world or the semi-supernatural plane of the P.B.D. church. As the resident Body of Christ on earth, it has its own lifestyle. It exists to edify its members, to penetrate Satan's kingdoms, and to bring the power of Christ into direct encounter with the power of Satan.

Such a Gathering Requires People with "Listening Rooms"

Consider the spirit of those who gather together for such a cell group. Each one present has spent time in the Listening Room, communing with Christ and meditating with deep love on the other members of this special family. The writer of Hebrews captures the spirit of it all:

> And let us consider how we may spur one another on toward love and good deeds. Let us not give up meeting together, as some are in the habit of doing, but let us encourage one another — and all the more as you see the Day approaching. If we deliberately keep on sinning after we have received the knowledge of the truth, no sacrifice for sins is left, but only a fearful expectation of judgment and of raging fire that will consume the enemies of God.[5]

The assembly's motive is clearly stated in the first phrase: "to spur one another on toward love and good deeds." The last sentence in this passage speaks of accountability to Christ. If truth is rejected, there is nothing left but judgment.

With their cell group in mind, members go to their private places, their Listening Rooms. Edification is inescapably supernatural. For believers to be channels for edification, they must first be in touch with the Source.

What pastor has not experienced the direct connection between time spent before the Throne and the anointing of the sermon when preached?

So it must be for every saint of God. Listening precedes ministry for us, even as it did for our Lord. His nights of prayer prepared him for his days of ministering to others. Personal seasons with the Lord in prayer and contemplation open up the channels of edification.

Elizabeth O'Connor describes the experience of prayer as preparation for ministry:

> . . . community is not programmed into an evening, but becomes possible only when there are those who have done the essential, preliminary, inward work of prayer. . . . When the work of prayer has been done, we can see and hear in each other what otherwise comes to us distorted or is entirely blotted out. We do not have the same need to be confirmed by others or to find a place for ourselves in the scheme of things. Prayer frees us to be for the other person. It is preparation for the event of community.[6]

An attorney who participated in an Anchorchurch group in Fort Worth, Texas, said to me: "I begin to prepare myself for the next gathering of our cell at the close of each meeting. The longer I stay in the group, the more time I need alone with the Lord contemplating what He wishes to do through me for the others. My prayer life has taken on a new dimension as I have learned how to intercede and to hear the Lord speak to me about how I should minister to others in the group."

Many keep a little diary to use in the personal Listening Room, containing the names of all who have ever attended their group. Prayer times can then focus on what God has already done with and through others in the cell and on strongholds already invaded and overcome. In addition, specific needs which have been shared can be targeted for intercession and listening. Keeping in contact with others in the cell between meetings is almost automatic if such intercession is taking place. Often a word from the Lord comes to make contact right away with a person; such guidance should be readily obeyed. Doing things that show mutual love for one another may include remembering birthdays, anniversaries, etc.

In addition, these personal times should focus on seeking the very best from the Lord for each member of the cell. Lifting up the other members to experience the highest possibilities of Christian experience is worthy of extended intercession.

Praying about sin in the life of a fellow cell member is an entry into the battleground where Satan has strongholds. Such a sin should be seen as a reproach upon each cell member, and all should bear the sorrow as if it were personally committed. What does Christ want to do about it? What spiritual gift does He want to flow to restore a fallen brother?

Above all, one result of time in the Listening Room should be a resolve to point the way by personal obedience. Paul wrote in 1 Corinthians 11:1, "Follow my example, as I follow the example of Christ."

In addition, time listening to the Lord should include seeking ways to let the cell share in one's own life needs, including doubts and burdens, dreams and aspirations. The closer people come to one another in love and understanding, the clearer all personal faults are seen. In this way, edification becomes a mutual ministry.

Prepared People Create Powerful Cell Group Meetings

As each member performs this spiritual "homework" in preparation for the cell meeting, the work of the Holy Spirit prepares each person to be a channel for spiritual gifts to flow, and also to be the receiver of edification. There will be a topic for the meeting, but edification will be its purpose. Writes Elizabeth O'Connor,

> Contemplative prayer is communion with a sphere that is beyond the world we know, but that communion makes possible an authentic, healing community in the here and now into which people can come and be renewed and find out what it is they are supposed to be doing. . . . it is about being commissioned. It is going some place because one is sent, and then it is being a contemplative person in that place until one knows or is told what to do next. Much of our unease comes from not knowing where we are supposed to be. . . . Whatever our path, we do not feel right inside. The same dilemma is evident in the church's corporate life. . . . she is engaged without having been sent.[7]

Gifts Flow in Precious Interaction

In 1 Corinthians 12:7, Paul says, "Now to each one the manifestation of the Spirit is given for the common good." D. A. Carson points out that this verse and the ones that follow do not exalt one gift more than any other. Their application to life needs within the Body is the issue, not the exaltation of gifts seeming to be more significant.[8]

Here is a couple with a heavy financial debt: the message of wisdom is manifested. In another case, a person is struggling with a significant decision to be made soon: the message of knowledge is manifested. For another family, deep despair over a son on drugs has overwhelmed them: through the Body, the gift of faith is given for them. The parents are enabled to trust God to bring about his salvation.

The gifts of healings may be a focal point on another occasion. Countless illustrations document the way this grace gift has brought joy to cells that have seen God restore the sick through prayer alone.

Discerning between true and false spirits is needed more and more; demonic manifestations have become commonplace. Those who have tampered with the occult in the past are rampant in today's society. Bringing them freedom from their oppression calls for this gift to be exercised in the cell group from time to time. Zone Pastors in Singapore are frequently called by a cell group to assist them in an idol burning service for a family they have recently brought to Christ. Stephen Khong has prepared an expository message he uses on such occasions, helping the converts understand their new life and the power of the Christ who has come to indwell them.

The gift of support is mentioned in 1 Corinthians 12:28. I recall a teen-age cell group who took up an offering for the abandoned mother of one of their recent converts. The Internal Revenue Service was about to confiscate their furniture for back taxes the errant husband had never paid. After their meeting, the group taped an envelope filled with small bills to her front door, rang the doorbell, and hid in the bushes. As she opened the envelope, she must have heard a cough in the darkness. She called out with a quivering voice, "Thank you, whoever you are!" It was through that event she followed her son into personal faith in Christ.

Also in the same verse is the gift of direction, which uses a Greek word primarily used for piloting or steering of a ship. It's a powerful gift which is needed by the Shepherd and Intern, among others, for the building up of the Body.

Paul summarizes the manifestation of these gifts by saying in 1 Corinthians 12:11-12,

> All these are the work of one and the same Spirit, and he gives them to each one, just as he determines. The body is a unit, though it is made up of many parts; and though all its parts are many, they form one body. So it is with Christ.

It has amazed me that book after book, commentary after commentary, ignores the transparent teaching of Scripture about the manifestation of these gifts as the focus of Body life in cell groups. It is the result of minds entrapped by centuries-old traditional thought patterns. No matter how much Greek or Hebrew a scholar knows, he still writes in terms of his church being a large group, gathering on a campus with buildings used for worship or Bible study. It's reflected in page after page of his writings.

Why can't he realize that? *If spiritual gifts are to be manifested by every believer for the building up of the Body, what possible form can the church take except the cell group, the Basic Christian Community?*

In the same way, the 36 books in my library on prayer never even touch the concept of the Listening Room as a part of a corporate lifestyle to prepare a believer for ministering the gifts. Nothing I can find has been written to prepare believers for the edifying event so beautifully described by Paul in 1 Corinthians 14:26-33. It is obvious that, to him, this was a normative event for church life.

Applying spiritual gifts for edification is a lost truth in our generation! While controversy rages over the least of all the gifts, the thrust of this fourteenth chapter is buried and forgotten. We neither edify one another, nor witness to unbelievers by doing so, as depicted in verses 24 and 25. This is reason enough for us to focus more earnestly on the importance of listening to God for His direction for the Body of Christ. Lord, bring on the Second Reformation!

12

Children in Cell Churches

The Context and Conditions for Children's Learning as Discovered in the Bible

In the Old Testament, children are viewed within a group of people, most often their primary family. God's plan in creation was not just that man should not be alone, but that children should not be alone, either.

A child enters the world in the midst of a ready-made group of people on whom he is dependent. *The child's physical and spiritual welfare is the prime responsibility of the family which brought him into being.*

The Hebrew family was not an isolated unit. It was part of a larger community, the tribe, which was in turn part of a still larger unit, the chosen people of God. The network of community reached out from the child to the boundaries of the nation.

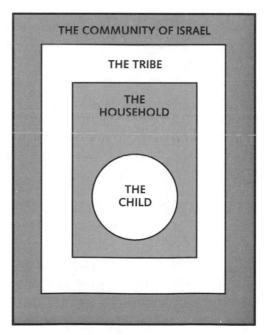

THE COMMUNITY OF ISRAEL

THE TRIBE

THE HOUSEHOLD

THE CHILD

The Hebrews did not see the child as the chance result of a physical human act. They regarded children as a gift from God, the sign of God's favor.[1] God knew each child from the time of its conception and his life was planned out ahead of time.[2]

When a child entered the world he belonged to God first, especially in the case of the firstborn.[3] The responsibility for the spiritual nurture of the child lay squarely in the context of the family, with the father having the duty of teacher and leader.[4] In Deuteronomy, the command to the family is to remember and teach.[5] The family is the context in which to retell the deliverance from Egypt and the greatness of God.[6]

The family was not alone in this enterprise. In a real sense, the individual saw much of his personality as being involved in the corporate personality of the nation. The individual's life was linked directly with the life of his ancestors and with the life of his living contemporaries. When the individual sinned, Israel sinned.[7] When the nation sinned, there was guilt upon every individual.[8] Israel could be described as:

> . . . a group of persons whose lives were so bound up together, in
> what must be called a physical unity, that they could be treated
> as parts of one common life.[9]

With this understanding, it was impossible that a child could be taught to know God outside the framework of the community of Israel, and especially in isolation from his immediate and extended family. Religious education was the responsibility of the community because the community was the arena in which the religious life would forever be practiced.

Furthermore, the way in which a father cared for his children and taught them was a symbol and illustration of the way God cared for his people and taught them.[10]

The Hebrew Child Was a Living Picture of the Nation's Relationship to God

Religious teaching for the child was not a matter of formal education until quite late in the history of the nation. From an early age, the young Hebrew child was involved in the daily and weekly prayers of his family. He watched the preparation and observance of the Sabbath. He

THE COMMUNITY OF ISRAEL

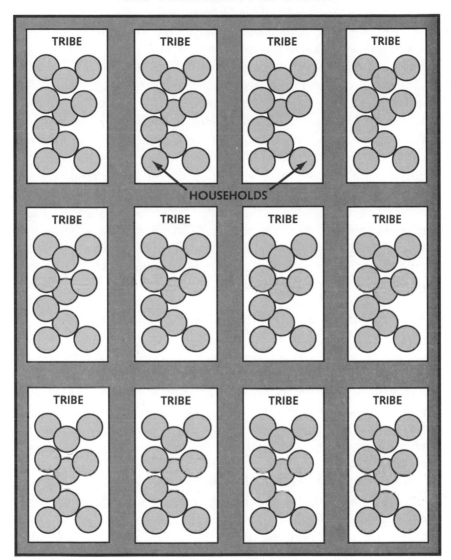

THE IMPACT OF THE COMMUNITY OF ISRAEL ON THE CHILD

- Modeling of Daily Life
- Passovers and Festivals
- Rituals and Sacrifices
- Commandments
- Sabbath

- Celebration of Events (Births, Entering Adulthood, etc.)
- Hearing the Law
- Drama and Signs (Prophets)
- Prayer, Witness

witnessed the sacrificial patterns of his family, and he would have understood that sin carries a death penalty. His parents were responsible for living the faith in open view, answering his questions as they arose. Speaking the words and commands of God to the next generation was not optional. The life of the nation depended on it.[11]

As each year passed by, he would share in the round of festivals, the Passover, the Feast of Tabernacles, the Feast of Weeks,[12] not as an onlooker, but as an active participant with an important role to play.[13] In some places, the child would see a memorial of the mighty acts of God, like the cairn of Joshua, and would ask to hear the story of the event.[14] At various times, the young child would meet the prophet of God, or a holy man who spoke the message of God and performed strange signs. It was such an experience as this which gave the Hebrew slave girl confidence to speak to her mistress about the prophet Elisha. Samuel, who entered the service of the temple so early in life, had a very special relationship with the old priest, Eli. In another passage, the young king Joash followed the instructions of the priest Jehoiada.[15]

Unplanned Modeling Shaped the Children

Apart from all these more obvious educational situations, there was the unplanned and unintentional modeling by the people who shared the child's world. The parents were specifically reminded that religious education was a day-by-day thing which happened at any time, in any place, even at the times when they were most unaware of it.[16] The teaching of the Lord was supposed to pass from one generation to another so "that they would put their trust in God."[17]

Not all the things which the children learned in this way were beneficial.[18] Sin in parents and grandparents carried its results into the lives of children to the third and fourth generation.[19] At times the children had to be protected from the idolatrous practices of their parents.[20]

Children Were Not Identified with the Nation's Sin

Yet, God did not always consider that the children were identified with the nation's sin. When the people of Israel refused to enter the Promised Land out of fear, God forbade all except the children to enter. The people had claimed that their fear was on behalf of their children, but ironically God transferred their inheritance to the children.[21]

Much later in Israel's history the prophet Ezekiel condemned this idea of community guilt. The righteous son should not die for the sin of the guilty father.[22] This suggests the New Testament idea that each person must find forgiveness for his own sin, but it does not invalidate the community nature of the child's nurture. Perhaps the most encouraging aspect of the Old Testament view of the child was the affirmation that he was capable of spiritual understanding and that his praise was acceptable to God.[23] God called the child, Samuel, and revealed his word to him.[24] Curiously, Samuel as a child is described in very similar terms to Jesus as a child.

> And the boy Samuel continued to grow in stature and in favor with the Lord and with men.[25]

Others who were called to be prophets from their birth were Samson and John the Baptist.[26] Apart from the book of Deuteronomy, Proverbs is the book which says most about the education of children. Once again the responsibility for training the child lies with the parents.[27] The father's authority over the child was closely allied with the authority of the Lord.[28] Probably the key verse for the nurture of children is in Proverbs 22:6:

> Train a child in the way he should go, and when he is old he will not turn from it.

This is not a promise that the children of godly parents will always turn out well. But it does suggest that the training a child receives does profoundly affect his later life.

The Childhood of Jesus

Probably the best example we have of the nurture of a Jewish child is the early life of Jesus. Even the sketchy evidence we have reveals the pattern of a godly Jewish household. After His miraculous entry into the world, God chose to provide Him with a family to guard Him and train Him. Even before His birth, His extended family relationships were strong.[29] Jesus was the oldest in His family, and probably carried the responsibility for His younger brothers and sisters from an early age. He participated in all the Jewish rituals[30] and began His worship in the temple festivals from the age of 12. We know that He was a part of an interacting community, because when He was absent during the return journey from Jerusalem it was three days before His parents missed him. Like many close-knit communities, they would have assumed that He was in the care of other adult friends.

Like all children, Jesus loved to ask questions; unlike some children, He listened to the answers. He felt completely at ease in the presence of adults, even learned theologians. By the age of 12, He already had a strong sense of relationship with God as His Father.[31] His life was also characterized by obedience. I do not think we should regard this pattern as exceptional. It is still possible for a child to grow up in a community of faith, to be mature (as a child) and obedient, and to have a relationship with God from an early age.

The Gospels do not record many direct encounters between Jesus and children, but some information can be inferred. It is certain that Jesus had close contacts with younger children in His home and community. He could describe their games, including playing as though they were attending weddings or funerals.[32] Perhaps He had even played with them.

He was sensitive to the needs of children. He knew they could be afflicted with demons or disease like any adult, and He healed them.[33] When He raised Jairus' daughter from the dead, He was most gentle and sensitive as He brought her back to life — like a mother waking her child in the morning.[34]

Jesus' teachings were not so boring that children could not appreciate them. At least one small boy appears to have followed Jesus all day, even forgetting to eat his lunch. The story method which Jesus so often used was intergenerational. A child might be able to perceive the point as quickly as the adults, sometimes even faster.

Children were never far from Jesus during His public ministry. When Jesus called a little child and placed him in the midst of the disciples, He did not need to search for one. He smiled, beckoned, and the child came. When He was at the busiest point of His ministry, Jesus gave the children His priority time and became angry when the disciples tried to exclude them. Like many adults today, they had assumed that Jesus did not have time to waste on children.[35] Jesus was glad to receive the praise of children even when some adults wanted to silence them.[36] (Children typically praise noisily and without suitable discretion.)

Jesus reveals the attitude of God towards children in a variety of contexts. He sees their relationship with their father as a model of the relationship between God and man.[37] He believes that God can reveal truth to a simple child which is hidden from their more learned and sophisticated elders.[38] He is so identified with children that to welcome a child in His name is the same as welcoming Him personally.[39] Conversely, the person who causes a child to turn away from God may as well destroy himself as face the terrible anger of the Lord.[40]

We have tended to lightly apply this verse to non-Christian parents or atheistic schoolteachers. We should not forget that many children have been turned from God by Christians who have acted in a harsh or insensitive manner towards them, or by Sunday Schools which have bored and insulated the children against the dynamic of the faith.

Children have special access to God in that their angels represent them before God. For this reason, no one should despise or overlook children.[41] God does not want any child to perish.[42] This surely says something about God's attitude to children who die before they are capable of making a responsible choice.

A child has something to offer God. It seems ironic that when the disciples were unable to meet the needs of the hungry multitude, a small boy was able to offer all that he had.[43] Jesus quoted the Psalms to remind the priests that praise from children was perfectly proper and acceptable.

Probably the most difficult area of Jesus' theology of children was their place in the Kingdom of Heaven. Jesus reminded His disciples that the citizens of the Kingdom must be like children in their nature.[44] This does not mean that childhood is a specially sanctified time of life. Jesus was a realist and did not romanticize childhood. It does mean that certain characteristics of childhood should also be characteristic of the Kingdom citizen.

A child has to receive the Kingdom by trust. He has nothing of his own that he can offer to buy his way in. He cannot earn his right to anything. The Kingdom is given to him freely.

The child is also a model for humility in Kingdom living. A child lives essentially in a state of total dependence on others. The only appropriate return he can make to his parents is obedience. Trusting and obeying is his required way of life. Later, adults imagine they have grown beyond that stage into independence and personal decision-making.

This does not mean, of course, that a child cannot be aggressive or self-centered. It does mean that in our society a child is without personal power and authority. His significant adults assert their authority over him, and many children attempt to resist that authority. In contrast, the child of God accepts his earthly father's authority, is secure within it, and uses it as his proper guideline.

This is an illustration of the nature of authority which Jesus envisaged within the church. Jesus would not accept a dominating, hierarchical system of authority. In fact, He expressly forbade it.[45] The authority of the Kingdom belongs to the Father. All citizens of the Kingdom have the role of servants or children, powerless in their own right, with their own authority being derived solely from their relationship and likeness to their father.[46]

There is one further indirect comment from Jesus on the nature of children's education. When the rich young man wanted to follow Him, he could claim perfectly honestly that he had obeyed the commandments of God from his earliest years.[47] However, he had missed the heart of the matter! His religious education had not altered his attitudes towards his possessions and his stewardship of them. Today, many children who have been well taught within our churches have also not seen the relationship of their Christian education to significant aspects of their lives. There has been no dynamic transformation.

Children, then, have a unique place in the Father's Kingdom. They are under His special care and are under His protection. Jesus identifies Himself with them and takes into Himself the attitudes with which people treat them.

Perhaps the most significant phrase in passages related to children reflects the place Jesus gives to them. He takes a child and places him "in the midst."

That's where children belong — in the midst of the learning community of God. They have two reasons for being there. First, they will learn best if they are in the midst of a vital community of faith. Second, the community needs to see the children visibly in their midst as a reminder of the nature of the Kingdom and their own attitude within it. The child is a living visual aid to the whole church.

The Child in the Early Church

In the history of the early church, children are notably absent from the scene. We can only infer the place of the children in the events which occurred. In Peter's first Pentecost sermon the promise of the Holy Spirit is extended to the children and descendents of the present generation of people.[48] The reference to household evangelism and baptism also seems to include children within the household, though we cannot be certain of the level of children's participation.[49]

The description of the nature of the church at that time gives a clearer picture of what children must have experienced. Churches met in homes for the most part, small homes where children must have witnessed what went on. They saw the believers meeting together often, sharing their goods with those in need. They must have heard the prayer meetings and watched the miracles which were performed. They must have been acutely aware of both the goodness of God through the merciful ministry of people like Dorcas,[50] and of His power, through the judgment of Ananias and Sapphira. They were probably present at the shared meals and saw the believers remembering the Lord's death. Much of their learning must have come through *being there*, witnessing the life of the church first hand.

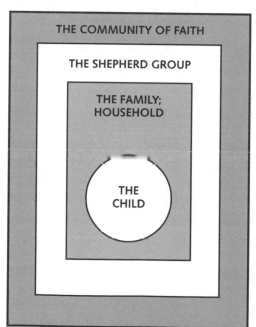

For some, there was an even more immediate learning experience. Some children were orphaned or saw their parents imprisoned because of their faith. They must have come under the immediate care of the Christian community.

For some children the influence of their family was crucial, even if one of the parents was an unbeliever as in Timothy's case.[51] Paul covers that point in

THE COMMUNITY OF FAITH

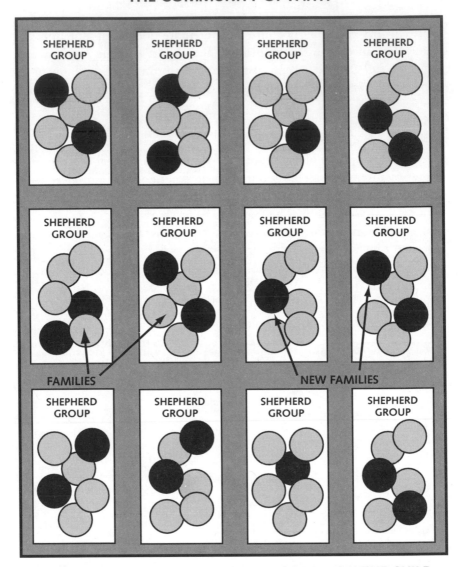

THE IMPACT OF THE COMMUNITY OF FAITH ON THE CHILD

- Modeling of Daily Life
- Festivals
- Rituals
- Scripture
- Worship

- Celebration of Events (Births, Entering Adulthood, etc.)
- Fellowship, Other Children
- Power Encounters, Healings
- Prayer, Witness

1 Corinthians 7:14, when he argues that the presence of a Christian partner in a marriage has a covering effect both on the other partner and on the children of the marriage. Paul's teaching on the stable family relationship is at the core of his view of the church as a community. The family is vitally linked with the church and the relationships in the church are based on the family model.[52] Children have a Christian duty to obey their parents, but the new element of the family relationship is the responsibility of fathers to treat their children with respect and not provoke them unnecessarily.[53] This must have sounded strange in a society where the power of fathers over their families was absolute, even to the point of life and death. The overall impression of the New Testament evidence is that children basically learned their faith from their parents, with whom they had a special Godly relationship. That teaching was, however, reinforced by the sharing of the family in the life of the Christian community. The children saw the words of their parents being lived out in the lives of people they knew best. They had a first hand experience of the power of God and the cost of discipleship. They knew that, for their family, being a Christian was not a nominal allegiance, but a serious daily risk to which all their adult friends were wholeheartedly committed. Half-hearted Christians can never inspire a lifetime faith in their children!

Conclusion

The Old Testament and the New Testament concepts of child nurture show remarkable similarities, which are diagrammed in the illustrations included in this chapter. The cellular structure seems to have particular strength in holding the families together within the overall community. This framework is better than a hierarchical structure where the whole weight of responsibility rests on the family alone. In the cell structure, there is mutual support and understanding, with one cell reinforcing the pattern of another cell. A partial or shattered family can be sustained within the whole community with supplementary help from other families. The one additional element in the New Testament illustration of the church is the possibility of outreach as families reach out to other families who are not in the faith.

The following principles seem basic to the biblical view of children's ministry:

1. God intends children to be taught and nurtured within the family setting.
2. The immediate family is supported and surrounded by the extended family and the community of faith.
3. Children are capable of spiritual understanding, and can offer acceptable praise and service to God.
4. Children are needed in the church community as a challenge and an example of some basic elements of kingdom living.
5. Children learn best through first hand experience and participation. Merely teaching children the right ideas is not enough. The goal is that their lives should be transformed as they become followers of Jesus.
6. The ultimate goal is full maturity in Christ.[54]
7. The present goal is maturity at the level of the child's development and understanding.

(Note: this chapter was contributed by Dr. Lorna Jenkins of Auckland, New Zealand, lightly edited by the author.)

The Structure
of a Cell Group Church

Part 3

13

Cell, Congregation, and Celebration

There are three words beginning with "C" which summarize the cell group church: *cells, congregations,* and *celebrations.* The most important of the three is the Cell. For those who are conditioned to think of the congregation as the focal point of church life, this will require radical adjustments.

Cells

Cells are the basic building block of all life forms. Following biblical patterns, the cell is also the basic life form of the church. Participation in these new churches takes place by joining a cell. The "one another" passages of the New Testament come alive as believers literally obey the pattern of Acts 2:42-46. They move from house to house on a regular basis. They break bread together, sometimes reverting to the original pattern for the Lord's Supper, where the broken bread introduced the Love Feast, and the passing of the wine completed it.

The cell's fellowship often includes the voluntary sharing of assets, even as was done in the early church. This is best done by the givers remaining as anonymous as possible, channeling the gifts for those in need through the Zone Pastor.

And, *the cells pray* — not polite little tritenesses, but by reaching toward heaven and bringing divine power into the needs of people in the room. Half nights of prayer are often cycled into the lifestyle of cells. Seasoned veterans of cell group life have seen God work in many ways and in many lives and delight in opportunities to pray for others. Intercession, deliverance, and other ministries often call for prevailing prayer by cell members.

This diagram shows the people who will typically be found in a Shepherd Group, not because it is so formed but because experience has shown it works out this way. If you were to attend a Shepherd Group for the first time, you would be able to identity the people belonging to each category.

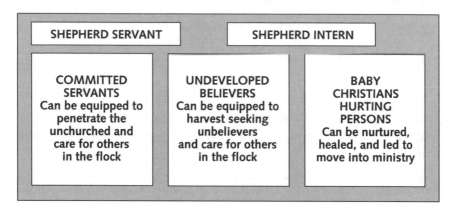

SHEPHERD SERVANT		SHEPHERD INTERN
COMMITTED SERVANTS Can be equipped to penetrate the unchurched and care for others in the flock	UNDEVELOPED BELIEVERS Can be equipped to harvest seeking unbelievers and care for others in the flock	BABY CHRISTIANS HURTING PERSONS Can be nurtured, healed, and led to move into ministry

We Are Going to Refer to Cells as "Shepherd Groups."

The Shepherd Group is the cell where people are nurtured, equipped to serve, and where members build up (edify) one another. It forms a community where believers are called to be accountable to each other, and where they can be totally transparent with one another.

Because the cell meets all the basic needs of the believer, it replaces the many "programs" that go on inside the traditional church. A cell group church has no Sunday School, Training Hour, Visitation Night, Midweek Prayer Service, or any of the other formal services which comprise other church calendars. In place of this, each cell becomes a true community, an "extended family unit" for Christians. A cell group church sees no need for other programs. Its basic needs are met in the Shepherd Groups. Adding further activities to its life dissipates the focus of believers and becomes counterproductive.

There are limits to the activity within a Shepherd Group. While it may begin its sessions with a brief time of praise and worship, that is not its primary purpose. While it will use the Bible freely in its lifestyle, it is not a place for Bible study. These needs are fulfilled at a different level in the life of the church, as we shall see in the paragraphs which follow. Thus, it is not necessary for the Shepherd to be a great Bible teacher, or even a strong communicator. Instead, the Shepherd must have a love for the flock and a desire to minister to their needs. He or she serves on a pastoral level, caring for the needs of the sheep. *The primary activity of the Shepherd Group is edification, building up one another.* This joint ministry of all is directed by the Holy Spirit, built upon scriptural teaching already received in an assembly of the cells meeting together in a congregation or celebration assembly.

In contrast, the traditional church collects people into classrooms in a church facility. Nearly always, members are insulated from closeness by involvement in a study of some sort, or a rehearsal, or a lecture, or a project. There are few times when members simply gather to belong to each other. They assemble to do something. Thus, people never really become close, and seldom visit in each other's homes. Their prayers are sincere, but they rarely expect immediate answers as they tarry together.

Cells Provide True Community

At one time, all people lived in family groupings. We now live among neighbors we barely know, where there are all sorts of beliefs, habits, and attitudes. In the cell group church, a strong focus is placed upon the development of relationships. People become responsible for, and to, each other. They sing, "Bind us together, Lord! Bind us together with cords than cannot be broken; bind us together with love." There is a deep-as-life sense of belonging to one another in the cell group church. That only exists when the group is small enough for intimacy to happen. All realize they are not there simply for themselves or their own sanctification, but for others who have parched hearts.

I am not talking about the creation of psychological therapy groups! The cell group church's point of reference is not on the emotional level, but upon the spiritual level. These people serve one another, edifying each other.

In contrast, the traditional church collects its members by rows in an auditorium or classroom. They sing the same song, put their money in the same plate, take notes on the same sermon. Their Bible study classes bring a sense of friendship, but not to a depth where the class becomes aware that Bill and Betty have a marriage in "white water." There are limited ways for each person to share spiritual gifts with others. Often, if the members of a traditional church create small groups for prayer or discipleship, they close the group to new people. The people who gather in them are there to receive, not to reach out. This is not true in a cell group church. Each cell knows it should multiply in a certain length of time. In Houston, for example, the cells should multiply in 22 weeks. In Abidjan, the time for multiplication is closer to 12 weeks! (One of the reasons is that 80% of Ivorians are unemployed, giving them many hours a day to focus on their cell group ministries.)

Share Group Cells Communicate the Gospel

Most significantly, the cell group church realizes they not only share the Gospel — *they are the living demonstration of it!* For them, "church" is never, never a word to use in referring to a building or activities which are held within it. The believers are the church, the beautiful bride, the body that lives in unity, the living stones, the holy and royal priests. The Gospel is embodied within them, not programs, services, or edifices. Thus, their cell groups are never, ever closed meetings.

To more effectively communicate the message of Christ's Lordship, a "sub-cell" of the cell group is formed, called a Share Group. In a later chapter, the structure of this subgroup will be explained in depth. Its purpose is to become a point of contact with "hard core" unbelievers who are totally unresponsive to gatherings of believers. The topics in a Share Group focus on the needs, problems, interests, hobbies, or inclinations of unbelievers. The Christians in the Share Group cell meet these persons on their own "turf," and on their own terms. I have seen a Jewess and an Arab student drawn to Christ by the same group at the same time. I have seen homosexuals face their lifestyle in a Share Group, and a lovely "Yuppie" with a razor-sharp mind confess her faith as she sat on the hearth of a fireplace in a group. Share Groups work!

More frequently than not, unbelievers will migrate from these sub-cells to the Shepherd Group itself. This is a result of a simple biblical concept taken literally: *every single child of God is a minister, and every one has a ministry!* Thus, all speak for God, and as a community they speak in a special way for Him through their community lifestyle.

Their evangelism is shaped by 1 Corinthians 14:24-25, which explains how harvesting is supposed to happen: when an unbeliever attends a cell group and witnesses the presence of the Holy Spirit among the group,

> . . . he is convicted by all, he is called to account by all; the secrets of his heart are disclosed; and so he will fall on his face and worship God, declaring that God is certainly among you.

A Shepherd Group had first-time visitors from a Share Group. They were not yet believers, but had developed a hunger to know more about Jesus. One was a Jewish woman, the other a man who, unlike the rest who came informally, was wearing a suit and tie. He was a banker with a Catholic background and had not attended a church in years. The group shared a common meal. One of the men briefly presented some powerful truths he had gleaned from his Bible study. A single woman parent had brought along her tape player with a background tape for "Surely the presence of the Lord is in this place," which she sang to the group. Her voice broke with emotion as she sang, and all were filled with a sense of Christ's presence.

The group took some time to get acquainted with the man in the suit, and he with them, by sharing the "Quaker Questions."[1] He shared that he had recently received a note from his wife telling him she had walked out of their marriage. *He was hurting!*

A lovely young wife shared with him how she felt when her father walked out of his marriage when she was only 16. She told how she and her mother's relationship with Christ had brought strength to them during that time. He felt Christ's edification coming to him through her. The Shepherd suggested the group cluster around the man and pray for God to bring him a deeper sense of His presence. Several prayed for him.

The cell then discussed another couple, not present that night. The husband had called. Their Chevrolet had blown an engine. It was his eighth week job-hunting, and they didn't have the money to fix it. He explained his wife was hurting too badly to attend the Shepherd Group. Someone suggested those present take up an offering for them. Checkbooks appeared, and a few moments later the total was counted: $765. The group gleefully planned how they would surreptitiously deposit their checks to the couple's account, so they would not know who had given the money.

A 25-year-old single had to make a decision about buying a house or remaining in his apartment. Some of the older ones asked some penetrating questions about his monthly budget. No one advised him, but he began to see that the choice to purchase a house at that time was unwise. He thanked the group for helping him. His own father had died a year earlier, and he shared how he missed being able to talk over things like this with him.

At the close of an hour and a half of such sharing, the group broke into pairs to pray. The Intern sat on carpeted stairs with the unbeliever, where they could talk uninterrupted. He said, "Shall we both pray, or shall I pray for both of us?" The unbeliever said, "I have another suggestion. Would you pray for me? I was deeply moved when the group prayed for me. But, I don't know how to pray for myself. And, for the first time in my life, I think I know why people get so close to God. I want to get close to Him. Pray I will learn how to share with Him."

The Intern probed more deeply. The man lacked all understanding of the basic truths of the gospel. God, Jesus, Man, Sin, the Cross, the Exchanged Life — these were all unknowns to him. He needed much more than a 20-minute presentation of the plan of salvation. He needed to share what he already understood, and the Intern needed to know what he was distorting when he used Christian words.

He was worth more to Christ than the reciting of a short speech. The men needed an entire evening alone together to really settle his decision for Christ. He agreed to set aside the next night for this purpose. They shared a meal to begin the discussion. It continued for several hours.

Do you understand? The evangelism "method" in that meeting was the presence of the Lord, operating through His Bride! He was "convicted by all; called to account by all; the secrets of his heart were poured out;" and he almost literally fell on his face as the men prayed together on those steps. He had discovered God was certainly among the people in the cell!

Once you have experienced such body life, it's agony to go back into a stuffy auditorium where strangers share a formal service, and no one even whispers a greeting to those seated around them.

How Do Cell Group Churches Differ from House Churches?

There is a distinct difference between the house church and cell group movements. House churches tend to collect a community of 15-25 people who meet together on a weekly basis. Usually, each house church stands alone. While they may be in touch with nearby house churches, they usually do not recognize any further structure beyond themselves.

There are tens of thousands of house churches around the world. Because there is no possible way to study them, there is no one pattern to describe them. Most of the time they grow slowly. Often they may not grow larger than their original number for years, having no aggressive evangelistic activity. They do not become a true movement of church expansion. Perhaps it is fair to say that some simply do not possess a vision for aggressively reaching the unevangelized, either in their own communities or abroad. It would also be unfair to say that's true of them all!

Many of Christ's finest people are to be found within the house church movement. One of their most celebrated writers is Robert Banks, who has written several important books. He and his wife Julia have authored *The Home Church*, an absolute treasure of information about house churches.[2]

In contrast, the cell group church recognizes a larger structure for church life. An assembly composed of cells which have networked under a common leader and ministry team is the norm. A good way to describe the cell group church is to think of a human body. It is composed of many cells, but no one cell would ever consider existing apart from the rest. There are links of love between all the cells in the church. Further, each one lives under the authority of a structure which services their needs and provides strong equippers to help them. Thus, the cell group church is a movement of God's people, always reaching out, always intent on drawing in the unconverted, always concerned about the equipping of every single member to function under Christ's Lordship.

Congregations

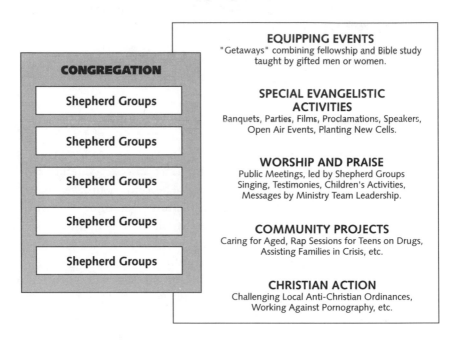

Cells aim to grow from seven or eight persons to 12 or 15 in four to six months. They then multiply into two cells. As the number of cells increase, the spiritual gifts of the body are called forth. Those who have the gift of teaching are discovered. Those who have the gift of "telling forth" are recognized.

The cells begin to form regional congregations, which seldom number more than 175 people. From within them, teachers and prophets come forth to share the Word and exhort, train and encourage. Thus, as the cells grow, many small congregations will be formed. However, they do not replace the cells as the most significant part of church life. For example, one never joins a congregation; *the only available link to its ministry is to join a cell.*

In some cell churches, the congregations have praise sessions. Large-group interaction takes place here. The congregation may set aside a half night of prayer, or sometimes several days for prayer or for teaching or training. Here the elder is one among equals, but loved and respected for the spiritual maturity which provides direction for younger servants.

I earlier referred to the cell church in St. Mary's District, just west of Sydney. Les Scarborough has seen a few cells grow to several congregations of cells in 5 years. He meets every Tuesday night with the elders and their wives who care for the cells in each congregation. I have attended some of those unforgettable gatherings. This dear pastor has multiplied himself sevenfold. He is greatly loved by the men who preach to those little flocks under his loving direction.

In contrast, the P.B.D. structure hinders those within the membership to exercise pastoral gifts. Some fear the pastor's prestige might be undermined. Sometimes the pastor jealously guards the office he holds, withholding significant preaching or teaching roles from the general membership. The traditional structure only allows a limited number of pastors.

As cells multiply, the need for pastors of various giftings also grows. Cell churches raise up "Zone Pastors" to oversee and care for the congregations. This person is often gifted in the areas of counseling, administration, and evangelism, but not in preaching or teaching. He is usually assigned to a congregation of cells and ministers among them. In no sense of the word does he become the "Senior Pastor" of the area cells and congregation he serves. His ministry is people-oriented, not pulpit-oriented.

The role of the congregation varies widely in cell group churches around the world. Faith Community Baptist Church has gathered its membership for a celebration, with weakly developed congregations. Others like Cornerstone Church in Virginia have strongly developed congregations. As I have studied these, it would seem that the vision of the pastors shapes the direction more than any other one factor.

Since all cell group churches are truly movements that have no geographical limitations, new congregations are needed as the years go by. Dion Robert has made good use of them for those who live too far away to conveniently travel to the main buildings. So has Yonggi Cho, who has auditoriums miles away from Yoido Island, where he is viewed by closed circuit television.

Celebration Life

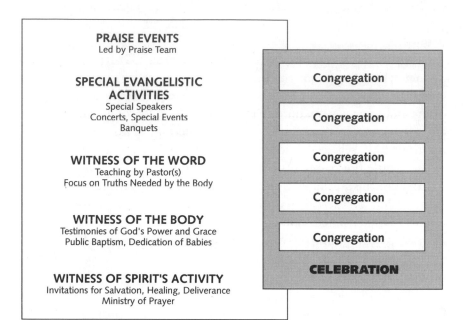

Finally, there are regular occasions when the cells gather for a demonstration of their life together in a giant celebration. These are "events," not services, and their length is of no consequence. They may last two or even three hours, with a break for refreshments.

Music focuses upon worship of the Godhead. There is much singing, often blending traditional hymns with Scripture songs. Slides or an overhead projector may display the words of songs; in some groups, hymnals are seldom used. Sometimes there is no song leader: the focal point is music projected on a screen. The room is charged with joy. A full hour of such praise time is not unusual.

Different traditions select different types of music. For example, in Dr. Cho's church the music is quite "Presbyterian." Nearly all of the selections are traditional hymns. On my last visit, the robed choir sang a beautiful selection from the Messiah. The audience recites the Apostle's Creed — most unusual for an Assemblies of God church.

Testimonies may be shared. Scriptures may be read responsively. The service may include public baptism of converts. An hour (and if I am teaching, longer!) of solid Bible teaching will always be included, often with the overhead projector used again. Scores of visitors may be present. At the close, the speaker (usually the senior pastor or elder) will invite those who wish to accept the Lord as Savior, or who have a special need, to raise their hands. In the place of an invitation to come forward, sometimes small groups of members encircle those who have raised their hands and minister to them. The hall then becomes one massive counseling room.

Most cell group churches must expand to two, four, even seven celebration services to minister to all the people. Rented facilities like ballrooms of hotels are often used, but eventually there is no facility in the city large enough to hold the people. By then, the numbers of members and the depth of their commitment makes it possible to pay cash for the construction of a facility to be used for these meetings, all-night prayer services, special equipping events, etc.

Why Not Just Divide into Smaller Units?

This is a frequently asked question in my seminars on cell group churches. The answer comes quickly when you examine the state of "parish churches" developed by denominations. They all believe the same doctrines and practice church life in lock-step with each other. Yet, their growth is erratic. It is caused by the different styles of leadership. The pastor of one church likes to counsel and does not teach very well. Another pastor is evangelistic, but does not feed the sheep. A third pastor is just downright lazy, while a fourth cannot manage well. A personnel director once told me that only a few people have an "automatic starter button" when they get up in the morning; most of the human race does better when they are supervised.

An effective cell group church must be a team effort. In nearly all of them I have visited, they have another important ingredient: *a truly anointed leader*. Many pastors are good administrators and preachers, but they don't have an anointing, a God-given vision that causes others to catch afire and burn for Christ in a special way.

When there is an anointed leader and a committed ministry team serving with him, honoring Paul's combination of pastor-teacher, evangelist, prophet, and apostle, there is much room for others to serve within the structures that form. Small churches which never grow larger than 250-300 simply lack the depth of vision and leadership that a city-wide or regional cell group church can have.

There is room in any city for more than one cell group movement, however. On one occasion I was visiting with Dr. Cho in his office in Seoul and he said to me, "I have been studying our Zone Pastors. I have two of them that I am going to sponsor to begin a work like ours. I will give them 5,000 members and $50,000 to begin their work. I know them well enough to know they can successfully carry out our pattern." As a professor of church planting, that made my mouth water!

When Cells Have Problems

A denominational missionary consultant in church growth said to me, "Cell group churches are only one method of church life. They don't always work." He then pointed out an illustration of a cell church in South America that failed to be successful.

I have spent many years examining the reasons why cell group churches grow, and why they have problems. I am convinced that the reasons behind the difficulties fall into these categories:

1. The cells are not based upon a solid theological understanding of why they exist. This is why so many pages of this book have been devoted to this area.
2. The pastors who develop cells are using them for the wrong motives. Cells developed to make a church grow will fail every time! Growth is never a goal — it's the natural byproduct of doing something right! Where there's true community, there will be growth.
3. The Shepherds were not properly equipped before being released for their ministry. The six-month period of apprenticeship for Shepherd Interns is critical. If the person isn't going to be effective, it will show up during that time, and the promotion to serving as a Shepherd should be delayed.
4. The cells had no zeal for the lost. Many of Yonggi Cho's cells triple their size through people won to Christ. If Dion Robert's cells go a month without a conversion, there are serious questions asked about its lifestyle.
5. A most common reason why cell churches stop growing when they reach 25 cells is that no attention has been given to the absolute necessity of providing one Zone Supervisor for every five groups, and one full-time Zone Pastor for every 25 cells. This is a maximum case

load for any one person. It's a major error, too, to assign a Zone Pastor another task within church life. The cells will suffer!

6. Competition with cell life leaks over from the P.B.D. mentality of the leadership. Other organizations compete for member's time. The cell is the Basic Christian Community, and it should have no competition!

Structural Options for the Cell Church

There are several successful ways to structure a cell church. Each structure shares the common elements of cell, congregation and celebration. Each one has been effective in equipping Christians for ministry and reaching unbelievers. All hold to a similar set of values, stressing that all Christians are ministers. All emphasize the supreme place of prayer. All have a similar goal, desiring to harvest the lost by penetrating society.

However, different cell structures develop and manage cells in very different ways. Each structure has a unique strategy for growth and oversight.

The 5 x 5 Structure

This is the "classic" system for cell churches around the world. Its major user has been David Yonggi Cho, who has built the largest church in the world in Seoul, Korea. It has been adjusted for use in El Salvador by the Elim church, which numbers over 110,000 members.

In this structure, a group of seven or eight believers reaches out to members of their *oikos*. They grow to about 12 to 15. During the time they are together, they sponsor incoming members who are trained to prepare them for ministry.

The leader of the Shepherd Group selects one or more members to become Interns to lead a portion of the group. Once maximum size has been reached, the group multiplies and two groups of seven or eight repeat the cycle.

It is called the "5 X 5 structure" because of the way it groups multiplying cells together to form Subzones. An overseer (often called a Zone Supervisor or Coach) serves up to five Shepherd Group leaders. This person is appointed to this task only after serving effectively as a Shepherd of one or two groups.

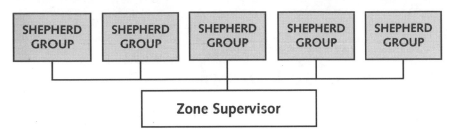

Five sub zones or 25 Shepherd groups form a congregation. The congregation is cared for by a Zone Pastor.

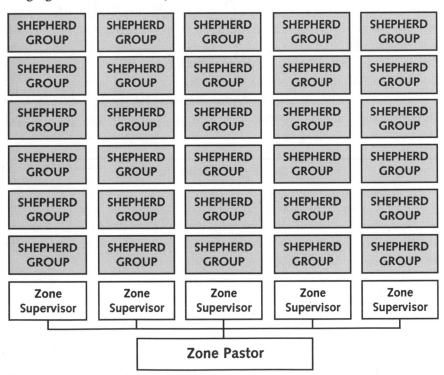

When there are five zones, these cluster to form a district, led by a District Pastor, who form a part of the Senior Pastor Ministry Team.

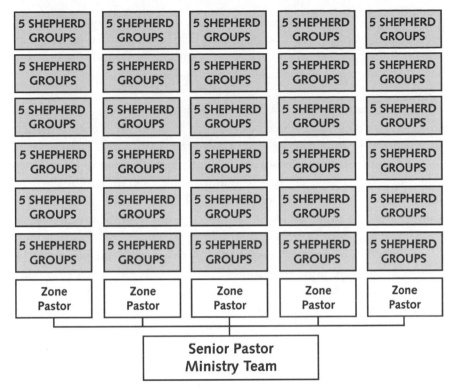

This basic structure can be found in Exodus 18. Moses was feeling the pressure of dealing with all of the issues requiring judgement and leadership within the entire nation of Israel. His father-in-law, Jethro, saw this and gave him some wise counsel. For this reason, this model is often called the Jethro model. Jethro tells Moses:

> What you are doing is not good. You and these people who come to you will only wear yourselves out. The work is too heavy for you; you cannot handle it alone . . . But select capable men from all the people — men who fear God, trustworthy men who hate dishonest gain — and appoint them as officials over thousands, hundreds, fifties and tens.

In this structure, the groups are usually formed geographically. Thus, there will be a North Zone, a Central Zone, etc. Some churches form cells by zip codes. Thus, cells match people who are not homogeneous but who live close to each other.

A zone averages about 250 people and 25 cells. A district will vary in number but averages 1,000 people in 100 cells. In this structure, there can also be homogeneous cells for children, youth, college students, etc. that may not always be geographical. Other non-geographical cells may form for those who are deaf, handicapped or who speak a foreign language.

Multiplication of the cells takes place when six or seven people grow to 12 to 15 people. Some cells can do this in about 26 weeks, although first generation cells may take much longer. As the cells increase, the installation of Zone Supervisors is mandatory. If the ratio of five cells to one Zone Supervisor is not maintained, the lack of mentoring and supervision can cause serious problems. There must also be a full-time Zone Pastor — the first paid position in the 5 X 5 System — to coordinate five Zone Supervisors and 25 cells.

In order to be successful with this model, these principles must be followed: 1) There must be a comprehensive equipping track that takes all new believers (and existing cell members) to a functioning level of maturity within one year. Without this there is a substantial breakdown in discipleship and leadership development. 2) Each cell leader must mentor two or three members with leadership potential to keep the number of interns higher than the immediate need. Without new leaders, cells cannot multiply. 3) A constant sense of urgency to see every cell member win a "Type A" unbeliever (a man of peace) for Christ within six months of cell life must be maintained. The cell group will ossify and eventually die if evangelism is not considered the primary purpose.

Benefits and Concerns about the 5 X 5 Model

The 5 X 5 structure is the most widespread cell structure today. It allows members who are not ready to become leaders to work in a productive cell environment and grow at a consistent pace while watching fellow members move into leadership. For many, this modeling is very productive. At the same time, it is a structure where "sit and soak" Christians can hide from issues and strongholds when the leadership is not strong or uninvolved in the lives of the members.

Relational evangelism between cell members has great potential in this structure. Many new Christians who join cells have solid friendships with three or more of the cell members. A concern is that when the "Type A" *oikos* contacts are exhausted, this structure can suffer long-term growth problems, observed in some cell churches around the world.

Cells multiply rapidly in this structure when cell members converted through relationship evangelism reach leadership. They are excited and have no traditional church baggage to discard.

A disadvantage is that close bonds are severed between cell members at the time of multiplication. For some, this is not a great issue when compared to the everlasting implications of Kingdom building. Others feel that working relationships should remain together for much longer periods of time.

Another benefit worth mentioning is that leadership comes from within. Successful cell leaders move into supervisory positions and then into full-time pastoral positions. At the same time when pastors come on staff, they may feel they are "out of the action" because they no longer have direct contact with cell leaders. However, ministry opportunities are always available.

The Interest Group Structure

The Interest Group structure has been developed through many years of testing. It is a development of the 5 X 5 structure and flows naturally from it. It is easier for those now in the geographical 5 X 5 structure to adopt it rather than moving directly into the G12 structure.

The Interest Group structure effectively converts geographical cell members into permanent leadership teams that focus on reaching affinity groups.

1 John 2:12-14 describes three levels of maturity among believers: little children, young men, and fathers (Of course, the gender designations are only related to spiritual maturity; John's description obviously applies to both sexes.)

The Little Children
In a typical cell in this structure, the little children undergo "transformation training." They are nurtured until they discover how to overcome the battles within their own lives. Few believers are effective in winning the lost until they have settled their inner struggles with sin, strongholds and soul ties. This is accomplished through a *Spiritual Formation Weekend* followed by the first 16 weeks of the *Year of Equipping* (explained in chapter 21.)

The Young Men

While the little children know they have a Father, young men also know the enemy and have "overcome the evil one." Young men are also virile, capable of fathering children. The *Touching Hearts Weekend* will launch the equipping of cell members to reach responsive (Type A) unbelievers and is followed by five weeks of daily study.

The Fathers

Young men then become fathers — those who have brought children into the Kingdom. Thus, the cell leader seeks to help each child become a young man and then mentors him or her to lead a lost person to Christ, thus becoming a father.

Fathers are then equipped to reach disinterested unbelievers. They are given training to penetrate people outside their *oikoses*.

Fathers form a team of three and target a specific group. They might reach out to the recently divorced, those interested in computers or who wish to learn a second language. There are literally dozens of contact points that can couple fathers to strangers through interest groups.

Interest groups meet for ten weeks. On the tenth week the whole cell becomes involved through a final activity. (This is fully explained in chapter 18.)

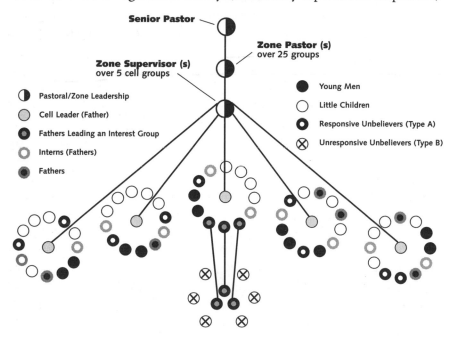

Implementation

After geographical cells have produced many fathers, they will form an outreach ministry creating 10-week interest groups to penetrate the lost. It is important for fathers to be called by the Holy Spirit into these target ministries. Christian A. Schwarz writes, "God sovereignly determines which Christians should best assume which ministries. The role of church leadership is to help its members to identify their gifts and to integrate them into appropriate ministries."[1]

As in the G12 structure, the geographical cells can gradually be restructured to target a specific interest group. For example, one person may have a burden to reach single women with children. Others can be given the opportunity to join in and form a new cell that will target this group. Fathers responding will withdraw from their existing geographical cells and form a new cell.

Over 20 interest group cells were formed using this strategy during the 1970's at West Memorial Baptist Church in Houston. They included: Divorcee Share Groups, Car Maintenance for Single Women, Teen Motorbike Repair Groups, Parents of Retarded Children, HOPE (Helping Others Practice English), etc.

When a 5 X 5 structure has reorganized so each cell group penetrates a special group, these cells begin to produce converts. They then form new cells that are homogeneous cells. They will not necessarily be geographical. Furthermore, it is possible for those in the penetration cell to remain together indefinitely, creating new cells with their converts. Close ties remain between these mother and daughter cells, since they meet regularly for strategizing new ways to reach their interest group.

When we first did this, it took about a year to see the results of restructuring cells to focus on interest groups. In our worship services, we had two rows for parents of retarded children, another row for teen bikers, Japanese families reached through HOPE, etc. In all, we had 21 different interest group areas that had naturally developed through fathers who had been led into ministry by the Holy Spirit.

One cell member had a vision for reaching people in apartment buildings. He manufactured a plastic holder for Christian booklets and installed them in laundry rooms where residents rested while washing and drying their clothes. Invitations to an interest group were placed in each booklet. Soon a large number of people had contacted him, and his cell began to swell with new converts.

Benefits and Concerns

The Interest Groups structure should not be implemented by cells that have not experienced a harvest of Type A unbelievers. Premature implementation could be harmful, much like running a marathon by one in poor physical condition. Cell members must overcome the evil one and sire converts and disciple them prior to launching an Interest Group.

Interest Groups require an abundance of cell leadership as well. Many cell churches move members effective in evangelizing into leadership, thus delaying Interest Group launches. This slows down penetration of the unreached. There must be a balance.

Interest Groups are very successful when disciple-making cell members have a passion to reach a segment of society. The addition of Interest Groups to a maturing 5 X 5 structure will foster body life evangelism.

The Groups of 12 Structure (G12)

César Castellanos is the originator of this system. He developed it for use by the International Charismatic Mission in Bogota, Colombia. He first launched his cell church using the 5 X 5 system and grew to a few thousand members. He then changed the structure, focusing on planting new cells instead of multiplying existing groups. The diagram at the top of the next page illustrates the system.

He selected 12 people from the church he personally wanted to disciple. He formed a "Group of 12" as a leadership team. Each person was assigned a segment of the community and formed cells within it. The G12 now meets weekly to report progress, pray, strategize, and edify one another.

César Fajardo, one of the 12, began to form youth cells. He trained teens to reach out to their friends and to form new cells. He then selected 12 successful teens to form his own G12. Thus, Fajardo belonged to Castellanos' G12 and pastored his own G12, with cells being planted through teens. In time, each of Castellanos' 12 formed their own G12, sponsoring cell members to become cell leaders. This "trickle down" effect has now mushroomed into about 20,000 teens in cells, and they are growing wildly! The adult cells are growing rapidly as well.

This structure is based on the model Jesus used to develop his disciples. Therefore, when you become part of a G12 you become a

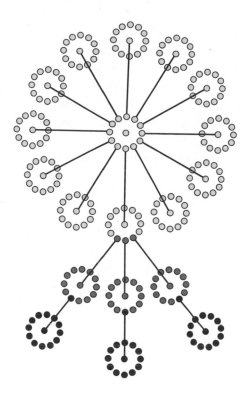

disciple of your G12 leader. When Castellanos was wrestling with how to lead his church, he felt God speak to him. He says:

> I began to see Jesus' ministry with clarity. The multitudes followed, but He didn't train the multitudes. He only trained 12, and everything he did with the multitudes was to teach the 12. Then the Lord asked me another question: "If Jesus trained 12, should you win more than 12 or less than 12?"[2]

In the G12 structure, every cell member is considered a potential leader. Each cell leader seeks to develop his or her cell members so that they will eventually lead a group. When cell members start new groups, the new leaders become part of the G12 of their cell leader. Therefore the new cell leaders' overseer is their original cell leader. This is one of the key principles — one is not a part of a G12 unless he or she is a cell leader. Therefore, the G12 structure is a cell leader care structure, not a structure that competes with the cells.

Because of this, cell leaders in the G12 structure of the International Charismatic Mission participate in three meetings per week. Each leader is involved as a member in a leadership cell (G12). They will also lead an open or evangelistic cell. In the leadership cell, there is nurture, care, and mentoring. In the open cell, there is edification and evangelism. Finally, the cell leader will lead a G12 meeting for his or her own cell members who have become cell leaders.

In this system, the cell leaders encourage the members to plant new cells rather than waiting for the original cell to multiply. When a cell member begins to meet with two or three other people, he has planted a cell group. When this happens, the new cell leader is invited to become a permanent member of a G12 rather than multiplying off as in the 5 X 5 system.

The G12 structure does not require Zone Supervisors, Zone Pastors or District Pastors. G12 leaders develop their networks, many having hundreds of groups under their care. G12 leaders mentor their G12 groups, who in turn mentor their G12 groups, and on and on down through the system. As a result of this highly relational network, the salaried staff is reduced dramatically. When a person has developed a network of 250 cells in Bogota, the church pays half the salary; to become a full-time staff member, the worker must have a network of 500 cells!

Encounter Weekends
Part of the success of this system is a result of their expectation that every person can become a leader. Therefore they have a plan to prepare everyone to lead a group. The first part of this process has proven the most powerful.

ICM regularly conducts a weekend retreat called *Encuentro* for incoming cell members. This is a critical part of their development. Multiple objectives exist for these retreats. For those attending, they experience deliverance from strongholds and soul ties, along with receiving the infilling of the Holy Spirit. It is an intense weekend of ministry, led by G12 members and fellow cell members who sponsor the new converts.

Benefits and Concerns
In the G12 structure, oversight is provided through relationships. Community is a priority. Cell members are constantly at each other's homes eating, playing, sharing the responsibilities of parenting and household chores. This fits perfectly in the Spanish culture.

Will Anglo Americans be able to duplicate this value? Living according to Kingdom values requires Christians to place relationships higher than personal freedom.

The G12 structure does not stress geographical structures. Instead, the homogeneous unit is the exclusive focus. Senior citizens, youth, doctors, business and professional streams are formed. There is a natural, relational linking of people to one another. At the same time, this may be difficult to sustain in sprawling metropolitan areas.

Because ICM requires their G12 leaders to participate in at least three meetings per week, this system can seem overwhelming to interested churches. Yet the G12 system is not defined by the number of meetings. Rather, it is a relational care structure where G12 leaders care for the cell leaders that they have developed within their own groups. Weekly G12 meetings are often not necessary, but weekly open cell meetings must not be neglected.[3]

The Department Model

A fourth major model for cell group organization has been developed by Dion Robert in Abijan, Ivory Coast. In this West African setting, *The Eglise Protestante Baptiste Œuvres et Mission* (The Works and Mission Baptist Church) has developed a strategy of war to come against the spiritual powers which bind people.

The son of a witch doctor in the village of Douleu, Dion made his way to Abidjan at age 21. There he joined the police force, and was so talented he shot up through the ranks to become a detective. At this point, he was sent to Senegal for a six-month training course. While there, he was led to Christ by a missionary and absorbed all this American could teach him in his free hours. Upon returning to the Ivory Coast, he set himself on a three to four hour sleep schedule so he could study the Bible undisturbed. With a mind like a sponge, he absorbed the Scripture until he was filled with its message.

In 1975, he went to see a missionary and asked him if there was a place he could preach out what was burning in his bones. He was driven to a residential part of the city called Yopougon and shown two small buildings with an "auditorium" added in the space between them. Dion moved into a couple of rooms with his wife, Helen, and their two children. They were the only members at the start.

A year later, the church had grown to 25 members. On May 1, 1976, during an all night prayer meeting, the people were deeply moved by the filling of the Holy Spirit and received a vision for the evangelization of the entire Ivory Coast nation. A year later, the church had doubled. Satan sought to destroy the church, and half of the 50 or so members left over Dion's biblical stand on the divorce issue.

In 1979, the missionaries who had sponsored the work wrote a letter giving the church autonomy. One year later, the little band planted a second church. In mid-1981, the group had grown to about 350 members, and realized they must build a better building for their meeting place. Dion still lived with his family in some side rooms off the small auditorium that would seat 100 westerners, now packed tight by the 350 who squeezed in "African style." It was in this year they decided to build a larger structure. They had extremely limited funds, since 80% of the people in the city have no full-time employment. Bag by bag, they bought and poured cement on a site a few miles away they purchased from the missionaries. Little did they know that this project would not be fully completed until 1990, and not entered for use until Easter of 1989!

Three more years of slow growth took place as Dion struggled to break from the P.B.D. model to the cell group church model. Dion took the limited information he gleaned from the Scripture and his reading to his nightly sojourns before the Lord, and divided his membership into cells. These were composed of separate cells for men and women.

Growth Began after Structures Were Fully Developed
Their next step was to organize the church structure into "Departments" which provided a root system to penetrate the community and win the lost to Christ. Responsibility was prayerfully delegated to Godly men and women. The graph of his growth does not explode until after he had taken this step to provide the superstructure for rapid growth. (See graph at the top of next page).

Within a year, the church had gone to four worship services and then exploded to seven — all preached by a man who was now sleeping on the floor of his own office because of the limited space available for the church's needs and the need for additional offices for the other pastors.

By 1987, there were 5,214 members and 232 cells. It was at this time Ras and Beverly Robinson visited the church, with the cloud of Bev's growing brain tumor threatening their future. The Lord flowed His

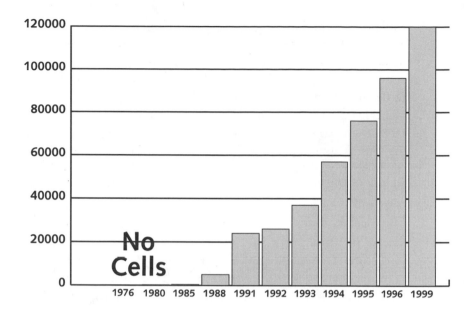

healing gifts into her while they were there; they returned to Fort Worth to discover she had been totally healed. This was one of many precious acts of God's power then being regularly experienced by the cell groups.

In January of 2000, there are over 120,000 baptized members in the church. Robert says these are the only ones they have reports from; he estimates there are more who do not turn in reports. Their ministry has literally covered all of the major cities of the nation.

The Cell Strategy

The cell groups are organized according to the homogeneous categories. There are five basic divisions: Men's, Women's, Children's, Professional's and Student's. This strategy fits their "at-war" mentality. In this setting it is easier to share deep needs and receive soul therapy. This also allows people to win their own kind rather than having to struggle to reach across social barriers.

Each cell group has a unique composition. Five different levels of commitment comprise the cell. First there is the cell leader or worker. Then he or she has three "disciples" that are being trained for future cell leadership. These people work together as the cell leadership core to follow up, heal, nourish, guard, and protect the sheep from the ravishing wolves.

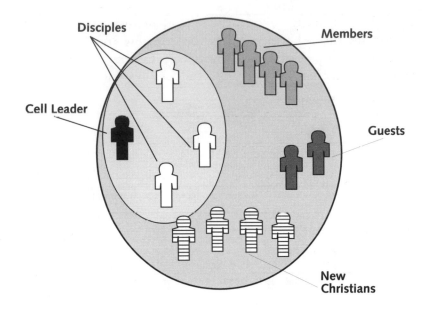

The third group found in the cells are called "members." These are believers who have been baptized, formally received as members of the church, and trained to work in various departments within the corporate body. These departments include ministries like evangelization, demonology, and others which will be explained below. The workers in the departments come out of the cells. The members are expected to be faithful to the cell and serve in a specific department. The "members" are trained in seven areas — discipleship, follow-up, structure of the house church, objectives of the church, soul therapy, vision of the church, and working according to the model.

The fourth group is comprised of new Christians in the group. These group members go through 16 weeks of follow-up and mentoring by one of the "disciples" from the cell. They are also preparing for baptism in a weekly course they attend for three to six months.

The final group is made up of guests. With these, the leaders visit in their homes to bring them to faith in Christ.

The Departments
The basic cell structure is supported by the ministries of other departments. This does not diminish the importance of the cell groups,

nor do they compete with them. These departments are support structures for the cell groups. These departments are classified under three categories — Ministries of Help, Central Ministries, and Specialized Ministries. The entire system looks like this:

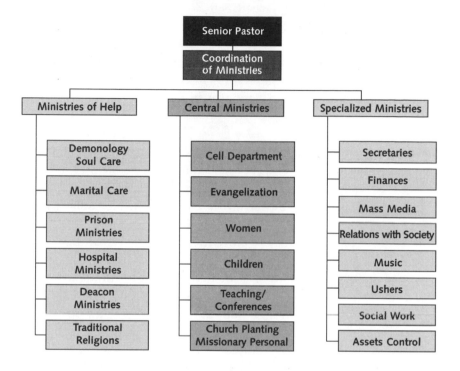

The structure within the Cell Department is very much like the "5 X 5" model.

The Evangelization Department is responsible for more than planning events or evangelistic campaigns. Remember, this is a strategy for war! This department is designed to win the battle against the enemy for people's lives.

When an unbeliever attends a service, a member from the Evangelism Department will make contact with him or her and set up an appointment to visit. After the person accepts Christ, another appointment is made for the new Christian to visit the Evangelism office during the next week. Four one-on-one meetings like this reveal the needs of the new Christian. He might be referred to the Demonology Department for Soul Therapy. If he has marriage problems, someone from the Marriage Department will follow up with him.

At Works and Mission Baptist Church, they do not consider someone a Christian on the basis of their public confession. They aim to raise disciples, men and women who are capable of doing something for the Lord. Therefore, each new Christian must go through this four-week evaluation in the Evangelism Department.

After regular meetings over a 30-day period with someone from the Evangelism Department, the person is assigned to a cell group as a "New Christian." At this point, he enters into the discipleship process for "New Christians," which includes 16 weeks of meetings with a cell group "disciple" and three to six months of training.

Benefits and Concerns

This model exemplifies a fully developed cell system. Through much testing, struggle and hard work, they have honed their system to meet the needs of the people in their cells.

Demon possession is rampant in the Ivory Coast. Not only is it the center for an evil blend of Rosicrucianism and animism, but the culture requires girls to produce a baby to prove they are fertile before they can be married. These girls go to witch doctors to be "blessed" so they will become fertile, and from birth the child is trained to worship the demon who "caused" the pregnancy. This church has responded to this with a full-blown Demonology Department with 24-hour ministry.

Many will see these multiple departments and conclude that evangelism is only done by those in the Evangelism Department or praying for the demon possessed is only done by the Demonology Department. This is far from the truth. Dion Robert records his first need for cell group ministry as: "It allows personal evangelizing."[4] Every cell member shares in the ministry of the cells.

Many churches must focus on building their cell structure and not all of the supporting systems. Adding departments only works when the cells are in place so the departments don't compete with the cells.

Cell groups form a part of their war strategy. Because their struggle is obvious and miraculous, the aggressive nature of this structure might not fit in every context. At the same time, one must not forget that "our battle is not against flesh and blood." Just because your battle is not as obvious as it would be in a culture filled with demonic possession, every cell structure must be made for fighting the spiritual war.

15

More about Shepherd Groups

Cell group churches worldwide use many terms for their cells. Bethany World Prayer Center in Baker, Louisiana has named their groups Touch Groups. New Hope Community Church in Portland, Oregon, calls theirs Tender Loving Care Groups. The name is awkwardly long, but it zeros in on the spirit of love and nurture which exists in each cell sponsored by that fine community of faith. Yonggi Cho speaks of his Cell Groups. In Cali, Colombia, the San Fernando Baptist Church selected Grupos de Amor. Some call them Life Groups and one church has adopted the name Friendship Groups. It really doesn't matter what they are called, as long as some thought is given to the way the description will be perceived by outsiders.

I have chosen to use the term "Shepherd Groups" in the guidebook I have written for cell servants. The main objection I usually hear to this term is that it isn't urban enough. One person commented, "What does anyone today know about sheep?" Of course, none of the other names mentioned above are particularly urban, either. My choice was made because the term is deeply rooted in Scripture. It makes sense to use it if one is looking for a theological base for a name. In 1 Peter 5:1-4, the apostle wrote:

> To the elders among you, I appeal as a fellow elder, a witness of Christ's sufferings and one who also will share in the glory to be revealed: Be shepherds of God's flock that is under your care, serving as overseers — not because you must, but because you are

willing, as God wants you to be; not greedy for money, but eager to serve; not lording it over those entrusted to you, but being examples to the flock. And when the Chief Shepherd appears, you will receive the crown of glory that will never fade away.

The name has a solid relationship to many, many Scriptures, which are reviewed in the first chapter of the *Shepherd's Guidebook* to emphasize that the pastoral role is not just leadership, but servanthood.

The New Webster's Dictionary gives this definition:

Shep•herd, n.: . . . one who exercises spiritual care over a community; a pastor or minister.

Choose whatever name you like for your cells, except "Care Group." (Ugh! More about that in a later chapter.) "A rose by any other name . . ."

Whatever the terminology, there are some very important principles which should not be ignored:

1. The attendance should never grow larger than 15 persons.
2. They should begin with three to eight persons.
3. They should always multiply when they reach 15 persons.
4. They should meet weekly, never biweekly.
5. They should be recognized as the Basic Christian Community of the church.
6. They should understand they are under authority, a part of a greater vision, and will be given assistance every step of the way by a vitally concerned pastoral team.

Shepherds Are Pastors of a Flock

A good shepherd is a revealer, not a teacher. Shepherds must be enablers, facilitators. They may or may not be effective teachers, counselors, or evangelists, but they must be lovers. They share their lives with transparency with those in their group, praying always that Christ will be formed in a new way within each life. They see three tasks as their primary assignments:

1. Each cell member should learn to exercise spiritual gifts.

2. Each cell member should be led to have a servant heart, edifying others through the exercising of spiritual gifts.
3. Each cell member should be equipped to minister to unbelievers, and personally experience bringing them to personal faith in Jesus Christ as Lord.

Shepherds Guide Each Person on His or Her Journey

I have written the *Journey Guide* for the Shepherd and the Shepherd Intern to use with all incoming members. It helps each believer chart the equipping steps needed for the journey into ministry and outreach. In the first year, the track makes it possible for the Bible to be surveyed from cover to cover and outreach to be experienced on two levels. (This is further explained in following chapters).

The family of Christ functions best when each Christian is led by someone who has walked a few steps ahead and at the same time is caring for others who are a few steps behind. It's a chain of caring. Thus, "discipleship" is replaced by "apprenticeship," as each cell member is responsible to someone and also for someone. This chain of caring extends all the way from the Father, through the Son, to the Shepherds. It then extends through the cell members to the newest believer.

It's pretty clear, isn't it, that being a Shepherd is not for the half-committed! It's a lifestyle of servanthood. It involves staying in close contact with the Lord and with the flock.

A good Shepherd doesn't ever drive the sheep. Instead, he lovingly leads them:

> He chose David his servant and took him from the sheep pens; from tending the sheep he brought him to be the shepherd of his people Jacob, of Israel his inheritance. And David shepherded them with integrity of heart; with skillful hands he led them.[1]

Some Christian groups look for "task oriented" personalities, who are then enlisted as cell leaders because they have a particular skill or ability to fill a particular job. Thus, most attention is given to finding the "talented." Without exception, every single Christian is gifted by the Holy Spirit and is expected to exercise spiritual gifts. There is no "hierarchy" among God's people. As we will see, this includes the children.

From time to time, a flock will include people who have severely damaged personalities. In some churches, they are passed along unhelped from one group to the next. That's not God's way! A Shepherd Group should pray over these problemed persons, asking God to help them become more than they now are. This may require special time with them, or perhaps a loving confrontation about their conduct. We shy away from such people . . . to their detriment.

The Three Spiritual Levels in a Shepherd Group

Consider the three levels in the Shepherd Group as seen by John:

> I write to you, dear children, because your sins have been forgiven on account of his name. I write to you, fathers, because you have known him who is from the beginning. I write to you, young men, because you have overcome the evil one. I write to you, dear children, because you have known the Father. I write to you, fathers, because you have known him who is from the beginning. I write to you, young men, because you are strong, and the word of God lives in you, and you have overcome the evil one.[2]

It's important to have a proper mixture of the levels of spiritual maturity when forming groups. To be an effective community, there should be "children," "young men," and "fathers." Note the levels of spiritual maturity in these three groups:

1. **Level One: Children — New Believers, Problemed Persons**
   The Children know forgiveness of sins, and know the Father . . . not with the deeper knowledge the fathers have of Him, but with a simple, childlike trust. These are represented by the first level in the diagram: New Believers and Problemed Persons.

2. **Level Two: Young Men — Outreach Team**
   The Young Men have overcome the evil one by their knowledge of the word of God. They are no longer tricked by the lies and accusations of Satan, who is described as the "accuser of the brethren." They can do battle with experienced eyes, knowing how he will attack. These are represented by the second level in the diagram.

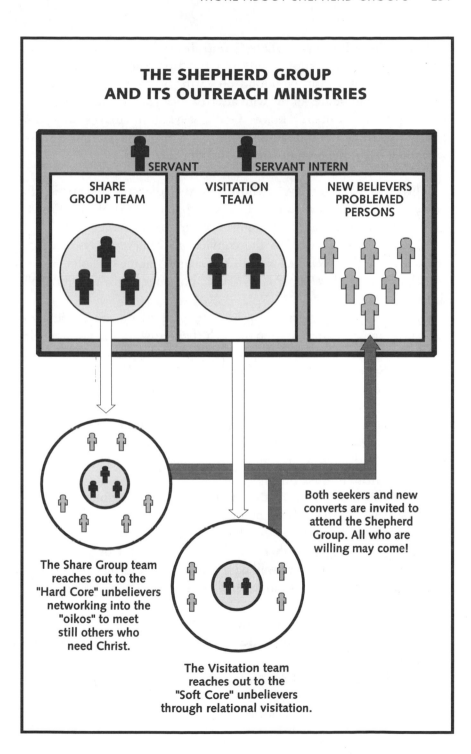

THE SHEPHERD GROUP AND ITS OUTREACH MINISTRIES

SERVANT   SERVANT INTERN

SHARE GROUP TEAM

VISITATION TEAM

NEW BELIEVERS PROBLEMED PERSONS

The Share Group team reaches out to the "Hard Core" unbelievers networking into the "oikos" to meet still others who need Christ.

The Visitation team reaches out to the "Soft Core" unbelievers through relational visitation.

Both seekers and new converts are invited to attend the Shepherd Group. All who are willing may come!

3. Level Three: Fathers — Share Group Team
    The Fathers truly know God, and function knowing whatever is bound in heaven can be bound on earth. As a husband knows the thoughts and desires of his wife after twenty years of marriage, even so spiritual "Fathers" know God's ways intimately. These are represented by the third and fourth levels in the diagram: the Share Group Team, the Servant Intern, and the Shepherd.

These divisions, or levels, shown in this diagram are artificially inserted. They are only used to help you recognize the levels of spiritual maturity suggested for effective apprenticeship to take place.

This structure is based on the conviction that every person needs someone else to help spiritual growth to occur. "Making disciples" is not the assignment of a few "super-Christians," but must be the activity of all Christians.

Many cell group pastors have said, "How are the other cell churches generating enough leaders to keep up with their growth?" It's not possible to use the traditional "discipleship" model which has been generated in the United States and achieve this objective! However, by using the "each one equip one" pattern of the Shepherd Group, there is a rapid development of equipped workers. Those who have first learned something, and then have had to teach it, know that this double process solidifies the grasp of the information as nothing else can. This is how people best learn how to live and change their values. The equipping chain is the answer!

At the "beginning end" of that chain of people equipping people is the brand new Christian. These newborns are to be treated as babes who "crave pure spiritual milk, so that by it (they) may grow up in (their) salvation." Beginning with them, a chain of caring for one another is established. Anyone who has walked a few steps ahead of someone else can share what has already been learned, and the journeys continue.

The First Level:
Working with New Christians and Problemed Persons

The first level in the Shepherd Group includes new believers and problemed persons. Neither type can become involved in ministry until after they are nurtured and matured.

**They helped every one his neighbor and everyone said to his brother,
"Be of good courage!"
Isaiah 41:6**

Each new believer is assigned to someone in the group who will help him become established in his walk with Christ. *The New Believer's Station* and *The Arrival Kit* help this take place. Over a period of 16 weeks, a new believer can usually mature enough to move into the middle division.

Problemed persons need the nurture of the entire group, but should be given special care by the Servant Intern. One type of person will be going through a temporary period of crisis, such as the death of a loved one, a divorce, loss of employment, etc. Like someone who has influenza, these persons must be temporarily helped until recovery takes place. They can then move into the middle level.

A second type in this first division is the chronically problemed person. These individuals are often "tolerated" until it is time for them to be "passed on" to someone else. Some are limited by their personality characteristics, and others never mature because people tend to avoid them. Their personalities are often anti-social. Sometimes they constantly say tactless things. In the *Shepherd's Guidebook* there are suggestions about how they can be helped.

The Second Level: Working with "Type A" People

Developing "Young Men" at the second level requires giving them experience. One characteristic of being immature is impatience. When children want something, they are not able to wait. They want it — now! This is also true with younger Christians who have not yet learned how to wait. It is best to give immature Christians a ministry which will produce quick results.

To do this, the Shepherd Group helps them to minister to "Type A" unbelievers — persons who are open to the gospel and to the church. These persons have visited celebration services and have asked to be visited. The names have been passed on to the Shepherd Group for further contact and ministry, perhaps because of age, geographical location, etc.

Additional "Type A" contacts will be found through *oikos* relationships — relatives, friends, neighbors, and work or school associates. "Young Men" must learn to pray for and minister to the people in their lives who are open to hearing about Jesus.

These contacts provide experience in meeting people, sharing in their needs, and inviting them to become a part of the Shepherd Group. If they are not yet Christians, it is often because no one has explained to them how they can receive Christ as Lord and Savior.

The Touching Hearts Guidebook has been written to equip those who will participate in this ministry. The course expects a team of two to work together, following the pattern Jesus established in Luke 10. This provides the accountability and the support needed to minister effectively.

The Third Level: Working with Type "B" People

"Fathers" are equipped by involving them with the hard to reach. The Type "B" unbelievers are not searching for Jesus Christ and show no interest in Bible study or other Christian activities. Only mature Christians are able to patiently minister can reach them. Like a mother with child, this "Special Forces" team must carry the burden of Type "B" unbelievers for many months before seeing them born again. Deliverance may be required as well.

This equipping is achieved by forming a second small group called a "Share Group." As shown on page 251, the Share Group meets separately from the Shepherd Group. These mature Christians will have two group meetings to attend weekly: their Shepherd Group and their Share Group. Each week, this Share Group team will move from house to house, involving "hard core" unbelievers in discussions chosen to bring them closer to accepting Christ as Lord and Savior. (More on this in Chapter 18.)

The commitment of time required to meet with both the Shepherd Group and the Share Group is significant. Only mature Christians who have "put away lesser things" can devote themselves to this dedicated life style.

Experience has shown that once a Christian has entered into Share Group ministry, he rapidly matures in the Lord. He will be thrust into new levels of faith which make possible God's further calling to become a Shepherd.

The Opening Hearts Trilogy has been written to equip these "green berets" of God's army. In the first of these three books, a team of three learns how to cultivate relationships with "Type B" unbelievers. The second book trains the team to lead a 10-week Share Group. The final book of the trilogy equips the team to penetrate the *oikos* relationships of the Share Group members to find the "man of peace" — the one open to the gospel.

When It's Time To Multiply

In all probability, in about six months a Shepherd Group will have grown to fifteen members, and it will be necessary to multiply it into two cells. At that time, the Shepherd Intern must be capable of shepherding half the group. From the very first week the cell meets, the Intern should be preparing for this time.

The pattern for this is found in 2 Timothy 2:2:

And the things you have heard me say in the presence of many witnesses entrust to reliable men who will also be qualified to teach others.

Consider the pattern of sharing which is described by Paul. His equipping was seldom if ever done using a "one on one" pattern. He refers to the "many witnesses" present as he worked with Timothy. Both Jesus and Paul discipled men in small groups, rather than "one-by-one."

Thus, the Shepherd Intern is equipped in the presence of the entire Shepherd Group. In this way, the members observe how the Shepherd equips the Intern. Since each of them is also developing someone, the Shepherd will be modeling how it is done.

The most ineffective way of developing your Shepherd Intern is by using one of the many discipleship courses available. Christianity in America, Australia, New Zealand, and Britain is saturated with notebooks, study guides, and lesson plans. Those who have spent months using this pattern of discipleship usually end up having good devotions, but few people have actually developed the capacity to shepherd others. The reason is obvious: shepherding is not taught; it's caught. That's why Paul wrote,

> . . . our gospel came to you not simply with words, but also with power, with the Holy Spirit and with deep conviction. You know how we lived among you for your sake. You became imitators of us and of the Lord; in spite of severe suffering, you welcomed the message with the joy given by the Holy Spirit. And so you became a model to all the believers in Macedonia and Achaia.[3]

Here's the pattern for apprenticing, taken from the *Shepherd's Guidebook*:

1. Your Intern watches you.
2. You explain what you did, and why you did it.
3. You observe as your apprentice does the same thing.
4. You objectively explain strengths and weaknesses you have observed.
5. You provide remedial activity to strengthen the weaknesses.
6. You turn the task over to the Intern.
7. You withdraw, using "benign neglect" as your strategy.
8. You closely monitor as your apprentice disciples a new Intern.
9. You remain a close friend, now treating your Intern as your equal.

How Do You Measure Spiritual Growth?

Measuring maturity is tricky! I have two grandchildren who live in California. We get to see them two or three times a year. When they come bouncing into the house, the first sign of change we observe is their physical growth. Grandma says, "Ruthie! You have grown three inches!" Little Ruthie beams with pride — as though she had personally triumphed over being smaller! We notice she no longer throws food on the floor. Mother lets her feed herself. She asks to go to the bathroom. Marvelous!

After a few hours with my grandson, I think: "Nathan's vocabulary has grown. He's writing new words, and he's also learning new facts. His little mind has grown."

At the close of a meal my son says to them, "Let's recite our Scripture verses for Maw Maw and Paw Paw." I listen as they speak the memorized words, rejoicing that spiritual foundations have been laid within them.

Then they get tired. Ruthie screams like a banshee when Nathan takes her favorite toy. He changes his cherubic facial expression, and glowers with selfishness. She throws another toy at him. Oh, dear! They are, indeed, still immature babies. I take Nathan to my office and say, "Nathan, you are a big boy now. Why do you still steal Ruthie's toys? You are too old to act like that."

He looks at me in stony silence. My mature words are not in his childish vocabulary; I am wasting my breath on him. Sadly, I realize such conversations between us are years away . . .

How do we measure maturity in these children? By knowing where they were, by seeing where they are, and by discerning where they must develop.

These same guidelines apply to those in the cell group. Where have they been? Are they responsible for their own lives, or are they controlled by circumstances? Do they know who they are in God? Do the decisions and choices they make reveal a God-centered value system? Are their jokes reflecting carnal aspersions to sexuality? Do they pray "on command," not at all, or with an appetite for fellowship with the Father? Edification is unique for all persons. It will be based on where they have been, and where they are.

Being Mature Is Measured by Being Responsible

The extent of a person's spiritual maturity is the extent of the commitment he or she has to Kingdom activity. This way of measuring maturity is most important. The Shepherd's assignment can be reduced to one simple statement: encourage flock members to be totally responsible for properly exercising their spiritual gifts.

The patterns of most traditional churches rob the believer of being responsible. The unstated practice is that the pastor must be mature and if others are mature the church is blessed. The pastor studies the Bible for the congregation, and shares his findings. The Christian is seldom exposed to biblical content in its entirety, rarely encouraged to purchase a basic set of books for personal research and study. When the believer has problems, he is given advice about what to do. If he has an illness, someone comes to pray at the hospital bedside. If a friend needs to accept Jesus, an appointment is made for him with the pastor.

In a cell church, the pastor does preach and teach the Word. He does counsel and lead people to the Lord. While he is responsible for using his spiritual gifts, he has the larger calling — to equip and encourage the entire flock to exercise their gifts. His job changes from doing the work of ministry to showing others how to do the work of ministry. While those in the traditional church often long to see this happen, they have yet to realize what can happen within a new structure.

Dealing with Strongholds

The weapons we fight with are not the weapons of the world. On the contrary, they have divine power to demolish strongholds. We demolish arguments and every pretension that sets itself up against the knowledge of God, and we take captive every thought to make it obedient to Christ.[4]

The word for "stronghold" used in this passage describes a well-established, strongly defended fortress. It guards the entrance to a territory or to a trade route.

Strongholds are the enemy of growth. With the Intern, the Shepherd will want to find private times with individual members to deal with strongholds. These times are crucial to the deliverance of Christians who have spent years wandering in the swamps of immaturity and defeat.

The use of the *Journey Guide* provides a perfect environment to discuss these areas of defeat in the life of the believer. It should be used as quickly as possible when a new member joins the group. Also many cell churches have developed a Spiritual Victory Retreat to minister to every member as they deal with strongholds. A vital part of the journey is challenging fortresses!

Daily Relationships and Shepherd Group Size

A Shepherd Group has a formal weekly gathering, but its life is actually embedded in the daily relationships and mutual sharing of life which is made possible by its existence. For that reason, its size simply must not exceed 15 persons, but that's not the critical factor. More important is participation. There must be an adequate involvement of all the members in the life of the group. When the community grows larger than 15, this becomes difficult.

The Shepherd Group is a Christian community. Jesus Christ has formed these living cells, and He is truly their Head. Perhaps you have experienced, or have observed, small groups in the church that sprang up quickly and disappeared just as rapidly. The reason? There was no true community: no renewal of persons, no ministry, no sacrificial love for others. These groups were simply meetings, regularly gathering on Sunday or Wednesday nights to "do their thing." Sometimes they piously reveled in their spirituality while ignoring the need-filled people around them. No room was made for the cross.

"Kinning" — As in "Kinfolks"

"Kinning" is creating true Christian community, where people become "Kinfolks" to one another. The cell must be a place where one is always welcome, no matter what stupid decision has been made in the past or the present. It's a place where crotchety, disagreeable, thankless old sinners are welcomed and challenged to be free from their inner strongholds. Praise and worship shape the cell's personality. The Lord's Supper, prayer, and the Word of God are vital to its lifestyle. It is missionary, reaching out to others until it must multiply and become two cells.

As people gather to form the group, there's no fixed pattern for how they will adjust to community life. All must start from where they are. Some will have had prior experiences of living and working together in the spirit of community, while others will find the entire experience a brand new lifestyle. Those who have never been a part of a warm family, who have lived lives of self-sufficiency for many years, or who have been betrayed in trust relationships, will need special encouragement.

"Kinning" takes many forms — as many as there are individual personalities. People cannot be developed by others; they must develop themselves. All others can do is provide the environment for this to take place. That's why it's important for the Shepherd to quickly provide specific tasks and ministries for all who are entering the cell group. Remember — becoming mature means becoming responsible. A person who is being useful is feeling worthwhile. Those who are simply expected to "be present" will soon fade away.

Like a marriage, after the honeymoon the group will have to work hard if the relationships are to be successful. The gold, silver, and precious stones in a Shepherd Group will not be found sitting on the surface. To discover them, there must be the digging out of deep spiritual relationships.

Shepherd Groups Multiply!

Only stagnation and spiritual bankruptcy can keep Shepherd Groups from growing! They will multiply, as we have said repeatedly, in about six months of time. As they do, Satan's domain has been penetrated and Christ has claimed His rightful ownership once again!

You are urged to read the *Shepherd's Guidebook* in conjunction with this chapter. Large blocks of this material have been reproduced from it, but there is much, much more in it for you to discover!

16

The Dynamics of Shepherd Groups

Architect Eugene Seow is one of scores of men who have caught a vision as he served as a Shepherd in a cell group. After months of experience in shepherding groups and seeing them multiply, he was made responsible for the equipping of incoming Shepherds. As he reflected on the challenge of imparting his experience, his architectural training took over. He developed charts that make the dynamics of Shepherd Group life clearer than I have ever seen them described. I joyfully share a series of charts with you, edited from his work, which show the pitfalls of not properly guiding the groups in their sessions together.

A lack of preparation for the Shepherd Group meeting is inexcusable! Each segment must be prayerfully, carefully developed using the concepts presented in this chapter. As Eugene Seow said to me, "If one cell group session ends at a low mood level, some will not desire to return. The Shepherd will pay a price for this, and will have to work doubly hard in the next meeting to build up the group again."

Mr. Seow has developed both a "micro" and "macro" look at the life of a cell. His micro chart presents the actual Shepherd Group meeting; the macro charts describe the stages the group goes through from the time of launching until it is ready to multiply. We are going to dissect the primary charts as we explain how things should go, and present charts which explain what will happen if things are not done properly. There truly is a skill in being a Shepherd — a skill which is caught, not taught.

Like anything else worthwhile in life, there is a "learning curve" before a person becomes effective in leading a Shepherd Group. While

Shepherd skills are developing, the preparation time required is greater than it will be when they are mastered. Shepherds who come to group meetings fully equipped in spirit and in mind will bless everyone involved. God honors preparation! In spite of the time required to develop into an effective facilitator, the true Shepherd will rejoice to see lives changed through his or her ministry to the cell.

Keeping a diary of the dynamics in the meetings and what happened during the weeks is extremely helpful in solving problem areas. These notes can be shared with the Zone Supervisor, who can give helpful counsel.

In a few months, what seemed awkward at the first will be mastered. Then the Shepherd can concentrate on the ministry side of his or her work without worrying about how to use the tools. In the beginning stages of launching a cell group church, it's important for the leadership to have previous experience in small group dynamics. While it's possible to read books on the subject, there's no substitute for experiencing the group process. Those who have done so will tell you

WHAT IS THE AGENDA FOR A SHEPHERD GROUP MEETING?

This is thoroughly covered in the
Shepherd's Guidebook.

It also contains examples of
how meetings should be
conducted.

It also shows the stages in Shepherd
Group life which are depicted in the
graphs which follow.

Order one from us today!
800-735-5865 • 281-497-7901 • www.touchusa.org

that groups build to a peak as the session goes on. In the case of a Shepherd Group, there are four important stages:

The first is called the "Ice Breaker" or "Welcome Stage." It has two parts to it. First, light refreshments should always precede the launching of the group meeting. As people arrive, this provides an informal gathering point. When all have arrived, chit-chat ends as the Shepherd calls the group to be seated. He uses a question which is totally non-threatening. My favorite can be used week after week: "Share the most important thing that has happened to you since we last met." It's important that all present participate in this, guaranteeing there will be no silent people in the group.

The second is the "Worship Stage." After relationships have been established between those present, there must be a bonding between the Body and the Head. It takes some skill and experience to create an effective worship period in a cell group. This is a topic so important it deserves a separate book! You will notice on the graphs which follow that the group hits its highest peak as Christ enters their midst in all His glory.

The third is the "Edification" or "Word Stage." The group focuses on the needs of those present, and/or the special work Christ wishes to do in and through the group. While Scripture is a vital part of this period, it must be stressed that the focus is on using the Bible as a tool, not the focal point. The people present are the focal point. The manifestation of spiritual gifts which build up the members present is vital, as is total participation.

The fourth is the "Share the Vision" or "Works Stage." This will always focus the attention of the group on their calling, the vision of the cell group church, and their ministry to unbelievers. As the first graph shows, this should be the highest point of bonding in the entire session. If people leave with a vision, they will feel Christ has been in their midst in a very special way.

Let's look at the graphs, described by Mr. Seow as "prescriptive, not descriptive." By helping the Shepherd anticipate both the macro and micro stages, problems may be avoided. They are designed to help in the planning for effective meetings and the effective multiplication of the Shepherd Group.

Figure 1

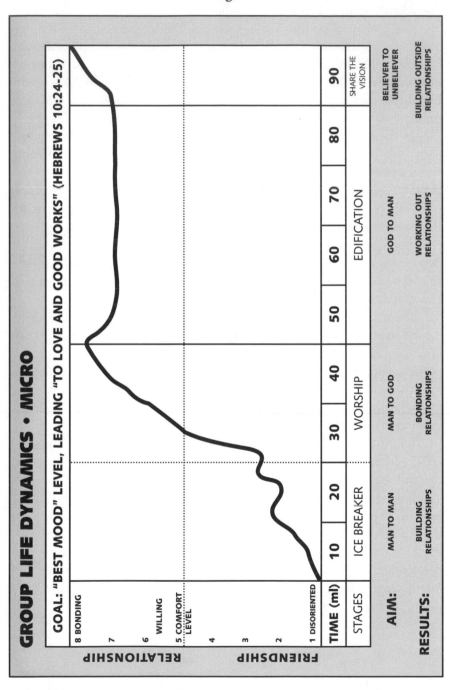

The Micro Look

A Shepherd Group session will pass through several stages — Welcome, Worship, Word and Works. Each is indicated on this chart as an example of a perfectly guided session.

The goal of the meeting is taken from Hebrews 10:24-25, which encourages the people of God to arouse fellow believers to love and active goodness, encouraging each other. The aim is to build relationships, not just to conduct a meeting by following a purposeless agenda. To be prepared for this task, there are two key steps which must precede the period of edification.

The first stage is called the Welcome time. It's a time for folks to feel comfortable together, to "shift gears" from whatever has been occupying their thoughts. It's a time of saying, "I'm here for you, and I accept that you're here for me."

After the relationships between those present have been established, it's time for the group to come into the presence of their King and worship him. Bonding the group to Christ is crucial for the time of edification which follows. "Man to Man," then "Man to God" are two phrases which will help you remember the pattern. Note the time frames set forth. The vertical lines which are dotted to indicate the flexibility of these two time frames.

When the group has been bonded with one another and with Christ, the level of edification can begin. To end the meeting on a high note, Mr. Seow recommends that the Works or Share the Vision segment of the agenda be placed at the very close. (Prayer, of course, has been a vital part of the edification period.)

His experience as a Shepherd verifies for him the importance of leaving the cell on the thoughts related to reaching out. He developed a barbecue every six weeks for his cell — a time for them to bring seekers or other unbelievers to be introduced to community. Such special events, along with the visitation ministry and the Share Group ministry, are the focus of the final period. As the chart shows, the meeting ends on the very highest level, and people are looking forward to their next get-together even as the present one ends.

Figure 2

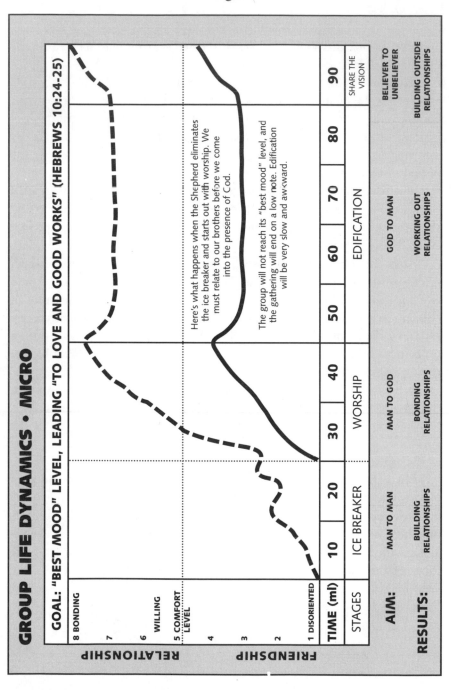

Figure 3

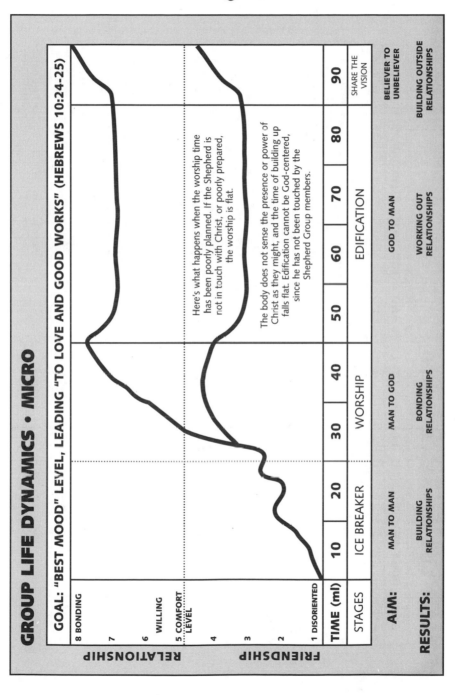

GROUP LIFE DYNAMICS • MICRO

GOAL: "BEST MOOD" LEVEL, LEADING "TO LOVE AND GOOD WORKS" (HEBREWS 10:24-25)

Here's what happens when the worship time has been poorly planned. If the Shepherd is not in touch with Christ, or poorly prepared, the worship is flat.

The body does not sense the presence or power of Christ as they might, and the time of building up falls flat. Edification cannot be God-centered, since he has not been touched by the Shepherd Group members.

RELATIONSHIP

FRIENDSHIP

8 BONDING
7
6 WILLING
5 COMFORT LEVEL
4
3
2
1 DISORIENTED

TIME (ml)	10	20	30	40	50	60	70	80	90
STAGES	ICE BREAKER		WORSHIP			EDIFICATION			SHARE THE VISION
AIM:	MAN TO MAN		MAN TO GOD			GOD TO MAN			BELIEVER TO UNBELIEVER
RESULTS:	BUILDING RELATIONSHIPS		BONDING RELATIONSHIPS			WORKING OUT RELATIONSHIPS			BUILDING OUTSIDE RELATIONSHIPS

Figure 4

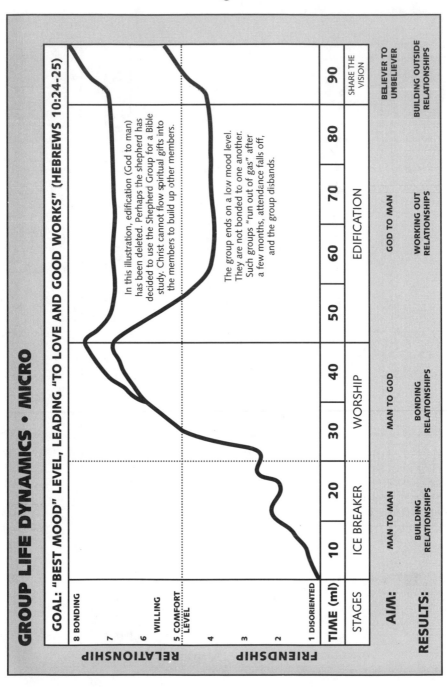

Figure 5

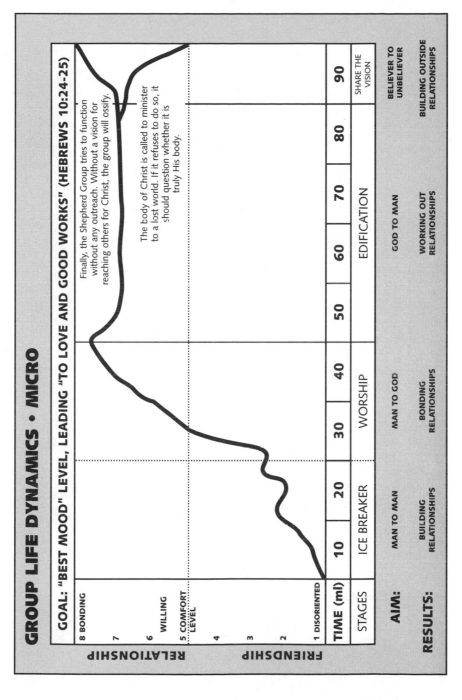

GROUP LIFE DYNAMICS • MICRO

GOAL: "BEST MOOD" LEVEL, LEADING "TO LOVE AND GOOD WORKS" (HEBREWS 10:24-25)

Finally, the Shepherd Group tries to function without any outreach. Without a vision for reaching others for Christ, the group will ossify.

The body of Christ is called to minister to a lost world. If it refuses to do so, it should question whether it is truly His body.

TIME (ml)	10	20	30	40	50	60	70	80	90
STAGES	ICE BREAKER		WORSHIP			EDIFICATION			SHARE THE VISION
AIM:	MAN TO MAN		MAN TO GOD			GOD TO MAN			BELIEVER TO UNBELIEVER
RESULTS:	BUILDING RELATIONSHIPS		BONDING RELATIONSHIPS			WORKING OUT RELATIONSHIPS			BUILDING OUTSIDE RELATIONSHIPS

RELATIONSHIP

FRIENDSHIP

8 BONDING
7
6 WILLING
5 COMFORT LEVEL
4
3
2
1 DISORIENTED

Figure 6

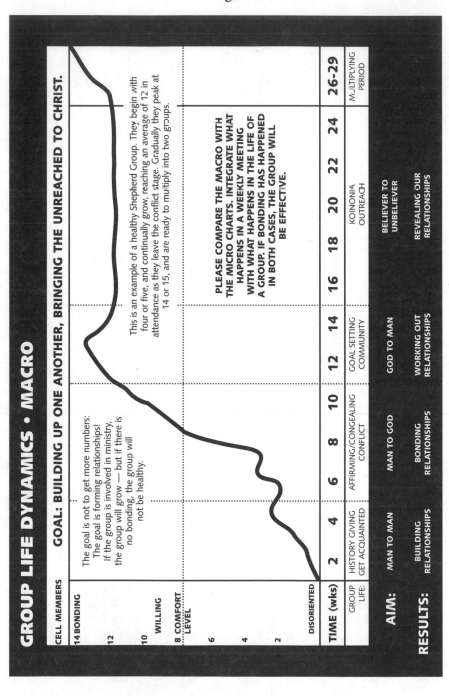

GROUP LIFE DYNAMICS • MACRO

GOAL: BUILDING UP ONE ANOTHER, BRINGING THE UNREACHED TO CHRIST.

The goal is not to get more numbers! The goal is forming relationships! If the group is involved in ministry, the group will grow — but if there is no bonding, the group will not be healthy.

This is an example of a healthy Shepherd Group. They begin with four or five, and continually grow, reaching an average of 12 in attendance as they leave the conflict stage. Gradually they peak at 14 or 15, and are ready to multiply into two groups.

PLEASE COMPARE THE MACRO WITH THE MICRO CHARTS. INTEGRATE WHAT HAPPENS IN A WEEKLY MEETING WITH WHAT HAPPENS IN THE LIFE OF A GROUP. IF BONDING HAS HAPPENED IN BOTH CASES, THE GROUP WILL BE EFFECTIVE.

CELL MEMBERS: 14 BONDING, 12, 10 WILLING, 8 COMFORT LEVEL, 6, 4, 2, DISORIENTED

TIME (wks)	2	4	6	8	10	12	14	16	18	20	22	24	26-29
GROUP LIFE:	HISTORY GIVING GET ACQUAINTED		AFFIRMING/CONGEALING CONFLICT			GOAL SETTING COMMUNITY			KOINONIA OUTREACH				MULTIPLYING PERIOD
AIM:	MAN TO MAN		MAN TO GOD			GOD TO MAN			BELIEVER TO UNBELIEVER				
RESULTS:	BUILDING RELATIONSHIPS		BONDING RELATIONSHIPS			WORKING OUT RELATIONSHIPS			REVEALING OUR RELATIONSHIPS				

The Macro Look

The macro charts provide signs to look out for, and goals to move toward as the weeks progress. In each case, the signs are indications of relationships being established and community being formed. There are five stages in the development of a Shepherd Group from birth to multiplication as is seen on the facing page.

A healthy Shepherd Group should multiply in about six months in the United States. It will vary with the hardness of the soil being penetrated, of course, and with the experience of the team leadership.

In this first graph, the left bar shows the number of cell members who are attending. Often the number of people who have attended one or more times may be double this figure. All should be contacted by phone each week, whether they are attending regularly or not. Note that there's a lot of "coming and going" in the first eight weeks. People decide whether they are in their "comfort zone" during this period of time. Gradually, the group stabilizes.

At the end of ten or twelve weeks, the group will have passed through the Affirming/Congealing/Conflict Stage and will move into the period of living in love together. This introduces the deep times of building up one another, with spiritual gifts exercised in a special manner.

It is at this time the cell seriously begins to reach out to unbelievers. The visitation team and the Share Group team are engrossed in their ministries, and growth is solidified as new people are brought into the "mix" of a stabilized community. The harvest replaces those who were earlier a part of the group but dropped out for one reason or another. These dropouts may be the result of a job change, moving to a new area, a death or serious illness in the family, etc. Although such persons do not now show on the attendance chart shown here, they may be considered a part of the ministry of the cell if they have not moved far away.

Shepherd Interns must be ready to guide half the group when it is multiplied in six months. This position is so important that no group should ever be launched without both a Shepherd and a Shepherd Intern from the very beginning.

Keeping a computerized record of the attendance and conversions of each cell group is mandatory! Only by examining the week-to-week develop-ment of a group can the Zone Supervisor and the Zone Pastor pick up trends and project when the group will be ready for multiplying into two groups. When that time approaches, very special attention must be paid to the cell.

Figure 7

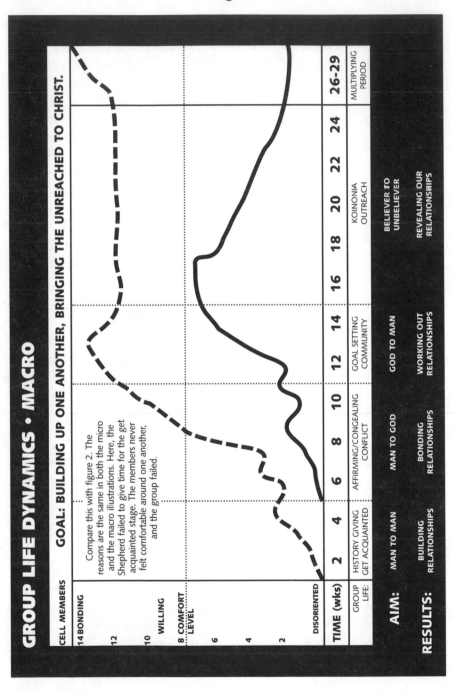

Figure 8

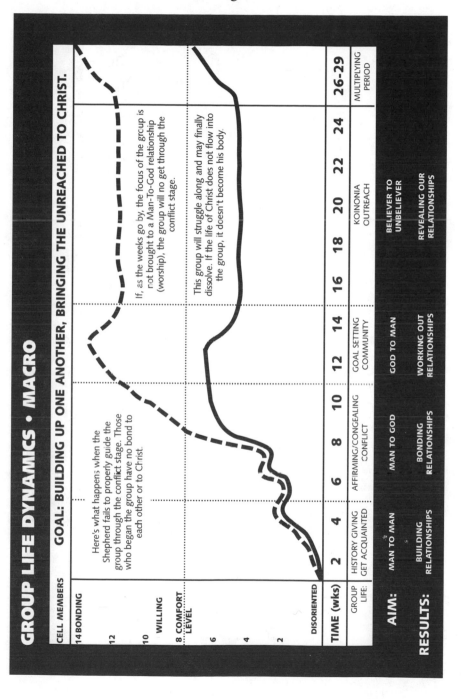

Figure 9

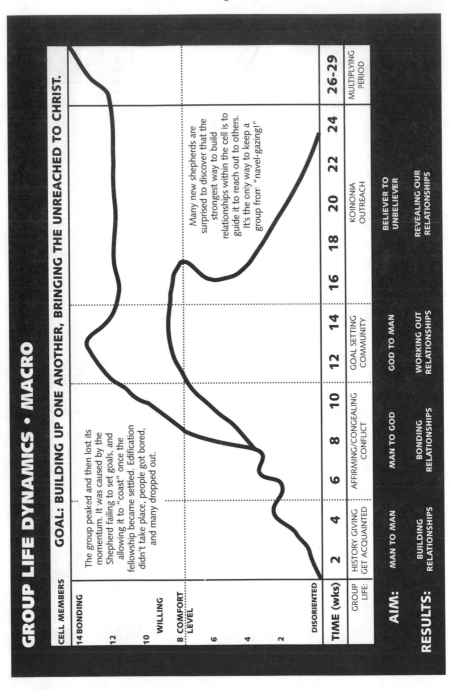

GROUP LIFE DYNAMICS • MACRO

GOAL: BUILDING UP ONE ANOTHER, BRINGING THE UNREACHED TO CHRIST.

CELL MEMBERS

The group peaked and then lost its momentum. It was caused by the Shepherd failing to set goals, and allowing it to "coast" once the fellowship became settled. Edification didn't take place, people got bored, and many dropped out.

Many new shepherds are surprised to discover that the strongest way to build relationships within the cell is to guide it to reach out to others. It's the only way to keep a group from "navel-gazing!"

TIME (wks)	2	4	6	8	10	12	14	16	18	20	22	24	26-29
GROUP LIFE:	HISTORY GIVING GET ACQUAINTED		AFFIRMING/CONGEALING CONFLICT			GOAL SETTING COMMUNITY			KOINONIA OUTREACH				MULTIPLYING PERIOD
AIM:	MAN TO MAN		MAN TO GOD			GOD TO MAN			BELIEVER TO UNBELIEVER				
RESULTS:	BUILDING RELATIONSHIPS		BONDING RELATIONSHIPS			WORKING OUT RELATIONSHIPS			REVEALING OUR RELATIONSHIPS				

Figure 10

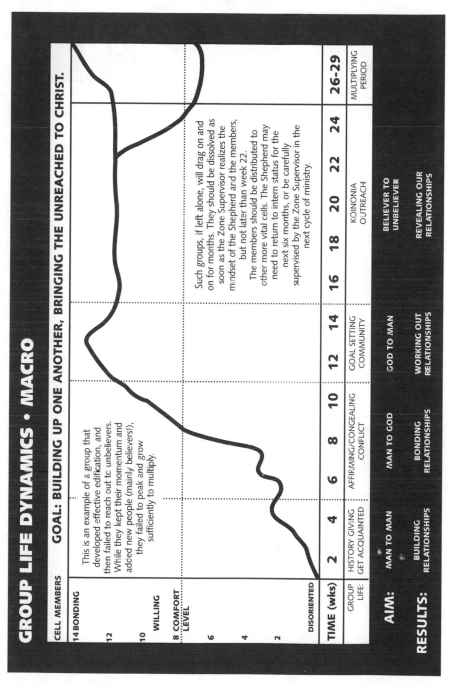

GROUP LIFE DYNAMICS • MACRO

GOAL: BUILDING UP ONE ANOTHER, BRINGING THE UNREACHED TO CHRIST.

This is an example of a group that developed effective edification, and then failed to reach out to unbelievers. While they kept their momentum and added new people (mainly believers!), they failed to peak and grow sufficiently to multiply.

Such groups, if left alone, will drag on and on for months. They should be dissolved as soon as the Zone Supervisor realizes the mindset of the Shepherd and the members, but not later than week 22.
The members should be distributed to other more vital cells. The Shepherd may need to return to intern status for the next six months, or be carefully supervised by the Zone Supervisor in the next cycle of ministry.

CELL MEMBERS
14 BONDING
12
10
WILLING
8 COMFORT LEVEL
6
4
2
DISORIENTED

TIME (wks)	2	4	6	8	10	12	14	16	18	20	22	24	26-29
GROUP LIFE:	HISTORY GIVING GET ACQUAINTED		AFFIRMING/CONGEALING CONFLICT			GOAL SETTING COMMUNITY			KOINONIA OUTREACH				MULTIPLYING PERIOD
AIM:	MAN TO MAN		MAN TO GOD			GOD TO MAN			BELIEVER TO UNBELIEVER				
RESULTS:	BUILDING RELATIONSHIPS		BONDING RELATIONSHIPS			WORKING OUT RELATIONSHIPS			REVEALING OUR RELATIONSHIPS				

17

Cell Evangelism Explained

As the illustration on page 251 indicates, reaching out to the unbeliever is as important to the life of the effective Shepherd Group as is edification. No true discipleship or spiritual growth will occur among Christians who are not involved in ministry to a broken world.

Since the Christian life is caught, not taught, imagine the impact made in an environment where even the newest Christians are reaching out to others. In a traditional church, it's quite difficult for a newcomer to actually observe others involved in evangelism. In a cell group, the focus is placed on personal growth with a motive — winning the lost!

The form of evangelism which is used is significantly different from contemporary styles of faith-sharing. It is important to grasp the contrast before proceeding further with our study of the cell church.

True Cell Group Churches Avoid Impersonal Evangelism Patterns

I have already shared my deep concern about the evangelism strategy within traditional church structures. Think about this fact: evangelism methods have changed very little in the last half-century. Denominations known for being evangelistic report steadily declining harvests. How long do we keep on doing what doesn't work before we admit we have a problem?

In my book *Future Church*, Os Guiness reminds us of an old Chinese proverb: "Never ask a fish what water is like." If you want to understand the limitation of evangelism methods used in traditional churches, don't talk to an evangelist or the instructors of commercially sold evangelism programs! Talk to the unreached pagan. Get out of the fishbowl and talk to those the traditional church has not touched. You will learn an important fact quickly: the evangelism strategy of the traditional church is totally out of sync with our society. It continues to assume everyone in America has a belief system similar to that held by we evangelicals.

Consider the problems we cause by the non-relational, insensitive use of personal evangelism methods now being used. A popular lead-in question demonstrates the issue clearly: "If you were to die today, and God were to say, 'Why should I let you into my heaven?' what would your answer be?"

I'm not critical of that question; I frequently use it myself. It's appropriate to use it with the "like us" people — the folks who will come on Sunday mornings to traditional church services. I sometimes use it with a stranger on an airplane. As have others, I have also seen strangers come to accept Christ on the spot. But always, always, I use that question only when I am sure I am speaking to a searching heart who is versed in Bible truths and open to God's good news.

It is the height of absurdity to assume that all unchurched people find that question relevant.

"If you were to die today . . ."

Tens of thousands of unbelievers do not believe in a life after death. The question assumes too much!

"If you were to die today . . . and God . . ."

What does this person think when you say the word "God?" Alcoholics Anonymous has recognized for years the wide variations in the way the word "God" is used in America. They skirt the problem by referring to Him as "your higher power, however you choose to define him." I strongly disagree with their approach as a Christian. Man doesn't have the freedom to define "God" by personal choice. *However, in a pluralistic society my definition of God is not necessarily held by others.* We are kidding ourselves when we use the word "God" and think every listener will define Him as Jehovah, our loving Father who has sent His son to redeem us from our sin.

I was in a Share Group with a number of students attending the University of South Carolina. Among them was a Japanese girl who had just arrived in the United States. We were sharing the "Quaker Questions" as an Ice Breaker. The final question asks, "When did God become more than a word to you?" She couldn't comprehend the question. A fine Japanese Christian in the group slipped into their mother tongue and explained what the question was asking. I shall never forget her response! She closed her eyes, shook her head to the right, waving her hand to the left. It was her way of saying, "I have nothing in my frame of reference on this subject."

". . . and if God . . . were to say . . ."

"Say?" God talks to mortals? To us, God is personal; He talks to us. Millions understand God as an impersonal force within an impersonal universe. The idea that He is relational is not believed by them.

". . . why should I let you into my heaven?"

Theological assumptions: there is a heaven, there is a hell, there is a judgment. I tell you from years of dialogue with unchurched unbelievers that thousands of them do not share any of those assumptions, particularly that there is a final judgment and an eternal hell.

I repeat: I am in full agreement with using that question with those who are living within a Christian orientation, and certainly with anyone at all who is searching for peace and is open to listen. But the idiocy of using it with the secular person who does not share our Christian orientation ought to be obvious. To talk to a stranger about a God and a Christ he does not know and to think that 20 minutes of memorized explanations without prior discussion will trigger a desire in that person to become a believer is patently absurd.

Would you agree to marry someone in that manner? Is not committing your life both now and forever even more important? Or, would you even commit yourself in advance to a lifelong friendship with a stranger? Then, why do we think disoriented unbelievers will respond in great masses to this approach? Nevertheless, this technique remains the primary "formal pattern" of evangelism in traditional churches. It continues because we absurdly hold the false assumption that all unconverted persons believe as we do.

As long as we remain in the traditional church and seek to evangelize only the "like us" people, this method presents little problem. However, the cell group churches are committed to touching the unchurched, and they have a big problem in using this technique!

What About Life BEFORE Death?

Have you ever wondered why the first question to the unbeliever has to jump from the here-and-now to life after death? Why does our offer of the Gospel have to start with life after death? Is it because what we have to offer the new convert in this life is a bit embarrassing to us? If the Bride of Christ is what it ought to be, life in Christ begins right now and the church will have great things to offer to the would-be Christian.

Jesus' focus was on the here, not just the hereafter. His concern was for those who are now poor, blind, imprisoned, and trampled upon. If we are His body to perform His work, *His power should be flowing through us to make this life new, right now!*

Look at the back page of any of the evangelism booklets or tracts. After the prayer of commitment on the inside back cover, then they suggest the convert find a good Bible-teaching church and join it. It seems we are a bit embarrassed at what we have to recommend to them between the moment of conversion and the Second Coming. Where Body life doesn't exist, the church is not a part of the Gospel message: it's a tack-on.

A Pure Church Has a Purer Evangelistic Message

In the cell group church, we have the rich treasure of the life of Christ being embodied in the here-and-now. So precious is it that one man in our congregation in Houston used to regularly fly in from California or New York to meet with his cell, returning the next morning to the tasks he left unfinished. Thus, the offer of salvation for the cell group evangelist is: "How would you like to experience the down payment of what Christ has reserved for you in eternity? You can begin to do so . . . right now! You can enter the Kingdom of God's love and discover what His family is like this very minute. It's awesome!"

A proper church life opens dimensions of evangelism not known in traditional church structures. The opportunity to first know an unbeliever in depth opens the way for the message of Christ to be inserted as a value, not just a piece of information. Bit by bit in the Share Group and in personal times together, the unbeliever begins to comprehend the joy of a life in Christ. He or she begins to question the

Christian about spiritual truth, and the flow of reality begins. It continues through both discussion and observation.

One of my favorite phrases to use in the last stages as an unbeliever comes to Christ is to ask, "Bill, knowing all you have come to know about the life in Christ, and considering all you have already come to accept as true, is it possible for you to turn around and walk away from Him?" One dear Jewish convert told me he felt like I had struck him in the chest when I asked that question. He thought for a moment and said, "When you put it that way, I see I am caught and there is no escape."

Instead of giving him a "canned presentation," I asked him, "Okay. Let's start with God. What do you believe about Him?" As we worked our way conversationally through all the biblical truths which are foundational to a conversion experience, we continued to dialogue. This was not the time for a lecture. It was a time for us to struggle together to find the pieces which were and which were not in place in his understanding.

When we finished, we found we had journeyed together to the Cross. I said, "Marvin, your last steps must be taken on your own. I will pray as you approach your Lord and exchange your present life for His eternal one. He will now indwell you, and His Holy Spirit will baptize you into His Body. When you return from the Cross, we will no longer be friends. We will eternally be blood brothers!"

Two General Classes of Unbelievers

Scriptures refer to "those who are far away, and those who are near." Unbelievers who are "far away" have no comprehension of the Gospel message. Unbelievers who are "near" are aware of the truth about God as shared in Scripture, and will be found filling out guest cards in the celebrations or congregations. They are two distinct groups, and must be ministered to in distinctly different ways. Their prior knowledge, or lack of it, is the key to classifying them in one of these two categories. For example, an unbeliever may say, "I believe all people who are sincere will make it to heaven. Buddhists, Baptists, everyone."

Two types of unbelievers: that's right — two types! Later, we'll subdivide them again into three stages of Type "A's" and two stages of Type "B's." First, let's learn about "A" and "B" types . . .

Type "A" Unbelievers:
The "Like Us" People, Easily Reached

1. They have attended a celebration or congregation meeting, and have been referred to you because they signed a visitor's card.
2. They already believe in God, accept the Bible, understand that Jesus is the Son of God, and have some awareness of Scripture facts (like Christ's death on the cross).
3. They may already have a church membership somewhere, but are inactive — perhaps have been so for years.
4. They are searching for something, and have come to our congregation in their search.
5. They may not have all the "pieces of the puzzle" in place as far as Christian knowledge is concerned.
6. Bible Study, and explaining the plan of Salvation, are appropriate activities to share with them.

. . . these people are reached through visitation!

Type "B" Unbelievers:
"Hidden" People, Needing Cultivation

1. They seldom attend church; have no desire to do so.
2. They may not believe in God, do not accept the Bible, do not understand Jesus is the Son of God, and have very little awareness of Scripture truths.
3. They have no active church membership.
4. They are not searching for the Lord's purpose for their lives, and have no intention of visiting church activities.
5. They have very few of the "pieces of the puzzle" in place as far as Christian knowledge is concerned.
6. Bible Study or discussing the plan of Salvation aren't appropriate activities to do with them at the start. There must first be a time of developing relationships — exposing them to the reality of the living Christ in our own lives.

. . . these people are reached through Share Groups!

This Pyramid Further Illustra᾿
Type "A" and Type "B"

Those at the Type "A" levels are open to the message we have to shaɾ
A special evangelistic Bible study called *The Handbook For Successful
Living* has been prepared to provide a "programmed learning" tool for
one-on-one Bible study that "fills in the blanks" for the unbeliever. It is
used by the person who has visited him or her, and has developed a
personal relationship as the foundation for close sharing. At the top of
the pyramid, the person is ready to make a commitment, and the cell
group member is trained to help in this wonderful moment.

The progress toward Christ is much slower with Type "B"
unbelievers. Patience and continued ministry through Share Group life
will bring many out of their spiritual blindness into the reality of
Christ's love.

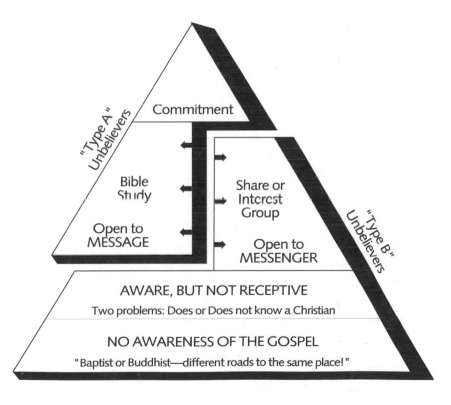

While there are many evangelistic patterns in the world of traditional churches, 99% of them focus solely on Type "A" people. This is logical: they are the only type who invade the private world of the Christians. Over 20 years of writing, testing, rewriting, and revising have been invested in the three books that comprise the *Opening Hearts Trilogy.* Along with *Touching Hearts Guidebook*, which prepares teams of two to reach Type "A" people, these books fully prepare a Christian to minister at all five levels found among unbelievers. It is possible, through the application of this equipping in the cell, to fully train a new believer in a year's time to sow, cultivate, and harvest. This is not done through classes taught by pastors, but by the members of the cell learning and then sharing what they have learned with other cell members. The pattern must be a tight combination of participating together in ministry, and studying the affective materials of the courses.

The "Oikos" Family of Words

Three words which belong to the *oikos* family are helpful to the cell group trainee in evangelism. The first is the mother word, *oikos*. It's the key to making contacts naturally, evangelizing those who are brought into our lives through the people we know.

The second word is our old friend *oikedomeo*, "building up," which requires the manifestation of spiritual gifts. It is a most powerful witness in a Share Group, where three Christians actually form community to be observed and entered by unbelievers.

The third word is *oikonomos*, translated "steward." It refers to a household servant who is entrusted with his master's wealth. He is to dispense it as a "proper ration at the proper time" to the members of the *oikos*, based on their needs. The Christian learns there are different "rations" for those at the five levels of the pyramid. Knowing that evangelism involves sharing the message of the cross is critical; knowing when to share it is also important. These details are carefully woven into the equipping materials provided for the cell group to use in the development of their outreach ministries.

These two tasks dominate the Shepherd Group life, and give a common task to all in the body of Christ. This common vision — reaching the lost and equipping believers for that task — provides the continuity between all the cell groups. It avoids the danger of the common direction being dissipated as different cells use different approaches to their lifestyles. There should never, ever, be a "skunkworks" community of cells, where each one does what is right in the sight of his own eyes.

The Oikos Strategy

A Type "A" unbeliever comes to a Celebration. A cell member, using *The Touching Hearts Guidebook*, has been trained to make contact on behalf of the cell. A special relationship develops between the visitor and the visited. In the proper way, a friend asks a friend about his relationship with the Lord. The person shares that the issue has never been settled. Using John 3:16 and a simple drawing done on the back of a place mat in a restaurant, a two way discussion takes place about the meaning of becoming a believer. The seeker fully realizes what it means to declare Christ as Lord, and then accepts Christ. He begins immediately to mature through attending the Shepherd Group.

The family of this new convert, along with friends and business contacts, is his *oikos*. The cell member who brought him to Christ meets most of them, introduced by the new convert and therefore accepted into the "inner circle" of their group. Following the principle of Luke 10:1-7, they search for others who are looking for the peace Christ brings. An oikos network of conversions begins.

The "*oikos* strategy" is built upon some important concepts Jesus gave the 72 disciples before He sent them into Perea in Luke 10:1-9. Let's examine it point by point:

> After this the Lord appointed seventy-two others and sent them two by two ahead of him to every town and place where he was about to go. He told them, "The harvest is plentiful, but the workers are few. Ask the Lord of the harvest, therefore, to send out workers into his harvest field."

Thirty-six teams of two are going to penetrate an area ignored by the religious leaders in Jerusalem. When each pair met a local person, there would be three — the starting place for community.

Our Lord doesn't paint a rosy picture. He says,

Go! I am sending you out like lambs among wolves. Do not take
a purse or bag or sandals; and do not greet anyone on the road.

"Lambs among wolves?" That's a sure way to get ripped to pieces —
unless you are certain the Shepherd is there to protect you! They need
neither money nor clothes nor extra shoes. They are to depend totally on
the Shepherd for both protection and survival.

Can you imagine what such total dedication does to a servant of the
Lord? Can you imagine what such commitment meant to those in Perea
who would meet these people?

When you enter an *oikos*, first say, "Peace to this *oikos*." If a man
of peace is there, your peace will rest on him; if not, it will return
to you.

Here's the strategy. They are to journey into a new territory where
they have no previous contacts. They are to find a person who will bring
them into his *oikos*.

They are to specialize in penetrating *oikoses!* No suggestion is made
of their doing "personal evangelism." Stress is to be placed upon this
point: their peace is to be offered not just to the first person they meet
who belongs to this *oikos*, but to every person within it. They are
"fishing" for a special type of person, called "a man of peace."

I. Howard Marshall explains these details:

. . . the word 'peace' is no longer an empty formality but refers to
the peace which is associated with the coming of the salvation of
God . . . . Luke speaks of the presence in it of a 'son of peace' . . . .
A 'son of peace' is an example of an idiom found in Classical and
Hellenistic Greek . . . . The saying does not refer to finding a
house in which there are already disciples, but to offering
salvation to those who are willing to receive it . . . Such a person
will receive the blessing offered to him.[1]

Oikos chain conversions happen all the time. In the same way that
the *oikos* can attack the new believer, there are many more occasions
when the opposite takes place. I have observed these networks of
conversions through my years of pastoring. First, a wife or a child is

converted, then others of the family, and finally the husband. In Singapore, I am always fascinated to talk with first-generation converts about the spread of the gospel into their family tree. From criticism or stubborn persecution, scores have told me of their persistence until other family members also came to know Christ.

This harvest principle must not be ignored! The initial contact with anyone should first be seen as a credential to meet an *oikos* of people, to live in their community of life, and to find the key person who is willing to receive the peace of salvation. Thus, cell group outreach is always to be seen as coming from the household of faith to those households who live in despair. For that reason, penetration is to be done by at least two believers from the Shepherd Group. Together, they model the love and fellowship which binds them together through their *oikedomeo* experiences they have had in the previous weeks. It's literally bringing the Kingdom of Christ into the kingdoms of Satan.

> Stay in that house, eating and drinking whatever they give you, for the worker deserves his wages. Do not move around from house to house [*oikos* to *oikos*]. When you enter a town and are welcomed, eat what is set before you. Heal the sick who are there and tell them, "The kingdom of God is near you."

The lifestyle of the believer is set for us in this passage. As Type "A" unbelievers are contacted, the penetration should deliberately be to all the *oikos* group.

The Same Pattern Works with Type "B" Unbelievers

Without faith bridges to cross over into an *oikos*, there must be another step before the hard core unbeliever will be responsive. Such people are intensely driven by their own desires and are best reached by "scratching where they itch." This is where the Share Group has proved to be powerfully effective.

Short-term, 10-week group encounters place the unbeliever in a group with three believers. The size of the Share Group is limited to nine persons. Thus, there are two unbelievers for every believer in the group. *The Opening Hearts Trilogy* shows how the Share Group contact is to be used to penetrate the *oikoses* of these two persons. Those who have taken this ministry seriously have discovered, over and over, that the "man of peace" is seldom the original person who comes to the group sessions. If the team focuses only on the six unbelievers they enlist for their Share Group, the harvest will be lost! They are taught two terms in their training: "In Visits" (entering into the *oikos* of the unbeliever), and "Out Visits" (inviting people out of these *oikoses* to enter their home for a meal, taking them to a birthday party for a Shepherd Group member, etc.)

Great impact is made by the "Out Visits." I recall an Italian lad who played with my son in Westchester, Pennsylvania years ago, when we were church planting. He always showed up in time to enjoy our evening dessert, so I taught him to read the Bible with us and share in our circle of prayer. Then, Ruth and I got acquainted with his parents. They were pure Type "B" pagans, totally out of touch with anything related to faith or religion. We shared a lovely meal together. When it was over, I handed the Bible to their child and asked him to read. We then invited them to listen along as we had our evening circle of prayer. When it was completed, the boys popped out of their seats and ran to play. I noticed the woman was wiping her eyes. In a moment she said, "That's the first time in my life I ever heard one of my children pray!"

Such relational *oikos* activities can penetrate the toughest hearts with the good news that "there's more!"

"Target Groups" Reach Different Segments

In order to expand contact with unbelievers further, many Share Groups will become Target Groups as they build relationships with people outside their current *oikos*. "Target Groups" divide into two types: those which attract unbelievers who are in crisis or struggling with deep problems, and those who are open to a relationship based on a common interest. There must be a balance between the sponsorship of these types. If this is not done, a church may collect a large group of broken people who will create a "Mash Unit" out of the cell.[2]

I have seen cells go overboard in attracting really sick people, only to be overwhelmed by needs which exceeded the capacities of the members. In addition, I have some personal battle scars from pouring hours into broken lives who were finally healed — and then "left our hospital group" to go to a church of "normal people." I'll never forget one woman schoolteacher who came to us out of an illicit relationship with a married man. Her daughter was into drugs and sex, and she was a basket case. After months of being together in the same cell, she suddenly joined a large church with a spiffy single's group — and never even bothered to say "Goodbye!" I went to see her and asked why she had dropped us like that. She said, "Ralph, I knew you guys wanted me to be healed, and leaving the group was my last step in that direction. I love you all very much, and now I can belong to a group where everyone is healthy." That happened years ago, and caused us to rethink our whole approach.

For that reason, a Shepherd Group should not have more than a couple of people who are in serious crisis. The Shepherd must guide the evangelism ministry of the Share Group in this matter, carefully evaluating the spiritual strength of the team before encouraging them to work with emotionally fragmented Target Groups.

Faith Community Baptist Church in Singapore has launched a number of Target Groups, relating to marriage, preparation for marriage, tennis, photography, hiking, lonely people, preparation for entering military training, personality development, and many more. These are the "root systems" which penetrate the world of the unbelievers. Share Groups can focus in any direction the members desire by making these "touch points" in the community.

During the life of *The People Who Care*, we had over 20 different Target Groups. They included a Share Group for parents of retarded children, a group for teens who drove motorcycles, "H.O.P.E" (Helping Others Practice English), another for divorcees, etc. Twice a year we had a "Touch Fair" on Sunday morning. Each cell would set up a booth explaining their target ministry, encouraging new cells to join them in their outreach. The fair was complete with pizza and activities for our children. The atmosphere of reaching out permeated the entire church, and the Target Groups were a key to this spirit.

In 1987, Houston's job market collapsed with a resounding thud! Rich and poor found themselves unemployed, and more than one person committed suicide. As the economy plunged and thousands of homes were foreclosed, I developed "LIFT Groups." Using the CARPOOL radio audience, I collected 119 unemployed listeners in a hall provided gratis by a local hotel and trained them. Free television and newspaper coverage got the word out to the city, and within a month we had over one thousand people involved in the 10-week target group ministry. Scores were won to Christ and channeled into nearby churches.

The opportunities to penetrate the lost world are endless! Each cell can find its target, and growth will be automatic. Try it: our Lord will be delighted!

The World Oikos Principle

Using the little diagram on the facing page, write in your own name at the top. Then, list four or five members from your *oikos* who do not yet know the Lord in the space shown for them. Next, think about the *oikoses* of your family or friends you have chosen. Is it not obvious that you already know something about each one?

God has designed a simple pattern to network each member of the Shepherd Group to an enormous number of people! The only "skill" it takes is a desire to be friendly, to care about others, and to limit the evenings spent watching TV so there is time for people who need your interest and your love.

Shepherd Groups who have such people in them find it easy to multiply in a hurry! Seldom will such a group take more than six months to expand into two groups in America. It's faster in Abidjan — multiplication in about three months, and slower in London — a tough place to minister. *Anywhere you go there will be a "man of peace" if you search for him!*

A JOURNEY INTO YOUR OWN "WORLD OIKOS"

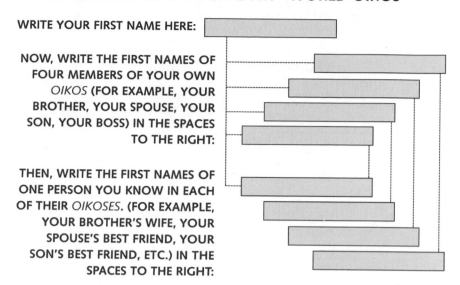

WRITE YOUR FIRST NAME HERE:

NOW, WRITE THE FIRST NAMES OF FOUR MEMBERS OF YOUR OWN *OIKOS* (FOR EXAMPLE, YOUR BROTHER, YOUR SPOUSE, YOUR SON, YOUR BOSS) IN THE SPACES TO THE RIGHT:

THEN, WRITE THE FIRST NAMES OF ONE PERSON YOU KNOW IN EACH OF THEIR *OIKOSES*. (FOR EXAMPLE, YOUR BROTHER'S WIFE, YOUR SPOUSE'S BEST FRIEND, YOUR SON'S BEST FRIEND, ETC.) IN THE SPACES TO THE RIGHT:

FINALLY, CIRCLE THE NAMES OF ALL THOSE WHO ARE UNBELIEVERS.

ARE THEY TYPE "A" OR TYPE "B" UNBELIEVERS?
IN A SHEPHERD GROUP USING THE TOUCH TRAINING MATERIALS,
WITHIN THE FIRST YEAR OF A NEW CONVERT'S LIFE,
THIS PENETRATION OF *OIKOS* CONTACTS MUST BECOME A WAY OF LIFE.

HAVE YOU OBSERVED THIS PATTERN?

Conversions often "travel" within *oikos* relationships. List below the names of people you know who came to Christ because the gospel moved through their *oikos*. (For example, a woman wins her friend to Christ; her friend wins her older sister, who in turn wins her husband, etc.)

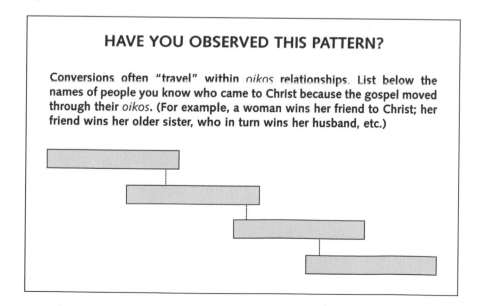

18

All About
Share Groups

A Bird's Eye View of "Share Groups"

The word SHARE is taken from 1 Thessalonians 2:8 (RSV):

> So, being affectionately desirous of you, we were ready to share with you not only the gospel of God but also our own selves, because you have become very dear to us.

While Paul wrote this to a specific group of believers, the verse accurately describes the ministry of believers to those who need their Lord. The word itself stands for "Sharing His Answer Regarding Everything."

Please, please don't change this name to "Care Group!" If you do, you will destroy the evangelistic impact of the cell. To an unbeliever, there is a great difference between attending a group that shares (equality is inferred) and one that cares (being "cared for" infers someone is better off than you are, or you are in need of group therapy). I have discovered many I have trained make this shift ignorantly, not realizing that such a simple thing as a name change can cut off people who could be reached. We must train ourselves to think like unbelievers think if we are to reach them.

SHARE GROUPS provide the contact between the unchurched and believers, using homes of Share Group members as a neutral meeting place. Three or four mature members of a Shepherd Group become the Body of Christ as a Share Group team is formed. As group members reach out, the group grows — both numerically and spiritually. Unbelievers become interested in the Gospel, leading to in-depth Bible study to explain the plan of salvation to them at a later time. Share Groups are a special arm of evangelism, reaching out from the Shepherd Group to the hardest groups to reach — the totally unchurched persons who have been ignored by the P.B.D. churches.

Facts about Share Groups

- They provide an informal, non-threatening time where unbelievers can experience sharing and Christian truth.
- They provide an atmosphere of trust, where people can truly be themselves without being rejected and condemned. Gradually, deep and abiding personal relationships develop between believers and unbelievers.
- They provide a setting where individuals can work through their problems with the help and love of the others in the group. Solutions based on the Scriptures are ultimately found.
- They provide a special structure for Share Group team members to learn how their spiritual gifts work together.
- They strongly emphasize the importance of prayer as the source of power and harvest.
- They are never a closed group, but are always seeking to grow through reaching out. "Body Life" is its method for sharing Christ's love and offer of salvation.
- They meet any time during the week. Each group sets its own schedule.
- Topics are relational, and apply to the "sting of sin" found among unbelievers. (Example: "Loneliness: What is it, and when do you experience it?")
- They may incorporate a "pre-believer's Bible Study," *The Handbook For Successful Living*, used either on a one-to-one or a group basis.
- They can be age grouped (e.g., high school, over 35 singles), mixed groups (singles and couples), or special groups ("Live Long and Like It").
- They move weekly from house to house. Thus, everyone hosts the group from time to time.

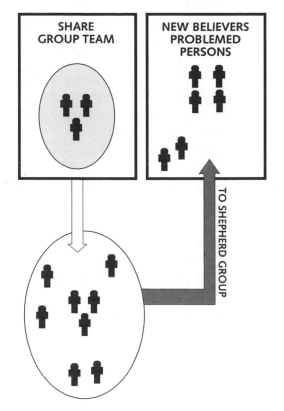

In this illustration, we see a Share Group team, three or at the most four, meeting together for prayer and training once a week. They then meet in their homes with unbelievers who are not open to Bible study. Soon the relationships deepen, and Bible study is developed on a one-to-one basis.

Either just before, or as soon as, a person has accepted Jesus as Lord, a new group is formed — the Shepherd Group. Nurture now takes place as the original team forms the new cell with the first fruits of their ministry.

The cell group church will focus on reaching out to others through the Share Group. The fellowship, prayer, and encouragement needed by the team members in the early stages is provided as they meet for their weekly equipping times. Working with unbelievers is the best way to keep the Shepherd Group from becoming an ingrown toenail!

Oikos Penetration Is Critical

The Opening Hearts Trilogy — comprised of three books called *Building Bridges, Opening Hearts; Building Groups, Opening Hearts;* and *Building Awareness, Opening Hearts* — have been designed to help with this type of development, but it must be learned in real life. The focus of this training is the penetration of *oikos* people.

The preparation for Share Group ministry begins with an equipping weekend called the *Opening Hearts Weekend.* It is designed to introduce the philosophy behind Share Group ministry and familiarize the trainee with the difference between traditional evangelism and cell group strategy. The seminar should be provided to the Share Group teams, not just to individuals.

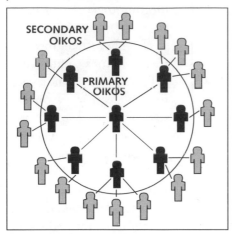

During the *Opening Hearts Weekend*, each person makes a list of all the people he or she talks to for a total of one hour in seven days. These are the basic members of the *oikos* for that individual. The list is classified by those who are not believers, and by those who are. This list becomes the primary mission field for each person. Then, the names of those who are in the secondary *oikos* structure are developed.

Obviously, each team member will have an entrance to these people through the members of their own *oikos*. Many people are surprised to discover that they actually have natural connections with as many as 100 individuals. These people should be the first to be reached and brought into the Share Group.

Before unbelievers become part of a regular group meeting, the team must prepare for their ministry. At this point, the group will work through the daily growth guides of *Building Bridges, Opening Hearts*. This book will help them develop the relationships required to form the group. The equipper should be heavily involved in supervising the untrained team members during this time, doing whatever is necessary to be sure each person has one or two people who will join the group. I usually spend time individually with each team member and meet with the entire group weekly for prayer and strategy planning. Because this is a new type of ministry, nothing can substitute for a seasoned equipper who has already done such a ministry.

A Share Group Usually Lasts 10 Weeks

In *Building Groups, Opening Hearts*, the team learns that the length of the Share Group is usually brief — 10 weeks on the average. The purpose is to develop a relationship with people who have no interest in spiritual things (Type "B") and meet the people in their *oikos*. A ratio of one team member to two unbelievers should never be changed. That "case load" makes it possible for quality time to be spent with each unbeliever and his or her *oikos* family.

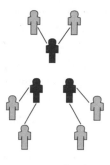

"In visits" and "out visits" are possible when the ratio is kept small. "In visits" are those times when members of the team enter into the *oikos* of the unbeliever. "Out visits" take place when the team members lead the unbelieving *oikos* members out to visit a cell group activity. This ministry is explained in *Building Awareness, Opening Hearts*.

Next, "Target Groups" Can Be Developed

After there has been time for the team to learn about the Share Group cycle and how the ministry is conducted with *oikos* contacts, a second strategy for penetrating can be presented. It should never, ever be used first of all with new trainees. They need to learn about penetrating *oikoses* and conducting the Share Group with friends before the second strategy is attempted. I have often explained the two strategies by comparing the difference between serving the Lord in your homeland, and serving Him in a foreign country as a missionary. If you can't do the first effectively, it's doubtful you will be successful in a strange new culture.

The second strategy is called targeting. In this case, people who are strangers, but who share common interests, needs, or problems are gathered for a Share Group.

For example, Ruth and I joined hands with two Godly divorcees to begin a group for women who had been recently divorced. Since such women are often financially limited, we assumed they would all read the local "For Sale Or Will Buy" bulletin board in the supermarkets. We stuck a card on several of them which read, "Recently Divorced? Need A Lift? Join Our Group! It's Free. Call 497-2420." We had so many responses, we had a waiting list of women who wanted to join us. We shall never forget the wonderful moments we had as we watched total strangers grow close to us, and become open to know the Christ who lived within us.

Another group I have personally targeted since seminary days in New Orleans are the men who frequent neighborhood bars. They always go to the same one about the same time of the day. I have made contacts with many families by first meeting a man in this way, then inviting him to have lunch with me. Gradually, the relationship would grow.

Cal Thomas, the journalist, worked with me as we targeted key men in the Houston professional world. His wife made the best breakfasts in town, and we always had a house full of lawyers, judges, and public officials for those early morning men's Share Groups.

One of the specialists in this type of group is New Hope Community Church in Portland, Oregon. It has about 96 different categories for targeting! The groups he offers include:

- Mr. & Mrs.
- Mothers of Excellence
- Self-Esteem
- Building Remarriage
- Grief Recovery
- New Life Victorious
- New Hope Seniors
- Overcoming Sorrow
- Total Healing
- WOW (Women of Worth)
- Separation Survival
- Divorce Recovery

The best way to decide what groups to offer is to talk to the Share Group trainees as they are working with the *oikos* contacts in the first phase of their training. Their hurts or interests or background will often trigger enthusiasm for a special target group. For example, Eugene Seow in Singapore has formed a Share Group entitled, "Cooking for Diabetics." He was packed for the first session!

A Target Group Strategy

As we saw in Chapter 1, there are more and more people who are completely turned off by religion. In Texas, the New Age movement is growing many, many times faster than churches. In fact, a recent survey revealed that a surprising number of new adherents are simultaneously attending churches in the mainline Protestant stream.

It's my conviction that a lot of reachable people are turned off by a religious connection when they are offered a group. Therefore, the church must create a movement that is very clearly grounded on the Bible, "Target Groups" that will be sponsored by well-trained believers who will penetrate *oikoses* and seek those who are searching for peace. These groups must appear and sound neutral and give believers the opportunity to interact with those who would never, ever respond to a group which is obviously church sponsored.

This strategy includes three types of groups. The first is for hurting people. With alcoholism, substance abuse, and depression all on the rise, there will be no end to the possibilities for group formation. Groups for the unemployed (LIFT groups) always provide an opening for relationships to be developed between people who are out of work and unable to find a new job.

The second type of group is for people who are not in crisis. These will focus on areas like jogging, photography, cooking, computers, how to study more effectively, etc. There are thousands of "Yuppies" who have good jobs and are bored to tears. In the past, we have snagged homosexuals, atheist school teachers, and many other segments of society that usually rebel against groups with a religious flavor.

In the place of celebrations, a very "churchy" event, this strategy calls for "Getaways." The contemporary culture has encouraged people to get out of town for the weekends. The freeway near my home is jammed with people getting away on Friday evenings. Corporations take their executives on getaways, where skiing, golf, tennis, fishing, or hunting is mixed in with seminars and lectures related to the work place. There is no reason the church cannot flow with this cultural activity. Living together in community for a couple of days and a night is very much in tune with the theology of the cell group church.

The third type of group, of course, will be the Shepherd Group. When conversions occur, those who have been turned off by traditional religion will be introduced to a new life form for the people of God. Thus, in this movement, the end goal is the establishment of new believers who are equipped and sent out to form new groups and penetrate even more deeply the millions of people who are being ignored by churchianity.

Actually, the idea isn't new. The Faith Community Baptist Church in Singapore has a separate ministry which feeds its cells. Lawrence Khong took the name "TOUCH" from me, and now has many ministries for outreach under that name. The TOUCH Singers have held concerts which have been attended by thousands. The follow-up by the cells of these musicals has brought many people into groups. They also created TOUCH Points, activities and services that connect the people of the church with the lost on neutral ground. One such service is a child care center. Many have come to Christ and entered the church through this ministry aimed at reaching people through the back door.

19

What About Finances?

Can you imagine a Body of Christ where nearly everyone is an *oikonomos* (steward)? Cell group churches approximate that to a much greater extent than do P.B.D. churches. It's quite easy to understand how that happens: where the person has come to terms with the Lordship of Christ and sees his or her role as part of a vision, stewardship is no longer a fund-raising word. It's a way of life.

To finally come to terms with the fact that everything inside my skin, and everything outside my skin, *everything I am is the property of my Lord*, is to settle the place He takes in my assets. This needs to be taught in such a way that it isn't connected to the institutional needs for another building or something of the sort.

The responsibility of the *oikonomos* to provide "proper rations at the proper time" is the key principle to be stressed over and over. We're dealing with an *oikos* concept. Those in Acts 2:42-46 generously cared for one another's needs because they were all in one accord.

When the believer realizes that becoming a Christian has made him or her a bondslave of Christ, nothing will ever be the same again. The issue is total ownership of our lives by Christ.

The exciting side of the entire issue is found in this trilogy:

It is the task of a servant to obey his Master.
It is the obligation of the Master to provide all his servant requires.
Therefore, that servant must never live in fear his supply will run
   out.

I often use the illustration of the master who told his servant to build him a house. The servant went to his wife and said, "How much money do we have in the bank? The master has told me to build him a house."

The wife replied, "Wait a minute! Did he tell you to draw out your resources to do it?"

"Well, no. He really didn't."

"Then you march right back to him and get the money from him!"

It's a great day when the people of God realize that a poor household servant who lives in the mansion of a millionaire wears better clothes, eats better food, and enjoys life more than ever possible if he were left to his own resources.

If an *oikonomos* sees one in the *oikos* with a need, and if that servant has received the Father's assets in order to meet that need, there will be again a condition in the church like that described in Acts 4:32-35:

> And the multitude of those who believed were of one heart and soul; and not one of them claimed that anything belonging to him was his own; but all things were common property to them. And with great power the apostles were giving witness to the resurrection of the Lord Jesus, and abundant grace was upon them all. For there was not a needy person among them, for all who were owners of land or houses would sell them and bring the proceeds of the sales, and lay them at the apostles' feet; and they would be distributed to each, as any had need.

Learning to live this way cannot be done apart from life in a community where believers have stepped into that faith walk. Rather than the "preacher getting off on money again," the issue of dollars is best left alone, and teaching about Lordship stressed.

Scrutiny of cell churches reveals they usually grow quite large before investing in a celebration center. It's inevitable that one will be needed. Nearly all of them I have visited can't find an auditorium in the city which will hold all the members. However, by the time they do build or buy a place, they are large enough that the payment is usually made in cash.

When and Where Are
the Offerings Taken?

This varies widely among the cell churches. Personally, I like Dr. Cho's plan. Each cell group member is given envelopes for the offering. The amount inside is marked on the envelope. They are turned in during the cell meeting. After being totalled by two persons, the separate envelopes are placed in a larger one. This envelope is then brought by the cell leader to the next worship service attended. Under the main auditorium there is a wall with pigeonhole boxes, where these envelopes are dropped. I have been deeply moved as I have watched one cell leader after another approach their pigeonhole in the wall, put the envelope to their heart and passionately pray for its use, and then drop it in a slot.

In addition, offerings are taken at every public service held. On one occasion I got in the way of the ushers after they had collected the offering from 25,000 people in the auditorium. They were using containers on wheels to roll the gifts into the counting room! Churches like this one seldom make special appeals for funds. When you have 800,000 people serving as *oikonomos* servants, there is no need to beg!

What Does the Budget
of a Cell Church Look Like?

In order to explain this, let's look at an illustration of how the funds must be utilized. First and foremost, the investment must be in staff workers. There must be one paid Zone Pastor for every 250 people, representing approximately 25 cells and five divisions of cells conducted by volunteer Zone Supervisors. Their gifts must also provide for secretaries, office space, rental of celebration facilities, the music staff, etc.

Using numbers in a book like this is not wise, so I'm going to do it using "Units" (U), which will represent currency in whatever nation this book is studied. Factor the units into the proper proportion for your currency, and see if it works out:

THE CELL GROUP: LARGE CHURCH STAFF

CELLS	CONGREGATIONS	CELEBRATIONS
S E N I O R P A S T O R		
MINISTER OF CELL GROUPS	MINISTER OF CONGREGATIONS	MINISTER OF CELEBRATIONS
DISTRICT LEADERS 1:25 District Pastors		CHOIRS
		PRAISE LEADERS
DISTRICT PASTORS 1:25 Zone Supervisors		DRAMA TEAMS
		ORCHESTRAS
		ETC.
ZONE SUPERVISORS 1:5 Cells	In the District, a mature cell church will develop and use these gifted cell members:	Those serving in this category are all involved in cell group life. Belonging to a cell is basic. Those who are musical are some of the most effective cell group members. Some cell churches organize their musicians by cells, others leave them in geographical cells.
ZONE SUPERVISORS INTERNS	EQUIPPERS	
	TEACHERS	
	COUNSELORS	
SHEPHERD 1:15 Maximum	EVANGELISTS	
	PREACHERS	
SHEPHERD GROUP INTERN		This is a model of a cell church with a Senior Pastor. Some cell churches use a team approach with a Leadership Staff, but there is always a key man who can be identified as the leader. Staff positions appearing in the shaded areas are paid positions. All others are volunteers. The number of people supervised is given as a ratio figure.
SHARE GROUP TEAMS 3 People: Minimum		

1. Income provided by Shepherd Groups:

Average number of persons in one Shepherd Group: 10
Number of households represented: 5
Annual support from each household: . . . . .U   3,000
Average annual support of the church
   from one Shepherd Group: . . . . .U   15,000
<u>Average annual support from
one District of 25 Shepherd Groups:</u> . . . .<u>U 375,000</u>

2. Expenditure of income provided by Shepherd Groups:
   (Please note: everyone in ministry is paid the same amount.)

Salary, Leadership Team (2 couples) . . . . .U   60,000
Salary, first Zone Pastor . . . . .U   30,000
Salaries, two secretaries . . . . .U   36,000
Rent, office . . . . .U   24,000
Cost of celebrations, including rent . . . . .U   95,000
Cost of equipping materials . . . . .U   9,000
Cost of retreats or "getaways" . . . . .U   19,000
Additional expenses, unspecified, including
   missions, care of members, etc. . . . . .U 102,000
<u>Average annual expenditure by cell group church</u> . . . .<u>U 375,000</u>

With the second Zone, the addition of one more Zone Pastor, plus a musician or two to be responsible for the Celebrations, and another secretary or two leaves a significant surplus for missions, the opening of a training school, and the creation of additional "root systems" to penetrate the community of unchurched people.

Actually, the only cell church in the world I have perused where money was a significant problem is Dion Robert's work in Abidjan. In that case, 80% of the members are under-employed! The principles remain the same, but he certainly deserves support from wealthier areas of the world.

Note: you are encouraged to read the chapter entitled "Too Much Month At The End Of The Money" in the *Shepherd's Guidebook* in conjunction with this chapter.

20

Developing A Penetration Strategy

Before launching or expanding a ministry, nothing is as crucial as the creation of an urban strategy. It is as important to the cell group church planter as is a business plan to the launchers of a new venture. In urban settings, a strategy is absolutely necessary if an entire metroplex is to be evangelized. While traditional church leaders tend to think in terms of parishes or "church fields," a cell group strategist seeks to develop a pattern that will be effective in reaching all the people groups present.

For several years, I taught M.Div. and D.Min. students in Columbia Biblical Seminary and School of World Missions classes using world-class cities as a laboratory. These students traveled the world with me, surveying church life in major cities. In each place, they were exposed to rapidly exploding cell group congregations. They focused on one major city for thirty days, learning the "tools of the trade" used by cell group strategists.

In 1962, when Dr. Leonard Irwin of the Home Mission Board, Southern Baptist Convention, introduced these tools to me, I felt something like Cinderella when she stepped through the looking-glass! After planting over a dozen churches without knowing what I was doing, a new way of praying and strategizing was opened to me through them. Those were the days when home computers were not in existence. We would rent a huge machine at $50 a day to do computations which now can be done ten times as fast with a little laptop!

Without any exception, I have found it possible to collect the necessary data to develop an urban strategy in every part of the world I have visited — even when local missionaries thought such data did not exist in their third world nation. Thus, reports have been created for Nairobi, Bangkok, Singapore, Jakarta, Brussels, Auckland, Brisbane, and London without any problem. In the United States, not only is data readily available, but special reports can be secured for a nominal sum which will give one, five, and ten mile detailed population reports from the intersections of any specific streets or highways.[1]

Developing an urban strategy includes the following steps:

1. Create A Prayer Base for Your Activity

Nothing is more fraught with danger than seeking to do the work of the Master without "Listening Room" time. Taking daily findings to the prayer closet provides spiritual insights not provided by the crunching of numbers. It is recommended that the strategy team spend periods daily in prayer. There will be moments in the study when there is simply nothing to do but weep and pray over the lostness of the neighborhoods being studied.

Without question, spiritual eyes will discern "strongholds" of Satan within a city as the study develops. When one evaluates districts of sin and evil in a city, it is necessary to remember that the battle we fight is not against flesh and blood, but against principalities and powers in the air. Let those who are spiritually blind to eternal warfare stay away from developing urban strategy!

2. Secure Data

The first step will be to collect all available census data, sociological studies, and previous reports which have been done about the city, suburbia, and the exurbia surrounding it. Sources include United Nations studies, national census reports, regional reports (including "Standard Metropolitan Statistical Area" data), city and county studies, and research materials completed through grants by local universities. Visits should be made to agencies developing highway systems for the area, and any Planning Commissions sponsored by national, state, regional, county, or city governments. Much information can be gleaned by interviewing utility companies in the region. Their forecasts of where telephones, electricity, and gas will be needed can be valuable tools for studying both suburbia and exurbia. Urban Renewal Commissions make recommendations about decaying inner city areas, and have much data available. Even the slums of third world cities have been carefully mapped, with lifestyles of inhabitants described. (In Bangkok, a huge multicolored set of maps has been published showing the location of hundreds and hundreds of slums.)

Basic questions to be answered about the city include:

1. How many children live here?
2. How many single-parent families are present?
3. How many retired and elderly, and where are they housed?
4. Where are the poor?
5. Where are the rich?
6. What ethnic groups are there, and where?
7. What are the educational levels and occupations?
8. What will the population be in five years? Ten years?
9. What urban redevelopment will take place?

One must enjoy being a Sherlock Holmes during this investigative step, making friends with officials at each office visited and asking endless questions. Often key documents will be "passed on," not usually given to the public, once the respect of the official being interviewed has been gained. In Singapore, I created the "Baptist Centre for Urban Studies" (that was just me!), had calling cards printed, and left them behind with each government official. I was soon being invited to all sorts of functions held by sociologists, demographers, and urban planners. Most of the best "leads" came by asking, "Who has additional information that might be of value to the study?" Offering to share the results of your own research when completed is greatly appreciated.

Include in this procedure visits to all religious headquarters in the region. Many denominational leaders have done studies which can be of great help. In doing an urban strategy for Brussels, interviews with the head of the state protestant church and a key Catholic cardinal provided significant data which influenced preparation of the strategy.

Include a study of cults and why they have succeeded in penetrating the society. In Singapore, we learned much from a study of how the Japanese *Sokka Gakkai* cult had exploded in size in just a few short years. The study of how the Mormons had deeply penetrated the Maoris in

Auckland, New Zealand gave insights into how that cult had tapped into their culture to get a foothold among them.

Secure listings of all known churches, synagogues, temples, shrines, etc., from all available sources. In some areas this is a simple matter: the research has already been done. In other cities, it will be the first time anyone has bothered to consider the matter. Your research will help you discover where ethnics and migrants have settled in the city: they are found by their faith and their food!

3. Create a Strategy Map

From a government or private mapping source, purchase the largest, most detailed map available of the region. For Singapore, I purchased segments of a map from a government office and had them mounted on a cloth base. The map was eight feet high and thirteen feet wide, and showed every street and track on the island. In Brisbane, we secured multicolored maps in sections about three feet by four feet in size, and developed each one separately, so they could be transported easily from place to place.

4. Separate the City by Neighborhoods

This has often been done by urban planners, but in many areas you may be the first person to delineate the actual boundaries of neighborhoods. Much help can be gained in doing this by scrutinizing the "Enumeration Districts" of the "Census Tracts." While the "C.T.'s" are shown on the census reports purchased from the Bureau of the Census, the "E.D.'s" are available only upon request. Expect to pay a special charge for this material.

The "E.D." shows the area assigned for one person to survey when a census is taken. It will be a "bite sized" area which can be covered on foot, not crossing any major highways or rivers to complete the task. This material is helpful in giving block-by-block reports of the number of residents, their incomes, education, religious preferences (in many countries), and even the number of toilets in their residences!

The boundaries of the city's neighborhoods should be carefully marked on the map, or maps, of the region. Use 1/16" bendable red ChartTape for this purpose, carefully pressing it over the streets which mark the edges of each area. As you do so, put a 1/4" round sticker in each neighborhood, with a number written on it. Create a list of these numbers, designating it with the commonly used name for that territory: e.g., "Woodlands, Section 1."

Also use round stickers to mark the exact location of all existing religious structures. In Philadelphia, doing so quickly revealed ethnic groups from Italy, Russia, Greece, etc., and where they had clustered. Of course, another way to do much of the above is with a computer and the vast amount of information availabe on the internet. I recently did a detailed report on Toronto from my desk in Houston.

5. Make Population Pyramids

Let's look at two population pyramids which help us decide what strategy to plant cells we should use in each area:

In this first pyramid, we see a slum area of Brisbane (Fortitude Valley). It includes prostitutes, night clubs, Chinatown, and a business district. Note the absence of children of either sex. A significant falloff of women in the 40-44 age group reflects the presence of the younger women of ill repute. Note also the large number of elderly people who are trapped here by their poverty. Here's a mystery: why should so many

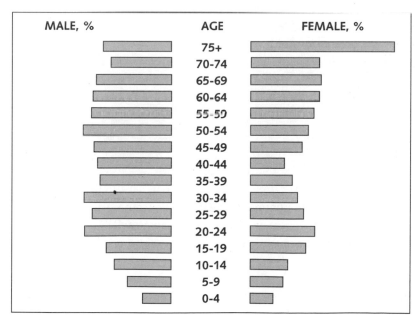

women above the age of 75 live in a place like this? In our research, we discovered that the Catholics had established a retirement home for nuns in this neighborhood generations ago, when Brisbane was young and the district was on the edge of town. The retirement center remains today, an imposing stone fortress in the midst of a hellhole called Fortitude Valley.

In the next example, we see a typical pyramid of a community settled by young couples with lots and lots of little children in the family (Ferny Grove, Brisbane). This would be a prime area for the planting of new work among young couples. Note the massive clustering of preschoolers, their parents reflected in the 25-39 bars of the chart.

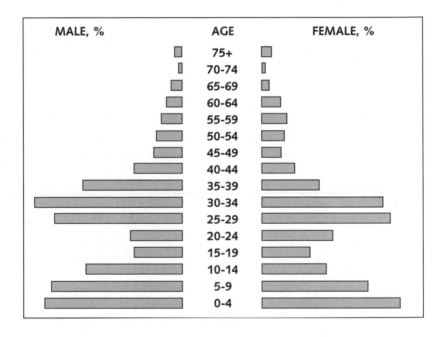

NOTE: A population pyramid is created by obtaining the percentage of each male or female age group in a census tract.

6. Create Templates for Your Report

Once the material has been collected, a special survey form can be created to collect the data for each neighborhood. A sample of this form is provided on the next two pages.

It is also possible for you to create a template for your actual report (see samples on the two pages which follow the survey form). I usually prepare a double-page spread for each neighborhood, showing the following information: population pyramid, small map showing boundaries of the neighborhood, housing information, immigration patterns, marital status of population, incomes, employment, religious preferences, brief description of the community, neighborhood category (see part 7), and recommended strategy for planting appropriate cell groups.

7. Develop Neighborhood Analysis

Using the survey form, fill in all the data for each category of each neighborhood. This requires simple compilations of statistics.

Once this has been completed, the charts are prepared for insertion into the template. The use of pie charts and bar charts give graphic overviews of the similarities and differences of the neighborhoods. Repeating the same format for all neighborhoods provides insights into strategies which can be used in similar settings.

> The six pages which follow are samples of forms used in the creation of urban strategies. You are welcome to use them as they are, or to create forms adapted from them.

WORKSHEET FOR: _____

POP. PYR. LOCATED ON DISK _____
NAME OF LARGER AREA (BOROUGH, CITY, U.A., ETC.) _____
TOTAL POPULATION OF LARGER AREA (MALE + FEMALE=TOTAL) _____
POPULATION PYRAMID OF LARGER AREA IS LOCATED ON DISK _____

RESIDENT POPULATION (TABLE 2)

MALE + FEMALE = TOTAL _____
TOTAL HOUSEHOLDS (TABLE 14) _____

THE FOLLOWING IS IN TABLE 5:
NEVER MARRIED,
   OVER 15 YEARS: _____

MARRIED   _____

REMARRIED   _____

SEPARATED   _____

WIDOWED   _____

DIVORCED   _____

DE FACTO RELATIONSHIP   _____

WITHIN THE TOTAL POPULATION ARE . . .

N. Z. MAORI (TABLE 4)   _____

POLYNESIAN (TABLE 4)   _____

NOT WORKING (TABLE 6;
   ADD MALE+FEMALE)   _____

BORN OUTSIDE N. Z.
   (USE TABLE 3)   _____

ADD M+F FOR **TOTAL:**   _____

ADD M+F FOR **N Z:**   _____

SUBTRACT: **USE THIS TOTAL:** _____

AMONG THE OVERSEAS BORN ARE. . .
(NOTE: SELECT THE 4 CATEGORIES WITH
HIGHEST TOTALS. THIS WILL VARY WITH
EACH AREA. USE TABLE 3)

AREA (USE CAPS ONLY!)   TOTAL
   (ADD MALE+FEMALE)

_____ _____

_____ _____

TYPES OF DWELLINGS (TABLE 15)
For the next two figures, use
Aggregate Number of Occupants:
Living in Private Dwellings   _____
In Non-Private Dwellings   _____
Separate Houses   _____
2 Houses/Flats, joined   _____
3 or + joined together   _____
Joined to business/shop   _____
Bach, Crib, Hut   _____
Temporary private dwelling   _____

INCOME (TABLE 11)
In all cases, add M+F to get one total.
Then, add together columns to produce
six totals:
E.G.: Add 5 columns to get $1-10,000, etc.
NIL OR LOSS: _____
$1 - $10,000:   _____
$10,000 - $15,000:   _____
$15,000 - $25,000   _____
$25,000 - $50,000   _____
Over $50,000:   _____

OCCUPATIONS (TABLE 8. Add M+F=Total)
Professional, technical   _____
Administrative, Managerial   _____
Clerical   _____
Sales Workers   _____
Service Workers   _____
Agricultural, etc.   _____
Laborers, etc.   _____

FAMILY TYPES (TABLE 14)
1 Family Only   _____
1 Family + Others   _____
2 Families   _____
Non-Family Households   _____
One Person Households   _____

WORKSHEET FOR: _____

WRITE A 75 WORD DESCRIPTION OF THIS AREA. INCLUDE FACTORS WHICH WILL IMPACT THE CREATION OF AN URBAN STRATEGY (Institutions present, geographical distinctives, hospitals, schools, factories, railways, comment about the pop. pyramid, your own observations from visiting the area, etc.) Type into proper area on book page when polished.

_____

_____

_____

_____

_____

_____

_____

_____

RELIGIOUS STRUCTURES FOUND IN THIS AREA

List the name in caps. Put the exact address of the church on the next line. Type into book page.

_____

_____

_____

_____

_____

_____

_____

_____

_____

_____

_____

_____

_____

RELIGIOUS PREFERENCES IN THIS AREA
(USE UNPUBLISHED TABLE 25)
ADD M + F = TOTAL

ANGLICAN   _____
PRESBYTERIAN   _____
ROMAN CATHOLIC   _____
METHODIST   _____
CHRISTIAN N. O. D.   _____
BAPTIST   _____
MORMON   _____
RATANA   _____
BRETHREN   _____
SALVATION ARMY   _____
PROTESTANT N. O. D.   _____
JEHOVAH'S WITNESSES   _____
ASSEMBLIES OF GOD   _____
OTHER   _____

ADD TOGETHER:
NO RELIGION   _____
OBJECT   _____
NOT SPECIFIED   _____
TOTAL OF ABOVE   _____

WORKSHEET FOR: _____

SURVEY DATA

As you work with 43 people in your area, list and tabulate the total results here:

Leisure Interests	Ch. Pref.	Attend.	Looking	Bible	Problems	Solutions	Group?	Seeker?
				THIS SUMMARY				
				PAGE IS USED WITH				
				THE SURVEY FORM				
				ON PAGE 325				
TOTALS								

WORKSHEET FOR: _____

WHAT COULD BE DONE?

Pray much about what you write here! This will be completed only after you have done all your field surveys and completed all other statistical analysis. Interviews with Pastors, residents, etc., will give you insights. Discuss your conclusions with your Team when you are in need of additional insights. Recognize that your suggestions may well influence the conversion of many people in the area. (Max. 400 words). Type into proper area on book page when polished.

_____

_____

_____

_____

_____

_____

_____

_____

_____

_____

_____

_____

_____

_____

_____

_____

_____

_____

_____

_____

_____

_____

_____

_____

PAKURANGA CENTRAL

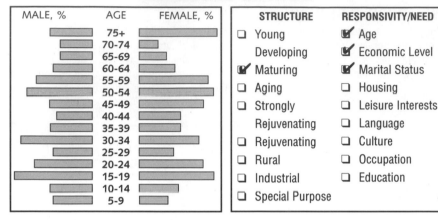

MALE, %	AGE	FEMALE, %	STRUCTURE	RESPONSIVITY/NEED
	75+		☐ Young	☑ Age
	70-74		Developing	☑ Economic Level
	65-69		☑ Maturing	☑ Marital Status
	60-64		☐ Aging	☐ Housing
	55-59		☐ Strongly	☐ Leisure Interests
	50-54		Rejuvenating	☐ Language
	45-49		☐ Rejuvenating	☐ Culture
	40-44		☐ Rural	☐ Occupation
	35-39		☐ Industrial	☐ Education
	30-34		☐ Special Purpose	
	25-29			
	20-24			
	15-19			
	10-14			
	5-9			

		Within the total population are. . .		TYPES OF DWELLINGS	
Resident Population	2820	N. Z. Maori	45	Living in Private Dwellings	2823
Total Households	894	Polynesian	15	In Non-Private Dwellings	24
Never Married-age 15+	684	Not Working	624	Separate Houses	735
Married	1179	Born Outside N. Z.	672	2 Houses/Flats, joined	99
Remarried	123			3 or + joined together	60
Separated	60	Among the Overseas Born are. . .		Joined to business/shop	0
Widowed	108	UK & IRELAND	393 persons	Bach, Crib, Hut	0
Divorced	75	EUROPE	102 persons	Temporary private dw.	3
De Facto Relationship	57	AUSTRALIA	48 persons		
		ASIA	39 persons		

INCOME

- Nil or loss
- $1-$10,000
- $10,000-$15,000
- $15,000-$25,000
- $25,000-$50,000
- Over $50,000

OCCUPATIONS

Laborers, etc.
Agricultural, etc.
Service Workers
Sales Workers
Clerical
Admin., Manag.
Prof., Technical

0   100   200   300   400

FAMILY TYPES

1 Person Households
Non-Family Households
Two Family Households
1 Family, Plus Others
1 Family Only

0   200   400   600   800

Generally, Pakuranga Central is made up of high cost housing estates 10 to 20 years old. There is a high turnover of residents in the middle cost housing bracket as jobs transfer people in & out of Auckland. Families may stay two to three years, then move on. There is a large young population under 24 years old which makes up about 30% of the population. Income is similar to that of greater Auckland, except for a slightly larger distribution of $25,000-50,000 incomes. It is also evident from the occupation chart that the labourers' & clerical categories are relatively higher.

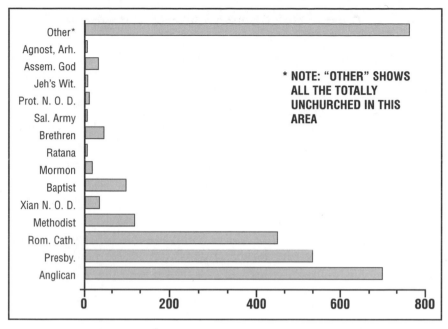

* NOTE: "OTHER" SHOWS ALL THE TOTALLY UNCHURCHED IN THIS AREA

REFLECTIONS ABOUT THIS AREA:

• There is a large commercial shopping centre here, which services the region.

• The Pakuranga Citizen Advice Bureau had the highest referrals of all the Citizen Advice Bureaus in Manukau City for the year ending May 1986. They had a total of 4,477 referrals. Of the calls they received, 29% were enquiries related to personal, family, health or welfare issues. The Bureau also reported, "the abuse of alcohol amongst women is causing concern... Relationships between parents and children is another significant area of stress... remarriage to new partners is common."

• The fifteen to nineteen age group is the largest age category in this community.

WHAT COULD BE DONE?

Ministries designed to touch whole families, using a household evangelism approach, are applicable here. Various leisure and social activities, such as neighborhood get-togethers and sports events could be initiated by resident Christians.

Unemployment has been a problem in this area. Ministry could include: assistance for job seekers, family counseling, etc. The percentage of teenagers is high in this community. Special interest activities, such as teaching guitar lessons, driving instruction, grooming classes and sports teams, could be used to gather these young people into Share Groups.

For young adults (20-34), evangelism strategies could include the development of

Share Groups around common interests. These might best be offered in a home, where young adults will feel relaxed and make friends with their peers.

Young couples frequently need relief in the midst of the stress of living with infants. Ministry to them can sometimes avert the danger of child abuse. They also need someone to give them reassurance and advice when things go wrong.

Another means to reaching these young families is through the neighborhood play centre. Strong relationships can develop these as Christian mothers meet other mothers once or twice a week on neutral ground as they supervise their children's activities together.

8. Cluster Neighborhoods into Categories

After creating all the data for the neighborhoods, they can then be broken down into these categories:

A. The Young Developing Suburb
These suburbs are still in the process of subdivision and construction. Their populations are, therefore, increasing rapidly as a result of in-migration and the establishment of families by young parents who are the principal buyers of the new houses. The population up to and including age 9 comprises as much as 27%, and always more than 15%, of the total. The age groups 60 years and over usually comprise less than 5% of the total except in those young suburbs containing a large senior citizens home. The social infrastructure needs of this type of suburb include kindergartens, child care facilities, primary schools, and playgrounds.

These areas should be targeted by churches, for they contain some of the most responsive segments of the city.

B. The Maturing Suburb
This type of suburb has been in the process of development for at least 20 years. The population total tends to be fairly stable although the composition of the population is undergoing change with a marked out-migration of young persons in the 15-24 age groups as families mature and grown children leave the parental home. Such out-migration is partially balanced by new births (but at a much lower rate than in the young developing suburbs) and, in some suburbs, a small net in-migration as the last remaining vacant lots are filled.

The population structure is characterized by a concentration of older families. The age groups 10-24 and 45-59 are usually predominant.

The social infrastructural needs of this type of suburb include a heavy demand for secondary schools, playing fields and recreational opportunities for older children and younger adults.

An aggressive ministry to young people, utilizing Share Groups led by themselves, can become a significant means of penetrating these areas. As adolescents and young adults seek to establish their own identity, they often search for a new set of values which contrast with those of their parents. If their peer group includes committed Christians, they will

SEEING THE CITY

Note: The "Rings" as described in this model are quite artificial. Terrain and historical events contribute to the actual locations of these areas.

Third world slums in cities always require: water source, government toleration, access to means of making an income. Slums are found along rivers, railroad track right-of-ways, public land, swamps, etc. Cells planted among them grow rapidly!

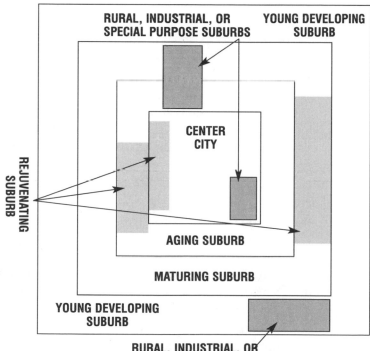

Find similar responsive segments in areas of the city that may be geographically separated. Use the same strategy in each area. Launch with the easiest group to reach!

often choose to follow Christ. At this age, peers have more impact than older persons who may seek to work with them.

In turn, when the young people in a family come to know Christ, they create a natural bridge to share their faith with other family members.

C. The Aging Suburb

This type of suburb typically consists of predominantly single family homes more than 40 years old. The population totals of all the suburbs in this category are declining, some by more than 5% per annum, because of grown children leaving the family home, and natural mortality or movement to retirement homes out of the suburb by persons in the older age groups who form a major proportion of these communities.

In these suburbs, persons over 60 years of age always comprise more than 12% of the total and in some cases as much as 26%. There is a marked lack of young children, the 0-9 age groups usually forming less than 12%, and always less than 14% of the total.

An important result of the population structure of this type of suburb is a low household size; many houses are occupied by widows or widowers living alone or by elderly couples whose children have grown up and left home.

The social infrastructure needs of these communities centre around the provision of services to the elderly such as meals on wheels, home nursing care and social clubs. These suburbs often contain underutilized school facilities.

The gospel has particular relevance to these persons when shared in the context of relational small groups. Quite often they are neglected by their younger family members, who are intent on pursuing their own agendas. They want people who will care about them, listen to them, and encourage them. The leisure time of the elderly makes it easier to reach them during the daytime. The effective church in these areas will offer the type of social and recreational life which is appropriate to senior citizens.

D. The Rejuvenating Suburb

This type of suburb is defined as one other than a young developing suburb in which the population of at least one young adult age group showed a net increase between censuses. A further distinction may be made between strongly rejuvenating suburbs, in which a decline in population has been reversed and the total population is now increasing, and weakly rejuvenating suburbs in which the population decline has been slowed but not reversed.

Rejuvenating suburbs include most of the old inner suburbs where the housing stock has been through more than one cycle of ownership. Their age structure is similar to that of the aging suburbs, showing a heavy concentration in the older age groups and very few children. One marked difference, however, is a concentration of people in the 20-29 age groups which usually comprise more than 20% of the total.

Household size in rejuvenating suburbs is small. As in the aging suburbs there are many elderly people living alone while the young in-migrants are most often single persons or childless couples occupying rental accommodations in old houses or in multiple dwellings.

The social infrastructure of this type of suburb will be those of the aging suburb supplemented with the lifestyle requirements of the unattached adult: dining and dancing venues, sports centers, clubs, theaters and other facilities for social intercourse.

Reaching this area must be done by two branches of Christ's body: one which focuses on the young adult, and another which concentrates on the aging persons. Many creative approaches can be used in these outreach strategies, including musical and drama groups, forum discussions, sports contests, etc.

E. The Rural, Industrial or Special Purpose Suburb

These areas are rural or semirural in character. They have a small population whose structure often cannot be characterized into any of the foregoing types.

To these suburbs may be added those which are of a primarily industrial nature with virtually no resident population, and those in which dominant residential institutions distort the pattern of the population structure. These would include such things as a prison farm or migrant hostel, a retirement village, nurse or student hostels, or military camps. They may also include seaside communities which contain many "second homes," often used seasonally or on week ends.

9. Take Surveys of Population Awarenesses

Once the neighborhoods have been systematically examined, there is a critical step which must follow: the interviewing of population categories to determine responsive segments. Local, cultural factors may influence this significantly in some areas. For example, those working in Belgium a few years ago discovered that young couples with their first baby and who spoke Dutch were unusually open to discussing salvation by grace through faith in Jesus Christ. French-speaking couples in the same condition were not as responsive.

On the other hand, some responsive segments exist in many differing cultures among the same groups. Youth and young marrieds are usually more responsive than middle and older aged persons. Better educated people may often be less steeped in the pressures of family religions than the poor. Conversely, in some cultures the elite are resistant, and the poor are more responsive.

These matters must be discovered by surveys taken within the population. There are at least two ways to do this:

1. Discover which population segments are turning to Christ in existing churches and parachurch groups.
2. Discover which population segments are most vulnerable to the evangelism of the cults, and what causes them to respond.
3. Interview people in different neighborhoods of the city. If it is discovered there is responsiveness in a certain segment of people, then use the previous research to locate where pockets of such people are located.

On the next page, a simple survey form is reproduced which has been widely used to gain insights into the needs and attitudes of people in different areas of cities.

District	Address			Apt.

NU HH	How long do you plan to live at this address?	Like it here?

ANYONE IN HOUSEHOLD BETWEEN AGES OF. . .

	M	F	LEISURE INTERESTS
0-5			
6-12			
13-17			
17-23			
35+			
Retired			

CHURCH PREFERENCE: _____

(Circle:) ALL   HUSB   WIFE   CHILDREN   OTHER

COMMENTS:

Have you considered looking for a new church in this area?

Would it have to be the same denomination you are used to?

When is the best time for you to worship? (Circle:)   AM   PM

Would you say you know the Bible. . . (Circle:)

Very Well   A Little Bit   Not well at all

What personal problems do people in this area face today?

What solutions do you see to these problems?

Would you be interested in a group which meets in the homes of its members and where folks can develop warm friendships?

Do you have an desire to know more about becoming a follower of Jesus Christ?

Family Name	Language Spoken

Surveyors:	Date: ____ / ____ / ____

10. Create Your Strategy Document

As shown in the sample pages in this chapter, this strategy report should include a population pyramid, basic information about the geography of the neighborhood, income, marital status, in-migration patterns, racial/ethnic mixes, types of employment, religious preferences, etc. Neighborhoods can be listed in several ways: by zones, census tracts, or alphabetically.

The entire presentation should be preceded by an overview of the city itself, providing the same data given for neighborhoods for the entire region. In addition, this introductory section should give population forecasts and other general information gleaned from the surveys taken and documents studied.

11. Select Key Areas for Penetration

With the strategy report available, it will now be possible to reach neighborhoods with similar characteristics. For example, young couples with young children may be scattered throughout the metroplex, but would be reached by a common strategy. Another area may reveal a large number of middle aged couples with teens; this would be of special interest to those seeking to reach youth. Through this selection, cell group churches seeking to penetrate an entire city will be able to plant cells appropriate to each area, targeting people with similar needs and interests.

In addition, much can be learned about specific population groups. Cells seeking to build around university students will be able to accurately pinpoint locations where they live.

When it is possible to include religious preferences in the strategy report, a further narrowing of the strategy can take place. Some nations regularly include information about religious preferences in their nationwide census (Australia and New Zealand, for example). In other areas, this must be developed by examination of membership figures from various denominations and religious structures.

When certain religious groups are open to the Gospel, they can be targeted through studying the report, and a strategy developed to reach them. For example, if there is a responsive segment of immigrants within a city, they will be located for evangelism activity. The strategy might include radio broadcasting in their language, as well as reaching them personally by direct mail and house-to-house visitation in the districts where they have clustered.

12. Use A Checkerboard Planting Pattern

Many years ago, I used this strategy to develop the ministry of *The People Who Care* in Houston, Texas. When we first began, the gap in our "checkerboard" was so large we would drive fifteen minutes or more between our homes for our cell meetings. Within a year, Ruth and I were walking on foot to our cell group gathering.

The Full Gospel Central Church in Seoul has done the same thing through the years with their "Districts." When I first began to study them, they had only fourteen districts covering the entire city. As their cells grew, they gradually reduced the size of each district and added new ones. There are currently several dozen — and they continue to plan for further ones as they move past the 800,000 membership figure. It is important to have a vision that reaches far beyond the primitive beginning stages. An urban strategy will be constantly reviewed and updated.

13. Create the Actual Strategy

Questions for the church planting or leadership team to answer may include the following:

1. Who are the responsive segments we have discovered? Do they have anything in common? If so, what are these things?
2. Should we seek to penetrate several groups as a test of receptivity before focusing on only one?
3. Which group, or groups, within the community should first be reached? How will this strategy lend itself to the expansion of the ministry into other segments of the community? Prepare both short and long range plans.
4. As we view the metropolis, where do these segments live or gather?
5. How should we seek to communicate with them? Should we use direct mail, word of mouth only, house-to-house surveys, etc.?
6. What will be our reason for contacting them? Should we offer special small groups which focus on their problems or interests?

(Examples: a Target Group for expectant mothers, or a group for lonely people?)

7. Where will we meet with them? Can we use their own homes? If not, what facilities in the areas where they live might be available for us to use? Can we use our own homes for this purpose?

8. How many groups can we launch in the first six months, given our manpower and their available time?

In most cases, the original strategy is only theoretical. As the ministry is launched, the church planting team will require many adjustments to their preliminary plans. Above everything else, the initial penetration of the unreached in the community should be given much higher priority than the establishment of a worship service on Sunday mornings. The many hours spent in preparing and executing this service may be better invested in ministry to the target group.

21

Equipping
All The Ministers

If everyone is a minister, then everyone must be prepared for the work of ministry. "Equipping all the saints for the work of ministry" is a nice sounding phrase, but it can be a real nightmare to implement in modern society. Time pressures upon urban Christians exceed anything experienced by first-century believers. With many people having to work 10 to 12-hour days, how can they be expected to be active in their cell group, spend time with unbelievers, and simultaneously devote evenings to attend discipleship classes?

Yet future leaders do not arise magically. They are developed. Unless pastors expand their vision of ministry beyond doing the ministry to equipping ministers, the cell vision will only be a pipe dream. If the vision is to expand and multiply many times, pastors must expand their vision even more. They must take the step from equipping others to developing a system that consistently equips every member for ministry. I call this a *taxonomy*.

A Taxonomy Is Required

Taxonomy comes from two Greek words: *taxis*, "order," and *nomia*, "distribute." A taxonomy expert would say, "If you are going to talk about C and D, it's necessary to first introduce A, and then B. Otherwise, the learner will not know what you are talking about."

Imagine a child being introduced to the death of Jesus on the cross without first knowing how He is God, and without understanding the meaning of the word "sin." Imagine a person seeking to know the will of God who has never been taught how to hear God speak. Imagine a believer seeking to build up a fellow Christian with little or no knowledge of spiritual gifts. Many churches train their people this way, but the cell church does not. The cell church trains with a purpose — to raise up people who can minister and lead others in holiness.

How Do People Learn?

To accomplish this task, we must take into full account the way people learn! Sitting people in rows in a classroom and speaking from a podium is an effective way to teach people information. But a classroom prepares other teachers and the cell church needs people who can do more than teach.

We must change the word "teaching" to "apprenticing." There are very few things we actually do unless we work with someone who both informs and demonstrates for us. We must begin with the premise that every true Christian is both in the process of being equipped, while simultaneously equipping someone else. This must begin with the first person entering a Shepherd Group and must continue right up through the Zone Pastors to the Senior Pastors! We must constantly be functioning on the philosophy that true equipping requires both activities to be taking place simultaneously.

The Place of Weekend Events in Cell Church Life

Most training in the church is spread over many weeks, using one-hour sessions attached to a worship service. However, equipping in the cell church is most effective when it is launched with "weekends." Think of them as camps on a hiking path. You must first go to a camp before beginning a journey. At these camps, there is intensive orientation to prepare you for the next stage of the journey.

Each weekend launches a study, a ministry, or an activity that further develops the ministries of those who attend. It is important to know that no weekend is complete without a journey to follow!

Some years ago, I was invited to a church in St. Louis, Missouri to conduct training for a church wanting to launch cell groups. The innovative pastor there advertised the eight-hour seminar as "Don't

Turn Out the Lights Night." The evening began at 10 p.m. and lasted until breakfast at 6:00 a.m. the next morning.

Having presented the same material many times previously, I expected the usual positive response but was overwhelmed at the paradigm shift that took place in the members of that traditional church because of the marathon style of the training event.

In the years that followed, the value of concentrated training became more and more obvious. Thus, the concept of a weekend event to launch each new stage of training in the cell church was introduced.

Weekends must always be followed by a "journey," where further input is provided. Tied to each weekend, there should be further training and experience to make it meaningful. Thus, the *Spiritual Formation Weekend* launches the study of *Beginning the Journey*, the *Touching Hearts Weekend* is followed by the *Touching Hearts* study guide, etc.

As you think of the equipping process, always keep in mind the value of a marathon event which precedes the ongoing equipping process. If it is too long for one evening, conduct it on a Friday night and return to the training on Saturday. Some cell churches who have Friday cells use a Thursday night through Saturday pattern. In all cases, the heart of the material should be included in the weekend, along with small group activity to process all input. Schedule these weekends as the main events in the church calendar.

How Weekends Coordinate with Harvest Events

Each harvest event (explained in the following chapter) in the church calendar should make maximum use of the weekends which prepare new people for the next step in ministry. Thus, the *Touching Hearts Weekend* is followed by a five week "journey" in the *Touching Hearts* study guide for the teams which have been trained. This weekend should precede by five to ten weeks a scheduled harvest event. For example a church might launch this event in January, culminating in the Let's Have A Good Friday! harvest event on the Good Friday before Easter. Soon after that, incoming cell members may be trained once again with this Weekend.

How Weekend Events Coordinate with the Cells

It is very important that these weekends do not "float in space!" They must be tied directly to the cell groups. Therefore, enlistment for them takes place in the cell group meeting, and the Shepherd must personally endorse each person to take the training.

The Shepherd should ask those who have been trained to share what they learned at the next cell meeting. In the case of the *Touching Hearts Weekend,* the team of two is to return and share the presentation with the entire cell group during the next two meetings. For the following three meetings a "round robin" is conducted. One person explains the first element of the illustration and passes the paper to the person on his/her right to explain the next element. In this way, the entire cell group will have a review of the diagram once or twice each year.

Your Equipping Journey

The Scriptural Foundation
1 John 2:12-14 describes three levels of maturity for the believer.

> *"I write to you, dear children, because your sins are forgiven on account of His name.*
> *I write to you, fathers, because you have known Him who is from the beginning.*
> *I write to you, young men, because you have overcome the evil one.*
> *I write to you, dear children, because you have known the Father.*
> *I write to you, fathers, because you have known Him who is from the beginning.*
> *I write to you, young men, because you are strong, and the Word of God lives in you, and you have overcome the evil one."*

The *children* discussed here are immature believers. They know the Father but are not far along in the journey. At this first stage, the discipleship path brings new believers into an understanding of what it means to live in the kingdom of God and raises their awareness of Satan's presence and motives on earth.

The second stage in this passage is that of *Young Men*. When believers have *overcome the evil one*, they will have won the battle over satanic strongholds and possess the Living Word within them. The discipleship path takes each believer through a mentor-led learning process and an encounter experience, providing the freedom to walk in Spirit and Truth.

The third stage in this passage refers to *Fathers*. By virtue of the name, spiritual *fathers* have sired children and are described as having a long-term, deep knowledge of God. This discipleship path trains up believers to reach the lost through relational evangelism and to mentor these new believers through the journey they have already begun.

The path will move group members through all three levels of maturity and create a growing number of discipled leadership candidates for your groups.

Hiking Up A Mountain
The following taxonomy for equipping can be illustrated by a mountain trail leading to four camps. Each camp supplies hikers with the tools they will need for the next part of their journey.

The Camps
The camps will be manned by pastoral staff members and mature lay leaders in your church. Any cell member who hikes up the discipleship trail will visit the camp, learn about the path ahead and pick up tools that will make the next part of the journey successful. The camps are as follows, in order of use:

1) **Spiritual Formation Weekend** *(Children)*
2) **Encounter God Retreat** *(Young Men)*
3) **Touching Hearts Weekend** *(Fathers)*
4) **Cell Leader Intern Retreat** *(Fathers)*

The Path
The paths *between* the camps provide the cell member with daily growth guides and mentorship. Each day, the member will spend five to ten minutes reading, answering short questions and praying about various topics: God, Christ's love, the importance of community and fellowship, overcoming sin, ministering to others and receiving ministry, relational

evangelism, taking a leadership role and more. The hiking tools are as follows:

1) **Beginning the Journey - 5 weeks.**
   (formerly The New Believer's Station)
2) **The Arrival Kit - 11 weeks.**
3a) **Touching Hearts - 5 weeks.**
3b) **Mentoring Another Believer - A reader.**
   (formerly the Sponsor's Guidebook)

These printed resources have been written carefully with a form of programmed learning designed to "overlap" important subject matter. As a set, they are powerful because they repeat key truths that readers will apply in ministry.

The first three resources have been designed with daily growth guides. The member will spend time in prayer and in the Word each day as well as read two or three pages found in the growth guides. Some pages ask questions, while others suggest discussing the content with a mentor.

How does mentorship work?

Certain parts of the discipleship path are difficult. A mentor who is ahead on the path or has walked the path before can be a great source of support and encouragement.

Cell leaders should assign a mentor to every new believer who enters a cell group. A mentor is usually the person who reached the new believer for Christ or has a strong friendship with the new believer. Mentors and protégés should be of the same sex, so if a man leads a woman to Christ, his wife or another woman in the cell may be asked to mentor the new believer.

If an incoming member has been a believer for many years, he or she should select an accountability partner from the group with whom to climb the mountain. The cell leader should make certain that this is a good match.

Once incoming members have completed their training and reached a friend or family member for Christ, each one of them will become a mentor and focus on discipling a new believer.

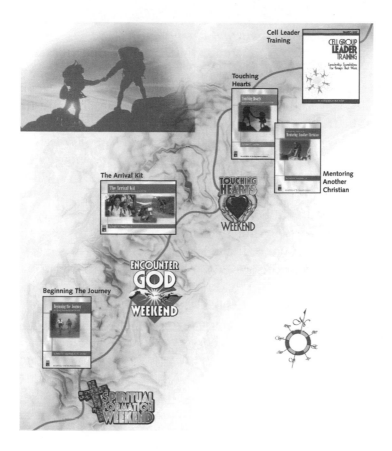

Let's Hike Up The Mountain Together!

Now that we've overviewed the camps, the paths and the mentor/accountability relationship, let's walk through each step.

Where does the path originate?

There are only two ways to begin the hike: as a new believer or as an incoming cell member. Typically, both types of people will become regular parts of a cell group before they begin the journey. If you already have established cells, encourage every cell member to go through the taxonomy. For some, parts of the training will be very basic, but everyone will learn something as they go through the process. If for no other reason, all of your cell members should participate so that they will be ready to mentor new believers through the process.

The First Camp — The Spiritual Formation Weekend
When new believers or members join a cell group, the cell leader should invite them to attend the next **Spiritual Formation Weekend**. This weekend is held at the church campus on a Friday evening and the following Saturday, concluding in the afternoon. With their mentors by their sides, they will:

- Share their life story through the use of *The Journey Guide for New Christians*, if this has not been done previously. (Existing church members entering your cell group ministry will use *The Journey Guide for Growing Christians*.)
- Learn about and be scheduled for baptism, if necessary.
- Learn about your church's history.
- Meet the pastoral staff and spouses.
- Be placed in or confirmed as a member of a particular cell group.
- Learn about their future at your church and the equipping journey they will undertake.

At the conclusion of this weekend, each participant is given a copy of the first discipleship tool, *Beginning the Journey*. When given, detailed instructions on its use and benefits must also be offered.

Also, schedule each participant for the next retreat, ***Encounter God.*** By doing so, everyone entering the cell ministry will understand that there is a unified discipleship system and that everyone will be moving through the system together.

The First Path — Beginning The Journey
Throughout the next five weeks, your cell members will take part in weekly cell group meetings, deepen their relationships with other believers between meetings and work through the daily growth guides in *Beginning the Journey*.

Each week, members will meet with their mentors. As they become friends, each pair will pray, talk about what they're learning and discuss ways to introduce the mentor to the protégé's lost friends and family. They will also discuss what they are learning through the daily growth guides. This includes current habits and lifestyles that do not glorify God, lordship, baptism, listening to God and experiencing freedom in Christ.

Beginning the Journey will bring cell members into a fresh understanding of kingdom living. When this happens, they will see the need for spiritual warfare and deliverance from satanic strongholds, which they will receive in the next camp.

The Second Camp

The Encounter God Retreat is ideally held at a hotel or retreat center within an hour's drive of your church's facility. This retreat is designed to take cell members out of their home environment (away from children and other distractions) to allow them to focus on deep spiritual matters. When they attend this retreat, they should be accompanied by their mentor.

Throughout the retreat, your cell members will learn how Satan uses strongholds to keep believers from being effective in ministry, bound by hurts, wounds and sinful habits from the past.

Then, your cell members and mentors will complete a supplied inventory card and confess their sins to one another after some training and testimonies.

At the conclusion of this retreat, present your cell members with the next "hiker's tool" entitled *The Arrival Kit*.

Then, each member should sign up for the next equipping event called **The Touching Hearts Weekend**.

The Second Path

The Arrival Kit will take your cell members through an eleven-week hike, examining worldly values with which they may struggle, such as spiritual warfare, a new life of servanthood, an examination of attitudes, the power of prayer and the priesthood of all believers. The wonderful thing about this part of the journey is that when it's completed, your cell members will be victorious over Satan and ready to mentor new believers they have reached for Christ!

The Third Camp

When your cell members arrive at this camp, they will have developed new "spiritual muscles" and will be ready to learn about strategic, relational evangelism. *The Touching Hearts Weekend* was specifically designed to teach people how to reach the lost through cell group relationships.

Your cell members should attend this weekend with a partner with whom they have been in a mentor/protégé or accountability relationship. The more teams from the *same cell group* that participate in this weekend together, the better! Before attending this camp, each participant should complete a *Journey Guide for Growing Christians.*

On Friday night, a brief overview of mentoring will be given by a church staff member or a coach over your groups. At the conclusion of the evening, your cell members will be given a copy of *Mentoring Another Christian* for reading at a later time. This is a great time for partners to discuss their *Journey Guide* results with one another.

On Saturday, the training for relational evangelism begins. Each of the cell members attending will receive a copy of *Touching Hearts*, which they will use as a workbook throughout the day. After watching video clips in the morning, your cell members will create a list of unbelievers with whom they frequently come into contact. Co-workers, neighbors, family members and friends will fill these lists. Using this list, each pair will determine who is most ready to hear the Gospel.

On Saturday afternoon, your cell members will learn to share the Gospel message with a unique version of a bridge illustration, called *The John 3:16 diagram.* Using their own changed-life as an example, each member will practice sharing the Gospel.

Now equipped with the right tools, your cell members will be sent out to reach their world for Jesus!

The Third Path
The next five weeks will be very powerful. Cell members will discover the power of Christian community to reach the lost and come to understand God's purpose in their lives.

During these days, cell groups will grow with new converts; the cell members who have been mentored (or who have been paired up for accountability) will be set apart to mentor the new babes in Christ.

The five weeks of daily growth guides within *Touching Hearts* will review the need to work as a team, the John 3:16 diagram, helping others find freedom from sin and allowing the Holy Spirit to speak through them as they share the Good News.

In the last daily guides, cell members will be challenged to examine their motives and to follow examples offered from the lives of Jesus and Paul. This will give them an in-depth understanding of the call on their lives and change them forever!

The Fourth Camp

As cell members reach the lost and begin to mentor them through the journey described here, mature, soul-winning leaders will emerge.

The pastoral leaders — along with your cell leaders — will determine which mentors are ready for the challenge of leadership. *The Journey Guide for Cell Group Leaders* has been developed to help pastoral leaders determine who is ready for leadership and how to assist future leaders in the weaker areas of ministry.

After determining who is ready for the leadership challenge, extend a personal invitation. Each couple should receive a personal phone call with follow-up printed information to go on *an all-expenses paid retreat to a nice hotel or out-of-town facility.* Arrange off-site childcare for the Friday to Saturday evening time through their cell group leader and members. If presented properly, your potential cell leaders will feel very special!

The **Cell Group Leader Retreat**, found in the *Cell Group Leader Training: Trainer's Guide,* is designed to bring information and inspiration surrounding cell leadership. This retreat should be described as a nice break from the hectic pace of life, where there will be time to fellowship and have fun on Saturday. The main point of this weekend is to thank your dedicated cell members for their hard work in the cells and to share the vision for their next step of ministry as an intern (or what some call an apprentice).

On Friday evening, pastoral staff members will cast the vision of the church and share the role of the cell leader. Testimonies by key cell leaders will help each person understand that leadership is not a superhero role but one of simple servanthood. Before the evening concludes, each couple will sign up to visit privately with a staff pastor on Saturday.

Saturday morning, after a not-too-early breakfast, your cell members will gather for more information about cell leadership. After lunch, the afternoon is free, with the exception of the individual, half hour appointments with the staff pastors. These private interviews are the place where your cell members will see their pastoral support and make a commitment to cell leadership. The concluding session is somewhat of an alter call, challenging couples to come forward if they sense God's call to move into leadership immediately. The entire group should gather around these and share prayers of thanksgiving!

On the Sunday following this retreat, present all the members and spouses who have agreed to become leaders to your church during your services. They will be brought to the front of the church and set apart for leadership, receiving the blessing of the congregation.

The Fourth Path

The top of the mountain is in view! Now that you have a new group of budding leaders (interns), they'll need special pastoral attention, guidance, and lots on-the-job training.

This hike can take a few months or half a year, depending on your church's leadership requirements. These are the basic requirements:

- A life free from habitual sin.
- A well-developed prayer life (alone, with spouse and family, and with cell members).
- The earned respect of cell members (from lots of servanthood).
- Faithful involvement in leadership training and ongoing events.
- A strong desire to share Christ's love with anyone who will listen.
- A dogged determination to help fellow cell members reach their friends for Christ.

If these basic values and disciplines are present, then it is easy to train a person in the skills of an effective leader. The training resource *The Cell Group Leader Training* covers eight topics that introduce a future leader to the needed skills. These are best taught over a period of eight weeks but it is also appropriate material for an intense weekend of training.

After a future leader attends the basic training, he or she needs a mentor, either an experienced group leader or Zone Supervisor to mentor him or her through the *8 Habits of Effective Small Group Leaders*.

Finally, as the leader develops, *Leading from the Heart* will reinforce and establish his or her ministry upon the foundation for true and impacting ministry.

Cover the Bible

A parallel equipping module to *Your Equipping Journey* is a basic survey of the Bible. This will equip every member to read and study the Bible competently. *Cover the Bible* will equip members to think about their Bibles as they learn how it was developed, about the authors of each book and how to understand the overall meaning of each book.

Zone Supervisor or Coach Intern Weekend

Those who are invited to participate in this weekend are hand-picked after much prayer from the cell leaders. It is a great honor to be selected for this event! The invitation to attend should come from either the Senior Pastor or the District Pastor. The entire weekend focuses on helping the Zone Supervisor and spouse realize they are very much a part of the "full time" pastoral team, even though they may not be drawing a salary for their ministry. The Zone Supervisor or Coach oversees up to five cell groups and as many as 125 people. As a result, this weekend communicates the special weight of their calling as they assume the pastoral role equivalent to 33% of all full-time pastors in the world. There is also the awareness that some of those who enter into this level of ministry will be called by the Lord to step into the life of a Zone Pastor in a year or more.

As with the **Cell Group Leader Retreat**, this event is held in a live-in environment, using a retreat center, hotel or nearby resort. The children may also be invited to attend along with their parents (optional). A spirit of comradeship must be developed. They are also invited to attend the next Intern Weekend as they complete their Internship. This gives them opportunity to better know the Interns they will be working with in the following months.

Also, as with the Cell Leader Intern, the Zone Supervisor Intern will be constantly tutored by a qualified Zone Supervisor for six to nine months, taking over half the cells at multiplication time. Upon completion of six months of Internship and six months of service beyond that stage, the Zone Supervisor is set apart for ministry by a special laying on of hands, witnessed by the entire church in a public service.

Reinventing the Wheel

The above equipping system has been developed over many years of trial and error. You don't have to make the same mistakes I did. The wheel is already invented. Start with the above taxonomy and begin equipping your leaders.

At the same time I want to warn you. I have used the following illustration for years. Each person swallows several ounces of saliva daily. Without this function, we would experience discomfort. Consider how you would feel if you were asked to spit several ounces of your own saliva in a cup and then drink it. Ugh! Why? It's your own spit, isn't it? Yet it now seems like a "foreign" substance. Now take it a step further. How would you feel if I handed you a cup filled with my spit to drink? Could you tolerate that?

I spent years developing the above models that equip believers and then usher them into ministry. To monitor their effectiveness, I served as a senior pastor in Houston and then as a senior associate pastor in Singapore. I rebuilt each module over and over, refining them as they were tested. I did this not to sell materials, but to provide working models of key principles for the next generation. My desire was that my work would serve as a platform for others, who would internalize and adapt the structure to fit their cultures and the Christians who would be equipped.

The above materials will get you started. Some you will use indefinitely as they will fit your church well. Others you will adapt for your own setting. Learn from them and develop your own "spit." We only have one aim: *Equip the Saints*.

See page 398 for more information or please contact the
TOUCH® Outreach Ministries office at
1-800-735-5865 or www.touchusa.org

22

Harvest Events

When you admire a tree in bloom, you see its leaves, its flowers and how its branches reach upward. Never, unless you are a botanist, would you think about the root system that produces this beauty. However, if you were to consider a tree's roots, how large do you think the circumference of the root system would be? Do you think the roots pierce the earth below exactly as deep as the tree is tall? Or do the roots spread under the earth exactly as wide as the branches have spread from the trunk.

The latter of the two choices is correct. If a tree develops a proper root system, it will be filled with strong branches and will bear fruit to reproduce itself in kind. The same applies to the church. A church only looks as good as the root system that supports it. In the cell church structure, strong emphasis is placed upon helping every cell member become a part of its "root system," as he is learning to reach another person for Christ within six months of joining a group. Each person then can be encouraged to sow, cultivate, and expect a harvest time in a continuing cycle.

Harvest events help develop this root system. If people know that the church expects and plans for a harvest, it is easier to commit time to it. Cell members know to look forward to what God will do in the lives of the lost.

Harvest Events Should Be Made
Cell Church Traditions

Think of harvest events as part of the traditions of your cell church. The word "tradition" may be seen as a derogatory reference to P.B.D.

church leaders who say, "We have our traditions. We never tried it that way before!" *(The Seven Last Words of the Church)*. Nevertheless, there is a need to create "traditions" in the cell church that are positive, leading to annual harvesting events.

In America's Southland, there were two traditional evangelistic meetings each year, called "Revivals." One was in October, the other in March or April. Around the turn of this century — without radio, TV, or transportation — these "Revivals" were spectacular events that drew even the town atheist to the public meetings. For example, the famous evangelist, Sam Jones, used to have a special seat for the town atheist on the front row of his meetings, and rousing debates would take place between him and the one who dared to sit in it!

In the past 30 years, "Revivals" have failed to produce — attracting few, if any, unbelievers and bringing little or no edification to the faithful core of the memberships who dutifully attended and put their "love offering" in the plate for the visiting evangelist. The times changed. People adjusted to a culture saturated with multiple TV entertainment channels, and the attractiveness of attending a "Revival" died.

As we think about lifestyles of people today, we recognize there must be a new approach to harvest events which attract the lost. Entertainment is no longer in short supply and this will not attract people to Christ. The church cannot out entertain Hollywood.

What will draw people to Christ? What can the church do better than anybody else? Relationships! As Christians, we have the power to love and reach out to people. Today's society is made up of lonely people. Most walk in inner despair, hungry for true friends.

In America today, the parachurch movement, "Promise Keepers," has exploded into existence. Tens of thousands of men gather in huge stadiums for men's rallies. These major events are fed from hundreds of small groups — each with three men who meet together and become accountable to and for each other. While it is primarily a gathering of Christians, many unbelieving men have been swept into the Kingdom by its impact. What is the drawing power of this movement? It offers intimate relationships.

"Body Life Evangelism" is a method which can best be utilized by the cell church movement. By building relationships with the lost, cell members will have the right to minister to them, leading them one step at a time to the Father. If this root system of cell groups is put in place, there should be times for harvesting the results as a formal activity of the church. These events should generate the annual church calendar.

The stronger the cell church grows, the more cell members are reaching out to the lost, the more critical it will be to focus on harvest events. The sign of a mature cell structure is the schedule of traditional events.

Believing that each community has its own distinctive needs and population mix, it is best to present you with models to stimulate your planning. Let us examine several illustrations of effective harvest events.

Church-Wide Harvest Events Used Successfully by Cell Churches

Come Celebrate Christmas
For several years, Faith Community Baptist Church has sponsored a special Christmas program for the people of Singapore. Every year, the 12,000 seat Singapore Indoor Stadium was reserved for four nights for the performance put on by hundreds of cell members. On some nights, hundreds were turned away! The conversions through that single harvest event numbered in the hundreds.

Heaven's Gates, Hell's Flames
This is a drama that is put on by the members of a church. Reality Outreach[1] has produced the script and sends a producer/team to direct the rehearsals for the church. The response to this nine-part drama has been phenomenal! Bethany Prayer Fellowship, Baker, Louisiana, presented this for 21 nights in February-March, 1994, and had 18,290 recorded decisions for Christ. In Modesto, California in 1995, there were 25,000 decisions when the presentation ran there.

Parent's Banquet
This event drew hundreds of Buddhist parents of FCBC young people to a special 12-course Chinese banquet held in a hotel ballroom. A Chinese movie star from Hong Kong who has accepted the Lord was the drawing card: she had been seen in movies by the parents for years. Many conversions were recorded on decision cards placed at each table.

Crusade

In El Salvador, the 110,000 member Mission Elim Cell Church packs out the largest soccer stadium in the nation for an evangelistic crusade. Cell members bring guests who are either unsaved or on the verge of making a commitment.

Stadium Rally

Each year, Dion Robert gathers the people who are in the cells of the *Eglise Protestante Baptiste Oeuvres et Mission* in Abidjan, Ivory Coast, for a harvest time. In the past, there have been so many decisions during this event that the church systematically multiplies all its cell groups prior to the meetings so there will be proper assimilation into the body of converts. People come days in advance to fast and pray in preparation for their ministries of deliverance. A team of over 200 set up a kitchen and feed all who attended. Miracles of healings constantly take place. Some of the highest government officials in the land sit on the platform, and many of them have been saved through attending this rally.

Holiday Excursion

When the Abidjan church had only 9,000 members, Pastor Dion took them by buses and boats to an offshore resort island. There the Holy Spirit began to draw the unbelievers who lived with the cell members. On another occasion, this church rented trains and took thousands of people from Abidjan to Bouake, the second largest city in the nation, for a special harvest event there. Unbelievers were glad to share in such an adventure as a trip to Bouake, and hundreds were saved in the meetings.

One Day Community Event

Fifteen years ago, a Florida pastor envisioned impacting Fort Lauderdale by sponsoring the feeding of 5,000 people on the church property. Newspaper ads publicized the date, inviting all who were poor or hungry to come to be fed roast chicken and many other dishes. The entire church participated as all the food was prepared in the homes of the members. Men with counter machines clicked those who received free meals, and true to their promise, 5,000 people were fed on that one day! The impact of this loving group caused many people to seriously investigate the claims of Jesus Christ. The impact made on the area was powerful.

Major Church-Wide Harvest Events

As a young man just graduating from college, I was employed by the Billy Graham Evangelistic Association. At that time (1950), Dr. Graham was forming his crusade team and needed guidance about crusade development. He contacted Mr. Hankamer, who had been with Billy Sunday years before. This gray-haired gentleman spent several months with the Graham organization. One of the lessons he taught us was that great stadiums were filled only when the crusade preparations involved at least one person for every ten who were needed to fill the stadiums. Thus, Cliff Barrows began to organize crusade choirs of 1,000-2,000 voices. The counseling training involved hundreds of people sitting in the stands. For several years as I worked in this crusade ministry, I saw the proof of his premise.

In order to successfully pull off church-wide harvest events follow these guidelines:

1. The calendar for the cell church should include at least one major church-wide harvest event each year.
2. This should be well planned to maximize involvement. At least 40% of the total cell group membership should have responsibilities in preparing for the event. For the event to succeed this high percentage must be honored because it creates high ownership. The cells are to be prepared to actively participate in the activity in every possible way.
3. Develop as many tasks as possible to involve people. Here is a list of ways cell members and cell groups have been involved by cell churches:
   a. Musicians: Bands, orchestras, dancers, drama groups, etc.
   b. Counselors: Prepare them by conducting a *Spiritual Victory Weekend* in advance of the Event.
   c. Ushers: use more than you need to build the percentage of involvement.
   d. Prayer Warriors: They might sit in a group. Have them begin to fast and pray one day a week for three months prior to the event.
   e. Greeters: Prepare shoulder sashes to identify them at the entrance doors.
   f. Technicians: Have volunteer crews using teens or young adults to assist in the moving of props, microphones, etc.

g. Parking Teams: Using flashlights, use teams to help guide cars to parking spots.

h. Food Support Teams: Arrange for food to be served to either the performers or, as will be shown below, to the people attending the Event.

District/Zone Events

Home Made Ice Cream Social

Tom Glymph was a Zone Supervisor in Houston, Texas. His subzone of five cells came together to penetrate a low cost housing estate in Houston, Texas. Tom deliberately moved into an apartment among these grass roots people to establish a Christian presence among them. The cells rotated, each spending a Sunday afternoon among the residents. Two ice cream making machines were purchased by the subzone, and each week home made ice cream was made in the middle of the courtyard in full view of all residents. It was then given away to all comers, and even taken in plastic cups to the doors of the apartments. After a couple of weeks, some of the unbelievers came out to "help turn the crank," and brought bananas and peaches for the mix. Out of this, the zone saw two new cell groups formed from converts. (The subzone would highly recommend this technique as a harvest event for you to try.)

Wild Game Night

One adult zone in Houston, Texas requested all their members who went hunting or fishing to donate a tithe of their game for a special banquet. The evening was called "A Wild Game Night," and it brought many chuckles as unbelievers were invited to participate. A film showing a "camera hunt" in Africa was presented, several men gave testimonies, and many decisions were recorded.

Foods of the World

In a zone with many different ethnic groups, there have been very successful events called "Foods of the World." The cell members in a zone or subzone invite all the friends of other ethnic communities. Each person coming is given the option of preparing an ethnic dish or providing a recipe as their "ticket" to attend. All the foods are placed on a long table and people are invited to taste as many varieties as they wish.

Little placards are put beside each dish giving the name of the dish and the country/ethnic group it represents. Costumes are encouraged, and get-acquainted games can be built around the different customs for doing common things (pointing with the fingers, greeting salutations, etc.)

Valentine Party
Special preparations for a valentine party include "ice breakers," decorations, etc. Couples are seated around tables in groups of six and share details of how they met, fell in love, etc. Towards the close, a speaker may share about the qualities of love and fidelity.

National Holiday Gathering
Some countries have a national day that attracts everyone's attention. This is a perfect time for a zone or subzone to have a special meal or party in connection with a parade with floats, etc.

Cell Group Events

"Mini-Harvest Events" will make a cell group come alive with vision for what can be done to win lost people to the Lord.

Evangelistic Cell Meetings
Located in the context of a nation with significant poverty and unemployment, the Elim Church in El Salvador has an astonishing record of conversions. They have grown to 110,000 members in less than a decade from approximately 3,000 at the time they transitioned. Their pattern is very straightforward:
- All cells multiply at 12-15.
- Each Zone Pastor has monthly "retreats" for his cells. This means they come to an all-night session which includes times of praying and times of marathon teaching. Most of those attending are grass roots people who do not learn by reading. Thus, this takes the place of *The Year of Equipping* in their context.
- Every cell leader is tightly monitored by the Zone Supervisor and he/she is often involved in visiting the lost with the cell leader, cell intern, or even cell members as evangelistic visits are made.
- The cell meets twice weekly. The first meeting of the week is for edification; the second gathering of the group is strictly for outreach.

Every single week, the group plans the activity that will put them in contact with unbelievers they know. This constant weekly cell group outreach is the main reason why they are growing so rapidly. They have a weekly harvest event in all of their cells!

Monthly Birthday Parties

Cell groups have at least one occasion each month when there can be a party — someone's birthday! Surprise birthday parties are always fun for both those who give it and the one who receives it. When the person having the birthday is an unbeliever, there is a special impact made by the thoughtfulness of the cell group that sponsors the party.

A cell group threw a surprise party for one of the young women. All her friends were invited, many of them unbelievers. After the big "Surprise!" was over and cake was being served, the cell leader said, "We would like you to give us a report of your past year and what your dreams are for the coming year." As the "birthday girl" shared, one of her co-workers began to think deeply. On the way home, she said, "Tonight I saw my need to think about where I am going. I was deeply moved by this evening. Thank you for inviting me!"

Celebrations at the close of Share/Interest Group Cycles

It is recommended that cell groups sponsor at least one Share or Interest Group annually. At the close of the ten week sessions, the special "celebration" is conducted. Each person in the group invites two friends. The three from the cell who have sponsored the gathering will invite all the other members of the cell to participate. This activity can often lead to a harvest of people so contacted.

TGIF

At FCBC in Singapore, we developed an annual cell harvest event for Good Friday. Because Friday is a time to relax after a hard week, it is a good opportunity to share with unbelievers why Good Friday means so much to Christians.

The format "Thank God It's Friday" takes on a party atmosphere. In fact, the first half of the gathering is called Happy Hour. During the Happy Hour, the cell members along with the invited guests participate in some crowd breaker games, eat together, play some more games and then sing karaoke.

The second half of the evening is called Agape Hour. This time is clearly scripted for the master of ceremonies to explain why Good Friday is so important to Christians. Then a short video is shown of the death and resurrection of Jesus. After this, everyone is invited to commit his or her life to Christ.

This is followed by a time of counseling. Shepherd Group members divide up with the guests and minister to them. During this time, everyone is invited to come to the Shepherd Group meeting the next week.

This kind of harvest event takes a lot of preparation to equip the cell groups to effectively pull it off. Yet it can be a powerful time of sharing Christ through relationships that reveal to the lost the love God has for them.

23

Transitioning a P.B.D. Church

After all the comments I have made about P.B.D. church life, I want to come to the end of this book and emphasize that the godly people on the staffs and in the pews of those churches have produced every reader of this book, *including the author!* On a scale of one to ten, you may rate the P.B.D. church structure as you will, but give the saints a great big "10."

Tribute must be paid to all those godly believers who love their Lord more than they love the next breath that fills their lungs. The world may be harvested more rapidly, and people may be edified in greater numbers by the cell church movement, but the saints of God have not been asleep. The dedicated men and women within the P.B.D. churches have poured their lives and their funds into doing the work of the Lord in the best way they knew to do it. It's overwhelming when you travel the world among God's people and see the suffering, the steadfastness and the devotion of their ministries. It's a tribute to them that they have accomplished so much using inefficient structures.

My heart goes out to all the wonderful people of God who now feel trapped inside church structures, and who don't see any way out. It also goes out to the tens of thousands who have left the church, who still believe in the Lord, and who wander like sheep without a shepherd to lead them.

We regularly take calls from pastors or church members who are saying, "Where do we go from here?" For those within the P.B.D. structure and who want to bring about change, I want to share some initial thoughts about how to transition a church into cell life. While these instructions will get you started, we have learned over the last 10 years that a complete understanding of the process of transitioning a church requires much more than can be covered in one chapter. The following instructions will help you assess your situation and set the course that your church should adopt.

Go to the "Listening Room!"

Before someone deeply rooted in P.B.D. life should attempt to bring change into an existing structure, there should be a very clear calling from the Lord about the matter. It's not something a person does because he is frustrated with the system, or because he is angry with a certain group. Negative reasons for causing change won't have the mind of Christ, and the work so established will not have his blessings.

The person seeking to bring a traditional church through a transition to become a cell group church must devote at least five to seven years to the task. He will have to unlearn much of what he thinks church life is and step into a new world where all things are new. That's not easy to do!

Many times I have felt like the Eskimo in the painting on my wall. As I stated in the Foreword, I have a picture of an Eskimo with a dogsled who had gone onto new ice to hunt seals. The weight of the dogs, the sled and his own body has caused the ice to crack away from the mainland. He is standing on the floe, his lead dog sitting pensively by his side, watching the water gap widen between them and security. When you feel like this, you don't want to go on.

I can tell you from my own journey that when you decide to leave structures behind, there is a price to pay. Every man since Martin Luther who has done so by choice or by circumstances can attest to the reality of this. Unless one has been to the Listening Room and has a clear word from the Lord, he will be unable to say as Luther did, "Here I stand. I can do no other. God help me!" One must know that his constant Companion has called him forth, and that he has little say in the matter of what comes next. Only then will the anointing remain when rejection comes from old friends.

Learn as Much as You Can

In the late eighties, not much was known about how to become a cell church. There were few models and those that existed were far from home. This is no longer the case. Thinkers have been writing on the cell church to expand your knowledge of the vision. Practitioners have struggled in the transition process and have developed models that will help you set a course.

Therefore read as much as you can about the cell group church. My books like *The Shepherd's Guidebook* and *The Year of Equipping* materials will take you a step further. Go to conferences while you are reading. I have also developed the material in the *Advanced Cell Training* conference that will go into further detail about the cell model. In addition, read the works of Joel Comiskey. He has done the most up-to-date research on the best cell church models in the world.

Read Larry Stockstill's *The Cell Church* and seek to understand his cell model. Read about Yongii Cho's church in Karen Hurston's excellent book, *Growing the World's Largest Church*. These will get you started.

While you are learning about the cell church, go see one in action. You do not need to travel to Singapore or Korea any longer. There are cell churches in Dallas, Memphis, Miami, Tulsa, Baton Rouge, Baltimore, Pittsburgh and Los Angeles. Buy the pastors of these churches lunch and pump them with questions. Ask permission to visit a cell group. Learn as much as you can from those who have taken a few more steps than you.

Ask the Hard Questions

As I reflect over the dozens of times I have been involved in the attempts of pastors to bring change to the church, the first thing I would suggest is that this hard question be asked: *"Is it really possible for this particular group of people to change? Should I attempt this?"*

There are thousands of churches who should simply be left alone. They are unable to change, and the attempt is a futile one. People gain their personal significance from their positions and power bases in church life as readily as they do in business life. To change the system is to threaten their worth and self-esteem, often developed at a great price of time invested by them during years of devotion and sacrifice to a church program. Unless a spiritual explosion occurs in their lives, they won't change.

There are truly devoted pastors who cling to the security blanket of the salary provided by a congregation. Should he risk all for a new concept of church life? That's a question for the Listening Room! He will invest years trying to bring change into that church. At the end, he may be no farther along than when he started — and stands a good chance of being sacked for his effort!

Sometimes it's better to just start over. Sometimes it's easier to take a "remnant," as Jehovah said He would do within Israel, and start fresh. It's a painful thing to draw out people who want to go on with God and leave the rest behind, but that's what God had to do with Israel in the desert. It is a viable option, and we are going to see more and more of this.

It's always something to be prayed over until the Lord provides the answer: *should the committed live in frustration because of the traditionalists who hinder the ministry, or should the uncommitted face a new future apart from them?*

In the early days of West Memorial Baptist Church, that's the situation I faced. My problem was the agony of loving everyone in the flock, and not wanting to hurt either the innovators who were excited about our new lifestyle or the tradition-bound folks who began to fight it tooth and toenail. My resignation caused the two sides to clash, and the result was the dissemination of the traditionalists into P.B.D. churches nearby. It was only then that we could make our changes in harmony and peace.

I understand how those feel who have close ties of love in a P.B.D. church family, and who are also torn by the idea of staying in the miserable structure. Such life-changing decisions are made slowly, with much grief, and must be done with love and not bitterness, in the Listening Room.

Have I properly conveyed to you my feelings about all this? If not, let me say again as clearly as I know how — I have the deepest love and affection for the saints everywhere! It's their entrapment in the traditional church I have sought to criticize.

If you are a church staff member or a church member, I would like to frankly say to you that you should not attempt to bring change to your church. Authority and responsibility are two categories which must exactly overlap. If the pastor is not going to endorse what you are doing, you will be a thorn in the church as long as you are there. Since you don't plan to be a part of the traditional direction of the pastor, it would be much better for you to move on. *You can't change a church without the spiritual oversight of it which God has assigned to its pastor. You are out of order when you attempt to do so!*

The rest of this chapter is specifically provided for a pastor of a traditional church who is trying to make up his mind about staying with the old or launching into the new. Please consider all the factors presented in this chapter.

Counting the Cost

"No one who puts his hand to the plow and looks back is fit for service in the kingdom of God" (Luke 9:62). It is better not to start the transition if you are not going to finish it. I heard about an Asian pastor who led his church through the first two years of transition. They had 135 cells. Then he discovered he could get a Ph.D. in London with all expenses paid. In a matter of a month, he left his church. This act left several hundred people disillusioned with Christian leaders. If he felt called to work on a Ph.D. he should have raised up a leader to take his place in the ministry before leaving the work unfinished.

When airplanes fly over the oceans, they mark a "point of no return" on their maps. From that point onward, there is no turning back. If you have yet to implement cell groups, you are not yet at this point. And before you do, please pray and consider the following issues before embarking on such a journey.

As you learn as much as you can about the cell church vision and strategy, evaluate the depth of calling and anointing for the task. It will require at least a five-year commitment of your life to lead your church through the transition stages and raise up and intern who could replace you if you should leave. If your spirit has been penetrated by the Spirit of God and you know you are called to cell church life in your church, you will work through many adjustments in the days ahead.

The following questionnaire will help you work through these issues:

1. How long do you plan to stay in your present church?

   _____

   a. What might make that answer change?
   b. If you were to leave in the middle of the transition, what would happen to this church?
   c. Who might you select from the start to become your intern to replace you if something happens?

2. Your typical reaction to stress (underline those that apply):
   a. I withdraw and become silent.
   b. I need to have face-to-face discussion as quickly as possible.
   c. I delay reacting until I have had time to think about it.
   d. I sometimes react strongly and with anger.
   e. Other: _____

3. Results of stresses you have faced in the past (underline all that apply):
   a. Sleeplessness
   b. Ulcers
   c. "Night sweats" (Sheets soaked as you sleep)
   d. Migraine headaches
   e. Other: _____

4. There is no set role for a pastor's wife in a cell church. It varies as widely as simply being a cell member and a homemaker to actively working in the development of the structure. Each pastor's wife will find far more freedom to be "real" in the church setting, since no formal role is demanded.
   a. Is she willing to either share in a weekly cell meeting or perhaps lead a group of her own? Or, will she be able to help you organize cells as a Zone Supervisor or Zone Pastor?
   b. Is your wife prepared to be your companion or co-worker as you enter into this task? How? _____
   c. Does she share the conviction for the cell church vision? _____
   d. Are you together sharing with your children the reasons you will be revising your personal family life to be more effective in ministry? _____

Change and the Church

How many times have you tried to introduce a new concept, only to be met by a brick wall — or given only token support by a few? Or, perhaps your suggestion was enthusiastically received, only to fizzle in six months or so. The main cause of these responses was a failure to properly initiate change.

No society in history has faced rapid, shattering change as has ours. We now expect change. We assume that tomorrow will somehow be better than yesterday, that new technology will bring "better" things. We expect our children to be smarter than we are. At the same time, there's a feeling that things have gotten out of hand.

Alvin Toffler called this feeling "future shock." Most of us by now are sure that we have had enough of it. Note the middle class American quest for oak furniture which was sold from Sears catalogues 60 years ago! The church has become, for most persons, the last bastion of yesterday. The church is the one institution which can preserve "the good old days," when nothing else has stayed the same. More and more Christians, when thinking about their local churches, resist change there — even though they would not think of driving a 25 year old car.

There's a good reason for this: *all change is perceived as loss*. Even when the change is an apparently happy occasion — like marriage, or moving to a new job — there remains the lingering feeling we have left something behind, something we'll never recapture.

Christian leaders should be change agents. We are in the business of leading people to higher ground, new ministries to the lost. We have been told that change needs to be carefully "managed." But too often as we seek to do this, we fail to take into account the anguish for which we are responsible.

We need to change. We need to move to higher ground. We need to mature in Christ. We need to right the wrongs that are out in the world, to change them for the better. But, in the midst of our quest, however noble it may be, we need a deep appreciation of not just how to accomplish the goal, but how to bring about change in a manner that will produce a minimum of distress.

Change only takes place in people when they are discontent. If we are satisfied with the status quo, why should we change? Skillful union organizers and other mobilizers of public opinion have traded on negative discontent. If one can find enough people who dislike the same thing, then one has a group with a common goal, namely to get rid of that which they dislike. The role of the change agent is then to provide a solution to the common felt need.

But there are also those who are in the business of creating what might be called "positive discontent." When a pastor calls people to maturity in Christ, he is creating in them a holy discontent — a discontent with the way they are, and a desire to become more than they are.

Resistance to change takes place in the same way. If people are presented with new situations which threaten their "comfort zones," their discontent will be aimed at removing the cause of potential changes. The amount of resistance to change will be proportional to the threat of losing vested interests in the system.

It's important to understand that resistance may not be against the change agent, or even against the change being proposed. Both may be intellectually perceived as excellent, but however good the program is, if it's going to result in changing the way things have always been, it's normal for it to be resisted. Church committees or departments can present programs which are beautifully conceived, and would produce excellent results for large numbers of people, but are often shattered by those who simply do not want change — any kind of change.

Your task as a facilitator, then, is to introduce change in a manner that will encourage people, not discourage them. Our culture focuses on individuality, not community. It is not the same in other cultures. Few other societies in the entire world pay as much attention to exalting the individual as does the British/American culture. This emphasis on rugged individualism can blind us to a basic fact about how change takes place.

How Change Takes Place in a Church

For a number of years, sociologists have described the change process within groups of individuals as "the diffusion of innovations." That is, a new idea seeps slowly through the soil of the total group, moving from one level of persons in the group to the next level. They have recognized that when an innovator poses a new idea or does something differently, there will be some who will see the personal advantages to them very early. Those who do so are called Innovators. The concept will next be accepted by the Early Adopters, followed by the Early Majority, the Late Majority, and perhaps never by the Laggard.

The important fact here is that, in all cases, each one of these groups of individuals accepts change because they observe its benefits in the lives of others first. They then see how it will be of benefit to their own lives. These important facts give us insight into how to plan for change in a "volunteer organization" like a church. People adopt a new idea by diffusion within the group, not by some formal vote where everyone is now prepared to simultaneously adopt the new proposal. It must be stressed that if people don't see benefits for their own situation, there will be absolutely no reason for them to adopt.

In Your Church, There Are Five Distinct Types of People

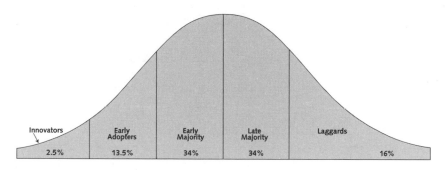

Note the five types of people in the graph above. Pay special attention to the fact that there are fewer people in the groups at the edges of the bell curve than in the center of it. Rogers and Shoemaker, in *Communication of Innovations*, describe them:[1]

Innovators

In your church, you have a group of 2.5% who are eager and ready to try out new ideas. Their lifestyle is characterized by a wide spread of friends, many living long distances away. These "risk takers" are usually more affluent than the rest of the group, since they may have to absorb losses resulting from innovating. These people are venturesome, creative and ready to try a new idea if it makes sense to them.

Can You Write the Names of Such Persons Here?

_____

_____

_____

Early Adopters

13.5% of your congregation fall into this category. They are usually the opinion setters in the church — certainly more than the Innovators are. Potential adopters in the next category, the Early Majority, will be friends of, and influenced by, these Early Adopters. They will be the "public relations" members, influencing those in the membership who ask them, "What do you think about this new cell group concept?"

Can You Write the Names of Such Persons Here?

_____

_____

_____

_____

Early Majority

These are the "deliberate" people, about 34% of the total, who wait until they are sure the idea has a good possibility of succeeding. They interact frequently with the Early Adopters. However, they probably subscribe to the idea, "Be not the last to lay the old aside, nor the first by which the new is tried." They seldom lead out, but will be the first to adopt after the Innovators and Early Adopters have working models of cell groups established.

Can You Write the Names of Such Persons Here?

_____

_____

_____

_____

Late Majority

These represent a significant 34% of the church, and can best be described as the "skeptics." This group will not adopt a new concept until most of the others in the church have done so. The weight of "institutional endorsement" must be present before they will agree to share in what is going on. Indeed, they may appeal to the denominational hierarchy to step in and stop a new "unapproved by headquarters" proposal. It takes the pressure of the peer group to motivate them to adopt, even after they see how they will benefit from the change. However, once they have accepted the new idea, it will be hard to ever eliminate it.

Can You Write the Names of Such Persons Here?

_____

_____

_____

_____

The Laggards

Traditional to the core, this 16% are the last to adopt. They possess almost no "world vision," and live in a tiny bubble of structured activity. They tend to seek out others who agree with their opinions about things and are openly suspicious of all innovations and all innovators. They can slow things to a crawl if they are in positions of leadership. Sadly, over the years of a church's life, as Innovators and Early Adopters move away and leave official leadership positions empty, the Laggards are added to the governing boards until they are in control. When the "pillars" of the church contain a majority of Laggards, there's little or no hope of that church body being changed. This trend builds up over years, and it may require many funerals before this group loses control. Unseating incumbents is hard to do, whether it is in politics or in church life.

Do You Dare To Write Any Names Here?

_____

_____

_____

_____

Power People

Before we proceed with practical steps for transitioning, you must understand the people you will be working with in this process, your primary leaders. I will call them the "Power People." List below the names of the "Power People" in your church.

1. _____
2. _____
3. _____
4. _____
5. _____
6. _____

No matter what you do, you will have to work with these people to transition your church. Any one of them can stifle the vision, no matter how great it is working. Now consider each person that you wrote down, placing each one in one of the adopter categories. Write the category beside each name. With this knowledge, you can be more realistic about your approach to leading change in your church.

How Long Does It Take the Change To Be Adopted By All?

According to Rogers and Shoemaker,[2] the length of time for change in each category is as follows:

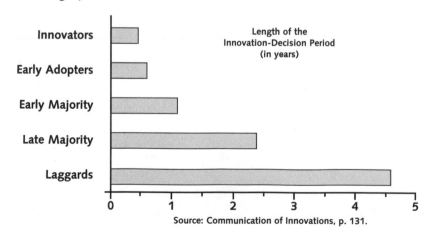

Source: Communication of Innovations, p. 131.

Indicators of Effectiveness Are Needed

How will the pilot project be judged? What indicators can be set up to measure the effectiveness of the ministry? What are the qualities we might expect to find? For example, if we are going to introduce a new form for the worship service in the local church, six months later there should be some indication that the new pattern is really bringing people closer to God. Or, if we are introducing a new policy on the use of offering envelopes, one year later there should be some increase in income as a result.

As you begin cell group life, how will you know, after one year, if your lifestyle evangelism ministry through the cell groups is effective? Why one year? While the Early Adopters may be very enthusiastic about the program shortly after it is begun, the majority of the staff or congregation will withhold judgment. They may even have negative feelings towards the ministry for a long period of time. How long is it going to take before all those who will eventually accept the innovation have adjusted to the presence of it? *About one year!*

Develop a Vision

After you have determined whether or not the cell church is for you, begin to put the vision into words. A vision represents a challenging picture of what the church and its members can be. It paints a picture of a possible and desirable future. The key leaders of the church should do this together.

A vision statement should include these characteristics:
• No longer than three sentences.
• Transferable.
• Includes all believers in its execution
• A timeline of five to ten years.
• Simple enough for an eight-year-old to memorize.

Once the vision is established, it will require persistent and enthusiastic communication to "sell" it through the ranks of church members so it will be embraced with commitment.

Develop Objectives

An objective is a long-term task that describes desired outcomes for individuals, cell groups and the church. Clearly thought out objectives will keep you on track. For every "yes" in your planning, there will be five "no's." Your objectives help you to say "yes" and "no" so you do not dissipate your ministry.

The church's vision is translated into specific objectives for each level. Those at each level participate in setting the objectives for what will be accomplished in their ministry area. Thus, the pastor does not set the objectives for cell leaders. The cell leaders set their objectives for growth and multiplication in consultation with the Zone Supervisor.

There are four important elements to consider when developing your objectives. First, the objectives must be specific. For example, "60% of all members will participate in cell groups by March 2002." Second, objectives must be set through participative decision making. The senior pastor must meet with the necessary leaders to set the annual calendar of activities and budget.

The third element is that objectives require a specific time period to complete the task. When setting objective dates, you will tend to "telescope" the time you think it will take to accomplish your objective if you have never done the task before. In the U.S. Navy Officer's Training, they teach that in these cases you should double the length of time you think it will take, and then be happy if you meet the deadline earlier than expected.

The final element is performance feedback. Each objective is divided into dated goals and the team should monitor the completion.

Sample objectives include:

1. All present church members will be in cell groups (date) _____.

2. All current activities of the church will be carried out by cell groups or will be made obsolete by the cell groups by (date) _____.

3. All existing paid staff and volunteer workers will be retrained and assigned to cell groups ministries by (date) _____.

4. All future leadership will be created within the cell group structure by (date) _____.

5. At least 60% of all cell members will produce at least one convert every six to nine months by (date) _____.

6. All cell members will be given a *Year of Equipping* to prepare them for a lifetime of service by (date) _____.

7. The church budget will be fully revised to reflect the life of the cell church by (date) _____.

8. The church calendar will be fully revised to reflect the life of the cell church by (date) _____.

Each of these objectives and others you will add should have a complete set of goals to back them up. Each milestone or event along the way should be thought through. If you are not inclined to this sort of disciplined thinking, create a team of people who thrive on this sort of thing to help you.

Set Goals to Meet Your Objectives

How do you eat an elephant? One bite at a time. In the same way, goals break down the larger objectives into workable units. Each goal must answer three questions:

1. Who will do the task?
2. When is the date it should/can happen?
3. Where will the resources (people, funds) come from?

Change the Values of the Existing Church Members

Values are hard to grasp. Unlike facts, values are constantly changing. Yet they are under our control. We can choose, modify, discard or replace them. Often our values are deeply rooted in emotions of guilt or love relationships from our past. These are the hardest to revise. For instance, "My mother hand sewed the cushions in our Sunday school class. How dare you suggest that we meet in homes!"

Not all values need to change. If you have a great worship service, this is a good thing. Cells will build on it. If you have a wonderful annual retreat, great. If relationships are strong in the church, you do not have to disrupt this to start cells. Friendships in church is an excellent value and it is important to the cell church.

But many values must be changed. For instance, some have a vested interest in the present church structure because they hold an office that gives them significance. If the Sunday school superintendent learns of the idea of cells, he or she could easily be threatened by this vision because they might lose a job. It will be difficult for people in positions like this to trade their secure role for one that is uncertain within a cell structure. Therefore, it is necessary to show these people the value of a cell group before taking away their ministry. If a child has a pair of scissors, you offer a piece of candy as you take it away. For early majority and late majority leaders, you must develop a prototype they can see before they will be secure.

Other values must also change. Many do not see themselves as ministers. They are only members who *observe* ministry. They will have to learn to value ministry. There are others who are longing to minister and have never had the opportunity. Identify those and pull them in quickly!

Values Change through Experiences not Teaching

We need not look beyond the ministry of Jesus to learn how he changed the values of his cell group. He did not sit and preach to his disciples about what they should be doing. His teaching arose out of experiences, miracles, encounters with God, exorcisms, and ministry to the poor and outcasts. You will greatly benefit by listing the experiences Jesus provided for His "cell group members" and seeing how you can duplicate them in your own setting.

Values change through stages of experience. When you are leading a group through change you must lead them through each of the following stages. They will not immediately arrive at the last stage of full commitment overnight.

Stage 1: Unaware, Uncommitted — At this stage, the person has no awareness there is any difference between a P.B.D. church and a cell church. The paradigm shift has not yet begun. It is important that there be no scolding or exhortations to "get involved" which will only create negative reactions. The persons problem is not resistance, but ignorance.

Therefore, the pastor must preach a series of messages on the topics related to Basic Christian Communities, *oikos, oikodomeo* and *oikonomos* lifestyles. Remember that theology breeds methodology. Provide a solid biblical grounding for the membership from the pulpit as you are forming your cell group. Use illustrations in your sermons taken from the group life you are experiencing. Use testimonies from converts.

Dig out messages that help the membership realize Kingdom life is much different than life in the kingdoms of this world. Carefully teach them the proper use of spiritual gifts, and that they are all to be exercising them. Share about strongholds in their lives and in the world about them. I preached a series on the word *segullah* (1 Peter 2:9), "a people for God's own possession," which was remembered for a decade by those who heard it.

Existing small groups (Bible study groups, prayer group, etc.) can begin to learn about the nature of a Basic Christian Community and determine what elements they do not currently embody.

Also church bulletins, newsletters, etc. should be used to create an awareness of what the cell church is all about.

Stage 2: Aware, Uncommitted — Here, the person knows there is a difference between the two church patterns, but is not interested in participating in the cell church. Some will see the change as too much work, or they may not see the value of adopting the new pattern of church life.

At this point, preach kingdom values. Call people to enter fully into the life of God. Like the rich young ruler, some will go away sorrowful. Others will just stare back at you. With many, you cannot do anything more at this stage. Not until some are surrounded by totally committed Christians will they be impacted by this new way of life.

At the same time, continue to give people experiences of community. Break up large group meetings into smaller groups for discussion and ministry. Encourage Sunday school classes to meet together in the home for a night of fellowship and ministry. Invite a group of people to your home for an evening of personal discussion and ministry. These kinds of activities will stir the desire for something more.

Out of these experiences, a remnant will arise. A remnant in Israel was found when the nation was at its lowest ebb. You must stir up those whose hearts are most tender and begin with them. It may take three or more years for others to move out of Stage 2.

Stage 3: Willing to Receive, Controlled Attention — At this stage, experiences are critical to the development of the person. The first experience should be a recruitment retreat. You should personally select and invite a group of no more than 14 people to this retreat.[3] The purpose is to evaluate potential leadership for the transition stage into cells. If some decline, do not attempt to "sell" them on the idea. They may be early adopters or even early majority who need to see the concept in action before they can make a commitment to participate.

It will be necessary for you to pray over the "pillars" in your church. Evaluate each person and his/her spouse. Which ones have potential to be leaders in cells and should be invited to the retreat? If some of them are carry-overs from the past and are unable to provide the leadership you need, this is a time to help them find a new position more suited to their capacities.

At the recruitment retreat, you will invite the participants to join a leadership core group. This will be the first cell group that you will lead. Remember the "monkey see, monkey do" principle! As I have worked with churches, it has become obvious that the biggest roadblock comes when the pastor and his wife are not personally touching the lives of the lost, and that the only people they ever led to Christ were those within the church walls. What can the members be expected to birth if the Shepherd and his wife are barren? There should be at least one growing group — the one led by the Pastor and his wife. That model is crucial to everything else. If there is one effective, working model led by the Pastor, in six months there will be two.

Pastors with multiple staffs sometimes tell me they are too busy to be involved with this, and they do not participate in launching a cell group. Every single time I have watched this happen, the pastor failed in his objective. Yonggi Cho has more pressure on him than any pastor I know, and he is adamant that the pastor must be involved in cell life! No greater priority exists than for the pastor to restructure his own lifestyle. He must personally be vitally related to the population around him who would not be caught dead in their own coffin listening to him preach.

This Leadership Core Group (don't call it a cell group) should only meet for three months and should include no more than 12 people or six couples who are being prepared to lead cells. It should embody all of the elements of cell life — prayer, community, and evangelism.

As the group meets for the first month and a half, the senior pastor models the life of the cell and involves everyone in different portions of the cell meeting. Each person should also begin going through an equipping track, beginning with the *Arrival Kit*. The pastor will be modeling and teaching about cells. As he trains in new concepts about the cell church, the members are delegated to participate in experiences to make each concept a reality.

During the latter time of this Leadership Core Group, some may not want to continue on. They may not be ready to enter into cell leadership.

Give permission for those who are not interested to step aside. Then work with those who remain and train them to be cell leaders. It will take about eight weeks to do this in weekly meetings or you can do it in an intensive weekend retreat. (The material for cell leader training is described in chapter 21.)

Stage 4: Committed, Conceptualization Completed — At this stage, the person has become fully aware of the new lifestyle and is prepared, with guidance, to help others move through these stages. You will divide the Leadership Core Group into cell leader and cell intern teams and reach out to other responding members of the church to form your first Shepherd Groups.

Stage 5: Characterization, Integrated Lifestyle — At this stage, the person is oriented to the cell church theology and methodology and is fully committed to sharing the vision with everyone in the church. This person's influence begins to penetrate the lives of those who are still at Stage 1. Pastors who have taken their churches through transition share that may take three to four years to get to this place. Once it has happened, the church has transitioned.

Remember: The Focal Point Must Be Upon God's Power

As the transition takes place in the formation of the cell groups, the greater transition will be the development of *oikodomeo* within the lifestyles of the people. In your leadership core group, you must be the first to discover how to receive and manifest Christ's power flowing through you as gifts are used. Forget about your role as a clergyman, and become a man who seeks Christ's direction for building up others through the "spirituals."

When your leadership core group experiences the power of God in its midst, healing of bodies and minds will take place, along with the discernment of strongholds and true and false spirits. Don't try to push this along: if He is not hindered, the Holy Spirit will make it happen. He has waited patiently for the opening in your church to show His mighty power!

Evaluate Teams Weekly

When the reports from cell group meetings come in, look them over carefully. They are indicators of what is happening. Do some attend one time and not return? Why? Is there inadequate follow up in person and by telephone? Are new people not being brought in? Why? Are some bringing new people, and others no one at all? Why?

Provide Contacts Where People Run Dry

Do not let a trainee fail! Helping each person be successful is all-important. One success leads to another, and self-confidence must be developed. Remember that you are asking people to do something they have probably never done before. They need to replace fear with faith, developing a personal vision of what it would be like to reach their world for Christ.

Bring Converts to Share Their Testimonies with the Church

Share the victories first hand with the entire church! Letting members talk personally with new converts will enforce their awareness that God has already started to do His work in their midst.

Make the Shift to Cell Group Church Life

When at least 50% of your membership are committed to cell group life, there will be a dissatisfaction and conflicts with the programs that are still running. Drop your organizations, one by one. Move to a pattern where everyone equips someone, while being equipped.

Those who are still gaining their significance and holding down a power base through controlling a program should be given special attention. It would be easy for these folks to just get angry and fight what you are doing, or leave the church in a huff. However, their mixture of ego with power in the church reveals a serious flaw in their Christian life. How much better it would be for you to minister to them, perhaps through small groups designed to work with you on their needs, until they are brought to a spirit of true servanthood and ministry. In a cell group church, no one should be declared to be "off limits" to the power of God.

Restructure the Church Staff

I really enjoy hearing Dale Galloway, the former pastor of Hope Community Church in Portland, OR, tell about the way he finally called in his staff and reassigned them to serve as Zone Pastors! What a day that must have been. From that day, that dear church has skyrocketed into a ministry that extends for miles and miles across the greater Portland area.

Here's A Chart To Show You What's Ahead!

The chart on page 374 will help you see the stages you are going to go through. Notice there's a cycle that causes you to return to the top of the chart and dream all over again. The mark of a true leader is his ability to get the mind of God for the next phase of cell church life and implement it before momentum is lost. No man in the world has done this any more effectively than Dion Robert in Abidjan! It requires more time in the Listening Room than most pastors have experienced. To have the mind of God is a glorious thing when guiding a church.

PROBLEMS	STEP	RESISTANCE
Lack of Knowledge Lack of creativity Lack of a model "Not invented here"	**CONCEPTION**	LIMITED AWARENESS
	Innovation ⬇	
No previous experience No expertise No guardrails	**DEMONSTRATION**	SKEPTICISM
	System Design ⬇	
Unawareness of requirements No previous experience No trained staff	**DEVELOPMENT**	LIMITED SUPPLY OF STAFF & FUNDS
	Developed System ⬇	
Development of training Trainers needed Expansion of management Cost-effectiveness	**INTEGRATION**	EXISTING WORK STRUCTURES
	Growth ⬇	
Expanded awareness causes cycle to begin again Reorganization threatens "turfs"	**TRANSFORMATION**	INERTIA INNER FEAR OF "LOSING CONTROL"
Triggers general unrest in denomination and generally intimidates "status quo"	⬅ CYCLE BEGINS AGAIN	

24

How To Plant
A Cell Group Church

As in the previous chapter, I am only providing initial thoughts on how to get started. Cell church planting is a growing field and you will need to glean from it as you explore the path that you should take.

If Possible, Apprentice Yourself to a Cell Church

I visited in Madrid with a fine young missionary. He is typical of what is taking place worldwide. His assignment is church planting. *He has never seen a church planted, and his seminary experience didn't provide a single course on the subject.*

A few years back, I was retained by a denomination to work with five church planter couples, all recent seminary grads, assigned to begin new work in Chicago and Pittsburgh. I was to make three trips in one year to "trouble shoot" for them. Their greatest trouble was that they didn't have the foggiest idea of what to do, where to begin, or how to break into the kaleidoscope of kingdoms of this world in these cities. Sadly, all five of them dropped out of their work in defeat. One moved to a small town church, and four of them quit the ministry entirely to go into secular work.

Study the book of Acts: there is a definite pattern for equipping the church planter. *The first step was to experience a church being planted.* This was the case with every single one of the men Paul trained. Indeed, it was also the case with Paul, who was placed in the Antioch church planting venture with Barnabas — who came to help Antioch get going after he had experienced the birth of the Jerusalem church!

The second step was to work with a church planter. We see the extent of this as we examine the names of Paul's travelling companions. I can just imagine the story-swapping of the seven apprentices who had seen churches planted in different places in Acts 20:4:

> He was accompanied by Sopater son of Pyrrhus from Berea, Aristarchus and Secundus from Thessalonica, Gaius from Derbe, Timothy also, and Tychicus and Trophimus from the province of Asia.

Phase One: Form a Leadership Cell

The Leadership Cell is a hybrid. It looks a lot like the Shepherd Cell, but also functions as the cell group church, not yet developed. All of the principle elements are able to function within it. It creates both Share Groups and visitation teams for outreach. This sets up a framework where core leaders can receive on-the-job training in every aspect of Shepherd Group life.

As you study the diagram on the following page, remember that diagrams on paper don't always work out the same way in real life. That's no reason to be cynical of them! Every good football team studies the coach's diagrams on a chalkboard. Their next step is to practice the diagram on the playing field until they are "picture perfect" in execution. They then face the opposition on the gridiron. Sometimes the play works exactly as in the diagram, and sometimes it doesn't. If it doesn't happen as anticipated, they go back to the chalkboard!

Begin the Leadership Cell with Six or Eight People

Duplication of strengths in the leadership cell may be necessary, but the best pattern would be to blend strengths so a wider ministry may take place. This would seem to be the pattern set in Ephesians 4, where the equippers of the saints include an Apostle, a Pastor-Teacher, an Evangelist, and a Prophet.

If the team members are moving to a new city, they should do an urban strategy study before deciding where to live. While this may require renting an apartment for the first few months, it's important that the selection of locations be made on the basis of the ministry, not the

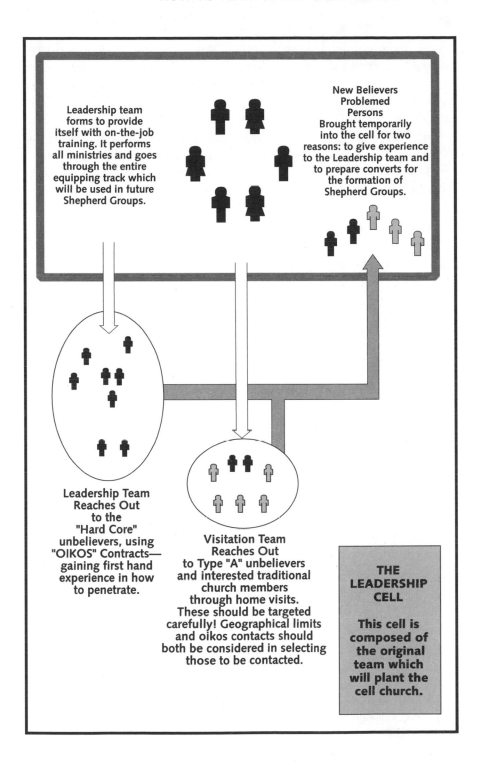

Leadership team forms to provide itself with on-the-job training. It performs all ministries and goes through the entire equipping track which will be used in future Shepherd Groups.

New Believers Problemed Persons Brought temporarily into the cell for two reasons: to give experience to the Leadership team and to prepare converts for the formation of Shepherd Groups.

Leadership Team Reaches Out to the "Hard Core" unbelievers, using "OIKOS" Contracts—gaining first hand experience in how to penetrate.

Visitation Team Reaches Out to Type "A" unbelievers and interested traditional church members through home visits. These should be targeted carefully! Geographical limits and oikos contacts should both be considered in selecting those to be contacted.

THE LEADERSHIP CELL

This cell is composed of the original team which will plant the cell church.

needs of the family. This may sound harsh, but those who begin by putting their own needs first seldom become effective servant leaders.

The financing of the Leadership Cell will take many avenues. Missionaries have support raised before they begin. Other church planters might seek employment outside their ministry position. The "upside" of that is the many *oikos* contacts that will be made — something a "full-time" worker cannot do without special effort.

The first purpose of the cell is to bond the leadership team. There must be a clear vision of what must take place, and a deep commitment to do whatever is needed to make it happen. There must be no question about the calling of each person to the task.

As it begins, the goal of the team should be to activate all elements of a cell group church. All members should become familiar with the lifestyle of a Shepherd Group, effectively performing all the tasks to be found within it. Thus, everyone should go through the materials used in the equipping track. All should be able to effectively visit and should bring a Type "A" unbeliever to Christ. All should participate in the life of a Share Group, and discover the dynamics which take place in that setting. All should serve as a Shepherd of the team for a period of time, evaluated by the rest of the group.

It really doesn't matter if this stage takes several months. There will be more growth in the future if the time is taken to bring the weakest member of the team "up to speed."

This, of course, must include the wives. Many a church planting venture has gone up in flames because the wife was treated as a "tag along," unable to effectively function. Excuses usually include the caring for the children, housework, etc. Our educational system commits a major blunder where wives of seminary students are concerned. The husband gets three years of education, while the wife remains dormant in her own development. I have witnessed many men weep as they have shared the burden of carrying on a public ministry while trying to carry their wives on their backs as a second burden.

The team should follow these guidelines for their initial times together:

1. Focus on God's vision for the work.
2. Develop an initial strategy.
3. Discover how to exercise gifts for edifying each other.
4. Be accountable to each other.

5. Target geographic neighborhoods.
6. Target special groups to be reached by Share Groups.
7. Form the first generation of Share Groups.
8. Form the first generation of Shepherd Groups.
9. Identify, enlist, and train the first Shepherds.

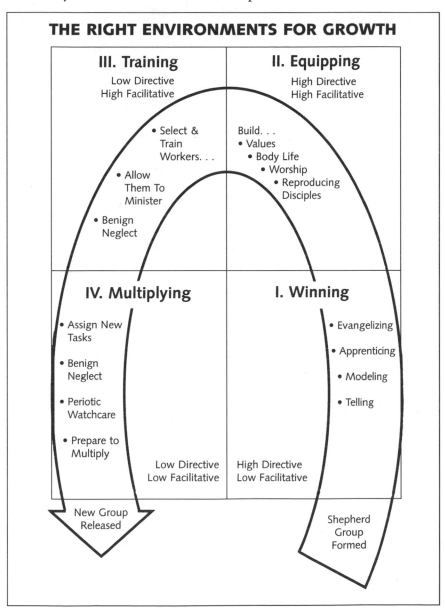

THE RIGHT ENVIRONMENTS FOR GROWTH

III. Training
Low Directive
High Facilitative

II. Equipping
High Directive
High Facilitative

• Select & Train Workers. . .

Build. . .
• Values
• Body Life
• Worship
• Reproducing Disciples

• Allow Them To Minister

• Benign Neglect

IV. Multiplying

I. Winning

• Assign New Tasks

• Benign Neglect

• Periotic Watchcare

• Prepare to Multiply

Low Directive
Low Facilitative

High Directive
Low Facilitative

• Evangelizing

• Apprenticing

• Modeling

• Telling

New Group Released

Shepherd Group Formed

Phase Two: Formation of First Shepherd Groups

Once the team has set a pattern of outreach to the lost, the converts will trigger the second phase. It is now time for the first Shepherd Group, or groups, to be formed. The Leadership Cell should continue to meet alone — perhaps forever! — but the members now try their wings at forming new groups.

The Leadership Cell members will, of course, serve as the Shepherd and the Intern of the first groups. Those who have accepted Christ will be moved through the equipping track.. They will complete the *New Believer's Station* and *Arrival Kit*, move on to *The Touching Hearts Guidebook*, and after winning someone to Christ will form Share Groups as they train using the *Opening Hearts Trilogy*. There will then be growth which will cause the second generation of Shepherd Groups to be launched.

During the first stage, the leadership team has been prayerfully evaluating each person. Initial Shepherd Interns must be identified and invited to be equipped. Each one will then serve as an Intern during this second generation, under the watchful eye of a Leadership team member.

Consider now a potential time line for all this to take place:

First Period (nine months?):
   Leadership team begins to function.
Second Period (six to nine months?)
   First generation of Shepherd Groups formed with converts.
Third Period (six to nine months?)
   Second generation of Shepherd Groups formed; some converts invited to serve as Shepherd Interns.
Fourth Period (six to nine months?)
   Third generation of Shepherd Groups formed; Shepherd Interns now move up to become Shepherds.

It is at this stage that the Leadership team must train themselves to serve in the role of the Zone Supervisor, assuming responsibility for the oversight of several Shepherd Groups. They no longer function as Shepherds. They move between the groups assigned, advising the Shepherds and Interns. By constantly attending all the cells as an advisor, they grasp the areas which need to be strengthened. By constantly spending time with the Shepherds, visiting and praying with the sick, or counseling a marriage problem, the Shepherds are given their "on the job training" by having a companion in their ministry.

The Leadership Team meetings are now devoted to sharing problems being encountered and strategizing for additional formation of cells in new areas of the society. They should stay at least one year ahead in their planning.

Finally, Establish Zone Supervisors or Coaches

Hand picking effective Shepherds to replace members of the Leadership cell members is the next stage. Since the only people qualified for this task are Shepherds, this usually requires his or her group to be distributed into other cells. While this may seem to be hard to do, if the entire movement has caught the vision of penetrating the city it is not traumatic. Friends go with friends when this reapportionment takes place, making the transition easier.

At this time, the Leadership Cell members must focus their attention on thoroughly equipping the Zone Supervisor. They will be heavily involved in working with each Zone Supervisor, being a participant in all he or she does for at least six months.

The more time the Leadership Cell invests in the launch, the stronger the cell church will be in the years ahead. It's much better to let the "rich young rulers" go sadly away in these formative stages, than accommodate their lack of commitment for the sake of numbers. And — by all means — send the traditional folks who don't want to change back where they came from!

Avoid the Temptation To Launch a Celebration

Something in the blood of those coming from a P.B.D. background cries out for the formation of a celebration, or a "Service of Worship," as the first step in church planting. Don't succumb to the thought! Imagine the countless hours which are required to hold a weekly public service. You must find the place to meet. Musicians are instantly needed. Song books, or at the least, song sheets, are required. Is there a sound system, or do you have to import one? What about a nursery for the children — and what will the young people do while the adults are meeting? Rented space means storing the furnishings required: does someone have a truck or a station wagon? How will we advertise it? Who will take the offering? Whew!

These remarks are not to disparage the place of the preacher and the celebration in impacting unreached people. Every strong cell church has weekly services that bless all who attend. These gatherings are an important part of the "root system" needed to penetrate the community. The combination of an anointed leader with anointed cell groups is the maximum way to gather in the harvest. The point is not to be so dazzled by the preacher that the more important ministry of the cells is ignored. Every cell group pastor preaches with power, saying in his heart even as he equips his people, "I am doing this to equip them; let them increase — and let my importance to our growth decrease in proportion."

The recommendation is that you delay any celebration for the cells until you have at least one hundred to participate. The assignments to develop the services can then be rotated among the cells, or certain cells can be asked to perform the same tasks in each service.

When you do finally create a public service, you'll focus them to build the life of the cells, rather than to attract people who may not be interested in cell group life. The more converts you gather in, the faster you will see your vision become reality.

Of course, in time the public services will require gifted musicians to be added to the Ministry Team.

Well, What Do You Do in the Beginning About Worship?

At the very start of the new work, meet as a small group on Sunday mornings to pray, to build up one another, and to train to effectively reach out through your Share Group. After you have gleaned your first harvest, change this Sunday morning time to become the Shepherd Group meeting. It will be a relaxed, precious time with all the families participating. Have an "Agape Meal" with covered dishes; begin it with the passing of the bread and ending it with the passing of the cup as the memory of Christ's death for His Bride.

Let those in the group bring messages God has given them from the Scripture. If you wish, listen to a taped message and then discuss it. Or, read a chapter from an inspirational book or expository Bible study.

Without Fail, Multiply Each Group at Fifteen!

As the first group develops from three or four to 12 to 15, it's time to do two things: form two Shepherd Groups and add a Share Group to the new Shepherd Group. From this time on, there should be about six to eight people in all Shepherd Groups that are launched, and about three or four on each Share Group team. The smaller the groups, the more involved they will be in ministering to each other. As you begin to form new groups, you or someone you designate will have to become a "Zone Supervisor" to minister to the special needs of these little cell churches. Remember — the maximum load for a Zone Supervisor is five groups.

The time to inform people they must multiply at fifteen is not when they have 18, but when they have eight! The longer you wait, the more static you will get when it's time to make two groups out of one.

The reason for this is plain when you learn a simple mathematical formula:

$$(N \times N) - N = CL$$

Which, being interpreted, means: multiply the number of people present by the same number. Then subtract that number from the total. This gives you the number of communication lines in the group. Note how fast it increases: I talk to you, and you talk to me: there are two communication lines. A third person joins us: there are six lines now. With the fourth person, there are 12, with ten there are 90, and with 15 there are 210 communication lines. In fact, after 15 persons you can no longer expect to have small group dynamics. It's a "large group" then, and must be treated in that way. Intimate sharing and interactive discussion is not possible. Save large group activities for the celebrations or, later on, for the congregations and celebrations.

Please — Move the Cell Meetings from House to House!

I have heard all the objections that can be used to doing this for many years: "People won't know where to come;" "It's too confusing;" "Why move around? There's security in having the same couple open their home every week for the meeting."

No, no, no! It's not true! I speak as one who has participated for many years in cell groups that moved every week, or at least every two weeks. In a Shepherd Group with only a handful of members, keeping in touch with one another is a simple matter. The mentality of people who make these objections is premised on the fact that the cell meeting is just one more weekly event in a church schedule. If the cell is what it ought to be, it will be the focal point of life for each member. If someone is out of pocket for a few days, it's a simple matter to call the Shepherd and find out where the group is meeting. On the other hand, either the Shepherd or the Intern should call every contact, every week. Affirming who will be present at the cell should be known in advance.

When the cell meets at the same house all the time, several major setbacks occur. The first is the miserable task of the poor housewife to get her place cleaned up for company every Tuesday night. After a while, that gets old!

The second setback is that the group quickly establish that this is "Bill and Margie's group." Mutual ownership is destroyed. Accountability for the gatherings is watered down.

The third setback is that people never get to really know each other until they spend time in all the homes in the group. This is a very important matter! If you meet Ruth and me at "Bill and Margie's house," you'll never know that we have chosen to live simply, and that our Houston home is packed with furniture and pictures which reflect our deep love for all things Chinese.

Finally, the Scripture plainly says that "they went from house to house." We never saw growth until we began to do that!

Your Second Biggest Problem:
Dealing With Frustrated P.B.D. People

(We'll get to the first biggest problem in a moment.) Avoid like the bubonic plague the temptation to grow by finding frustrated P.B.D. church members who want to join you, unless you have an opportunity to evaluate their motives. Those who depart from P.B.D. life with a grudge seldom, if ever, have a passion for the lost. Take it from years of experience with them — they will drag their feet and slow you down in your mission of becoming the real family of God.

One dear pastor who is in his third year with a clump of folks who pulled out of a P.B.D. situation recently shared his frustrations over this matter. Out of 89 people, seven families have dragged their feet from the first, reticent to abandon the "tried and true" ways of their pasts. They refused to participate in either Share or Shepherd Groups, attending only the public worship times. They finally insisted on a youth program for their teens, a regular Sunday school for their tots, and regular Bible studies for themselves where they could "get fed." At the same time, in three years they had made no move whatsoever to share their faith or make friends with unbelievers. *The rest of the cell group members finally asked them to please leave, and join a church that pleased them.*

We went through great traumas over this when I pastored *The People Who Care* in Houston back in 1970. Half of our original group wanted to enter our new lifestyle, and the other half fought it at every turn. I hated to split a church, so I split myself wide open emotionally instead. I resigned after one year with no place to go and six mouths to feed. I was hurting so badly that I actually chose the concrete pillar on the freeway I was going to drive into at 90 miles an hour. I resigned the church with nowhere to go. My dear friend Jack Taylor invited me to come to San Antonio to work with him. Those were terrible months for me!

In His providence, He spared me from my dark night of the soul and also arranged for a precious lady, a psychiatrist in the group, to confront the Houston congregation with their conflict. The P.B.D. folks all moved en masse to a nearby church. The little band of 42 who remained called me to return to the work again, and I moved back to Houston.

From that moment on, and for all the years that followed, we were extremely cautious about people who visited us from local churches. I used to say to them, "What you see when you come to our celebrations is not our church. You need to get involved in our cell groups for at least three months. If, at the end of that time, you are still interested in becoming part of our cell group life, we will provide a Spiritual Formation Seminar for you before you become a part of our lifestyle. Just remember that we don't plan to change who we are, and we are not looking for folks who want to try to change us." We didn't get large numbers from other congregations, and those who did join us were precious jewels. This also kept our focus on the growth which would come through targeting unchurched people.

Your First Biggest Problem: Helping Christians To Effectively Relate to the Unchurched

Expect it to be tough going when you form Share Groups to reach the unchurched! The problem is not that these folks are difficult to reach: it's that the Christians you will work with have spent years ignoring the pagan world. (Does that include you?)

Restructuring personal values is a slow and painful task, but it's much easier when you're in a cell with a desire to reach out. The first steps in learning how to *oikodomeo* each other will come as you struggle together with your barren lifestyles.

Making contacts is not difficult, but it will require a new way of spending your time. Friends require the investment of hours spent together. When one is free from the P.B.D. rat race, there is time for this.

How many on your Leadership team have personally brought at least one other to Christ? Let them build up the ones who have never done so, by modeling and explaining how it is done as *The Touching Hearts Guidebook* is studied.

Do one or two of the team have contacts ready to participate in a Share Group? Let them show the way they developed such friendships to those who have no contacts. It's "show and tell time," folks! There's no way to learn how to do this except by watching and doing what you see demonstrated.

Early in the life of *The People Who Care*, I took men who had been deacons and church leaders into apprenticeship. They were wonderful guys who had been so busy in the church they had lost contact with unreached men. One at a time, I took them out with me to visit on Friday evenings. We went to taverns, to pool halls, to bars in local hotels, to all-night doughnut shops packed with kids on drugs. After I showed them how to make friends with people in our area in this way, they began to go out by pairs without me. We would meet on Friday nights at my house for prayer in the early evening, and they would return late that night to share and pray about the new contacts they had made. After they developed a "case load" of three or four men, they temporarily used those Friday nights to entertain the men (and often their spouses) in their homes.

Developing a lifestyle that focuses on reaching the unchurched will take some time. Expect this! Look again at the chart of Yonggi Cho's church growth in the first chapter, and realize it will take a while before you get your cell group church under way. In the beginning, you are sowing a lot of seed to be reaped in later months. Keep reminding yourself that once the ministry takes off, the growth is exponential!

Most important of all, remember that the first person you must train is — you! Until you have personally been able to accomplish what you want to train others to do, you will not be successful. Remember Dion Robert: with limited education, without a day of Bible college or seminary, he has developed the largest church in the history of his nation. The three things that made him successful was determination, determination, and determination.

Tan Tien Sur was my student in Singapore in 1977 when I taught these concepts. After I returned to America in that year, he tried and tried to make the cells work among taxi drivers and factory workers. To do so, he forced himself to learn Chinese dialects they spoke. Months went into years, and he couldn't get the right combination to touch this semiliterate, unreached segment of the population. When I returned ten years later, I discovered his exciting ministry called Care Corner had reached hundreds of these folks for Christ. He has cell groups which meet right in the factories. His dream is to create a "Seminary" to train leadership among these new believers. It will have to be a "school" without books, for few of them can read. Although he, too, has never had any formal Bible school or seminary training, his cell movement has won more unreached people for Christ than scores and scores of churches in Singapore have done in a generation! With a multitude of cell groups, he has finally formed his own cell group church. The Chinese speaking congregations he tried to work with rejected these blue-collar people!

This chapter ends, then, with this recommendation:

How will you start your cell group church? With a vision so deeply rooted in your heart and soul by the Holy Spirit that it will not wane when the going is rough and you feel like quitting!

SELF-CHECK FOR YOUR OWN READINESS TO BEGIN

List five unchurched people you spend quality time with each week. They can be from your Primary or Secondary *oikos.*

1. _____

2. _____

3. _____

4. _____

5. _____

List those occasions when you have personally either brought a friend to accept Christ, or when you have tried to do so. It must have happened on a one-to-one basis, not just serving as a counselor in an evangelistic meeting, etc.:

_____

_____

_____

_____

SELF-CHECK FOR STEPS TO TAKE AS YOU BEGIN

List the names of three or four other persons who are willing to participate in forming the Leadership cell with you:*

1. _____

2. _____

3. _____

4. _____

- Give each of them a copy of *Where Do We Go From Here?* Assign them portions of it to read. Meet regularly to discuss the material. Work through all philosophical differences before proceeding.
- Spend significant periods of time together just praying and seeking the Lord's face about your project. "Significant" means three to four hour periods at least once or twice a week. Don't spend all your time talking; you did that as you discussed the book together. Learn to go into the Listening Room of prayer. Create prayer lists for each person to use in these times together. Share impressions the Lord gives you as you pray together. Take those impressions back to the Throne of God to discern whether they have been given by Him to you, or whether they are simply personal preferences. Learn to be a Body related to the Head—to be living stones, built upon the Foundation!
- List all unbelievers in your *oikoses* and include them in your prayer periods. Pray for openness and receptivity to your forthcoming invitations to join you in a Share Group.
- Actively seek to build up (*oikodomeo*) one another by permitting Christ's presence to flow through you for each other.

* If you have a larger number of people, divide them into cells of no more than five. Underline names of possible servant leaders in each cell. Be sure each group includes at least one mature person with *oikos* contacts among the unchurched. Repeat the above suggestions with each group.

Notes

Chapter 1

[1] John E. Cox, "Problems and prospects of shelter and human settlements to the year 2000 and beyond." EKISTICS 53, no. 320/321 (September/October-November/December 1986):266.

[2] The United Nations Population Division Website: http://www.undp.org.

[3] Available from the Population Reference Bureau, Inc. 777 14th St., N.W., Suite 800, Washington, D.C. 20005.

[4] Research done by the Home Mission Board of the Southern Baptist Convention verifies these figures, first recognized by Lyle Schaller. The author studied this phenomenon for the past 10 years in nation after nation. It is a worldwide statistic.

[5] The Gallup Organization Website: http://www.gallup.com/poll/indicators/indreligion.asp.

[6] The Barna Research Group Website: http://www.barna.org/cgi-bin/PagePressRelease.asp?Press ReleaseID=6.

[7] Charles Arn, Donald McGavran, Win Arn, *Growth, A New Vision for the Sunday School* (Pasadena: Church Growth Press, 1980), 25-27.

[8] Auckland, Resistant and Neglected (Houston: TOUCH Publications, n.d.), 9-18.

[9] *Emerging Trends*, Princeton Religion Research Center (Vol. 11, No. 9).

[10] Baptist Pastor Dismissals Rise. *New York Times*, March 15, 1989.

[11] Acts 2:42-46; 1 Corinthians 14:24-26.

[12] Jean Vanier, *Community and Growth* (Homebush, NSW, Australia: St. Paul Publications, 1979), 18-21.

[13] The address of this church is Yoido P. O. Box 7, Seoul 150-600.

[14] John W. and Karen L. Hurston, *Caught in the Web* (Seoul: Church Growth International, 1977), 11.

[15] Reported by Dr. Cho in his address to the Tenth Church Growth International conference, held July 25-31, 1989, in the facilities of the Yoido Full Gospel Church.

[16] Solhein Datin, "Church Planting Since 1945," Paper presented to the Twenty-Seventh Hayama Men's Missionary Seminary, January 6-8, 1986, 9.

[17] Stated in an address made by him to the 1989 Church Growth International board members, Seoul, Korea, August 4, 1989.

[18] Kenneth Dale, Circle of Harmony, A Case Study in Popular Japanese Buddhism with Implications for Christian Mission (South Pasadena: William Carey Library, 1975), x.

[19] Dr. Kriengsak Chareonwongsak may be reached at this address: Hope of Bangkok, G.P.O. Box 1390, Bangkok 10501, Thailand.

[20] Ben Wong and Tony Chan can be reached at P.O.Box 62263, Kwun Tong, Kowloon, Hong Kong.

[21] Dion Robert may be reached at this address: Yaye Dion Robert, Pasteur Principal, Eglise Protestante Baptiste Œuvres et Mission Int. Ext., 03 B.P. 1032, Abidjan 03, Ivory Coast.

[22] Pastor Harold Weitz may be reached at Little Falls Christian Center, P.O. Box 1206, Wilgeheuwel, South Africa.

[23] See Joel Comiskey, *Groups of 12: A New Way to Mobilize Leaders and Multiply Groups in Your Church* (Houston: TOUCH Publications, 1999).

[24] César and Claudia Castellanos may be reached at Mision Carismatica Internacional, Calle 22c NO. 31-01, AA. 50433, Santafé de Bogotá D.C., Colombia.

[25] You may contact Elim at Final Colonia Santa Lucia, Calle El Matazoano No. 1, San Salvador, El Salvador, C.S.

[26] You can contact Bethany Cell Church Network at 13855 Plank Rd, Baker, LA 70714.

[27] Larry Kreider may be reached at Dove Christian Fellowship Int., 1924 West Main St., Ephrata, PA, 17522.

²⁸ Bishop Bob Davis may be reached at Long Reach Church of God, 6402 Dry Barley Lane, Columbia, MD, 21045.

²⁹ You may reach Dr. Steve Bennett at Colonial Hills Baptist Church, 7701 Highway 51 N., Southaven, MS, 38671-5203.

³⁰ C. Peter Wagner, *Spiritual Power and Church Growth* (Altamonte Springs, Florida: Strange Communications Company, 1986), 126-7.

³¹ Charles H. Kraft, *Christianity with Power* (Ann Arbor, Michigan: Servant Publications, 1989), 8.

Chapter 3
¹ Jean Vanier, *Community and Growth* (Homebush, NSW, Australia: St. Paul Publications, 1979), 18-21.

Chapter 5
¹ M. Scott Peck, *The Different Drum* (New York: Simon and Schuster, 1987), 59.

² *Oikos* is used in this book to refer to the basic building block of community life. It is usually translated "household" in the New Testament. A later chapter will fully develop its importance to cell group life.

³ Servants Among the Poor may be contacted at: 691 E. Howard Street, Pasadena, CA, 91104.

⁴ Bruce Bettleheim, *Home for the Heart* (New York: Random House, Knopt Publishing Co., 1973), 41.

⁵ Matthew 16:13-20.

⁶ Matthew 18:15-20.

⁷ Anyone who has tried to pastor a traditional church realized the impossibility of following these instructions in a congregation made up solely of polite acquaintances! Discipline of members is either never done, or it is done with a blunt hatchet which leaves broken bones strewed everywhere.

⁸ Peck, 1987, 300.

⁹ Robert Banks, *Paul's Idea of Community* (Homebush, Australia: Albatross, 1979), 96-101.

¹⁰ 1 Peter 4:12-13.

¹¹ John 20:21-23.

¹² Luke 3:16.

¹³ 2 Corinthians 3:18.

¹⁴ Colossians 1:27.

¹⁵ Acts 2:41-47.

Chapter 6
¹ E. Mansell Pattison, *Pastor and Parish — A Systems Approach* (Philadelphia: Fortress Press, 1977), 19.

² Acts 18:8, Romans 16:5, 10, 11, 1 Corinthians 1:11, 1:16, 16:15, 16:19, Philippians 4:22, Colossians 4:15, 2 Timothy 1:16, 4:19.

Chapter 7
¹ Benjamin Tona, *A Gospel for the Cities* (Maryknoll, NY: Orbis, 1982). See Chapter 2.

² Charles H. Kraft, *Christianity with Power* (Ann Arbor, MI: Servant Publication, 1989), 20.

³ See Philip Steyne, *Gods of Power* (Houston, TX: TOUCH Publications, 1990).

⁴ Dominique Lapierre, *The City of Joy* (London: Arrow Books, 1986), 214.

⁵ Robert McGee, *Search for Significance* (Houston: Rapha Publishing, 1985), 11.

⁶ Tonna, 38.

⁷ Matthew 13:33.

⁸ Pattison, 19.

Chapter 8

[1] Encyclopedia Britannica, 1967 ed., s.v. "Blood."
[2] Ibid., s.v. "Circulation of blood."
[3] Ibid., s.v. "Arteries."
[4] Romans 12:7, 1 Corinthians 16:15, Acts 9:36.
[5] Romans 12:8, 1 Corinthians 16:2, Acts 4:32-35.
[6] Romans 12:8.
[7] 1 Corinthians 12:9, Romans 12:3, Hebrews 11:1.
[8] 1 Corinthians 12:10, Hebrews 5:14, 1 John 2:14, 4:1-3.
[9] Romans 12:8, Acts 13, John 17:18-19.
[10] Romans 12:6, 1 Corinthians 12:10.
[11] Romans 12:7, Matthew 28:18-20.
[12] Matthew 12:42, Acts 6:3, 7:10, 1 Corinthians 1:26, 2:6-12, 12:8, Colossians 1:24-27, 2:3, 3:16, 4:5, James 1:5, Revelation 5:12.
[13] 1 Corinthians 12:8.
[14] Romans 12:8, John 14:16.
[15] 1 Corinthians 14.
[16] 1 Corinthians 14.
[17] 1 Corinthians 12:10.
[18] 1 Corinthians 12:10.
[19] 1 Corinthians 14:24-25.
[20] D. A. Carson, *Showing the Spirit* (Grand Rapids: Baker Book House, 1987), 111-116.
[21] Ibid., 105. See 1 Corinthians 12:30 and 14:18.
[22] Ibid.
[23] Ibid., 103-104.
[24] 1 Corinthians 14:26.

Chapter 9

[1] 1 Corinthians 14:23.
[2] 1 Corinthians 14:12.
[3] 1 Corinthians 14:26.
[4] Kraft, 8.
[5] 1 Corinthians 10:24.
[6] 1 Corinthians 12:4-6.
[7] Romans 12:6.
[8] Romans 12:4-6a.
[9] 1 Corinthians 12:4-6.
[10] 1 Corinthians 12:11.
[11] 1 Peter 4:10.
[12] 1 Corinthians 12:7-10.
[13] 1 Corinthians 12:28.
[14] 1 Corinthians 12:30.
[15] 1 Corinthians 14:1.
[16] Hebrews 2:4.
[17] Carson, 59.
[18] Ibid., 60.
[19] Ephesians 4:15-16.
[20] 1 Corinthians 14:1.
[21] 1 Peter 4:8.
[22] Hebrews 10:24.
[23] 1 Thessalonians 3:12.

24 2 Thessalonians 1:3.
25 1 Corinthians 16:14.
26 1 Corinthians 14:12.

Chapter 10
1 1 Corinthians 14:12, 26, Hebrews 10:24, 25.
2 Ephesians 4:30.
3 Romans 6:3, Galatians 3:27, 1 Corinthians 12:13.
4 1 Corinthians12:7.
5 1 Corinthians 14:25.
6 Daniel 10:12-13.
7 Hebrews 5:13-14.
8 David Lowes Watson, *The Early Methodist Class Meeting* (Nashville: Discipleship Resources, 1987), 194.
9 Ibid., 200.
10 1 John 2:13-14.

Chapter 11
1 C. S. Lewis, *The Four Loves* (New York: Harcourt, Bruce & World: 1960), 192.
2 Carson, 179.
3 This is not to say that all who publically declare words of knowledge are frauds. I watched Sam Lai in Hong Kong hold a street meeting in the park on Temple Street. He walked up to a man in the crowd that ringed him as he preached, and spoke so plainly to him about the sin in his life that the man trembled with fear. The rest of the crowd became so afraid he would do the same to them that they literally ran away.
4 1 Corinthians 14:26-33.
5 Hebrews 10:24-27.
6 Elizabeth O'Conner, *Search for Silence* (Waco: Word Books, 1972), 87.
7 Ibid., 95.
8 Carson, 34.

Chapter 12
1 Psalm 127:3.
2 Psalm 139:15-16, 22:9-10, 71:6.
3 Exodus 22:29.
4 Deuteronomy 6:6-7, 11:19-21.
5 Deuteronomy 4:9-10.
6 Deuteronomy 6:20 21.
7 Joshua 7:11.
8 Exodus 32:31-32.
9 W. Robertson Smith, *Lectures on the Religion of the Semites* (new ed., rev, London: A. & C. Black, 1894), 273. Quoted in H. Wheeler Robinson, *Corporate Personality in Ancient Israel*, 28.
10 Psalm 103:13, Hosea 11:1-3.
11 Deuteronomy 32:46-47.
12 Deuteronomy 16:16, cf. Luke 2:41-51.
13 Deuteronomy 6:20.
14 Joshua 4:6.
15 2 Chronicles 24:2.
16 Deuteronomy 6:7, 11:18-21.
17 Psalm 78:5-8.
18 Jeremiah 31:29.

[19] Exodus 20:5-6, Deuteronomy 5:9, Numbers 14:17-18.
[20] Deuteronomy 18:9.
[21] Numbers 14:31.
[22] Ezekiel 18:18-20.
[23] Psalm 8:2, 148:12.
[24] 1 Samuel 3:7.
[25] 1 Samuel 2:26 (cf. Luke 2:52).
[26] Judges 13:3-5, Luke 1:76.
[27] Proverbs 1:8, 4:1-4, 6:20.
[28] Proverbs 3:12.
[29] Luke 1:42.
[30] Luke 2:39.
[31] Luke 2:49.
[32] Matthew 11:16-17, Luke 7:31.
[33] Matthew 17:14-18, Mark 9:14-27, Luke 9:37-43.
[34] Mark 5:41, Luke 8:54.
[35] Matthew 19:13-15, Mark 10:13-16, Luke 18:15-16.
[36] Matthew 21:14-16.
[37] Matthew 7:9-11.
[38] Matthew 11:25.
[39] Matthew 18:5, Mark 9:36-37.
[40] Matthew 18:6, Luke 17:2.
[41] Matthew 18:10.
[42] Matthew 18:14.
[43] John 6:9.
[44] Matthew 19:14.
[45] Matthew 20:25-28.
[46] Mark 9:36-37, Luke 9:46-47.
[47] Luke 18:21-23.
[48] Acts 2:39.
[49] Acts 16:33-34.
[50] Acts 9:36-42.
[51] 2 Timothy 1:5.
[52] Ephesians 5:32-33.
[53] Ephesians 6:4.
[54] Ephesians 4:13.

Chapter 13
[1] See *The Shepherd's Guidebook.*
[2] Robert and Julia Banks, *The Church Comes Home: Building Community and Mission through Home Churches,* revised edition (Peabody, MA: Hendrickson Publishers, 1998).

Chapter 14
[1] Christian Schwarz, *Natural Church Development: A Guide to Eight Essential Qualities of Healthy Churches* (Carol Stream, IL: ChurchSmart Resources), 23-24.
[2] Quoted in Joel Comiskey, *Groups of 12: A New Way to Mobilize Leaders and Multiply Groups in Your Church* (Houston: TOUCH Publications, 1999), 24.
[3] See Joel Comiskey, *Groups of 12: A New Way to Mobilize Leaders and Multiply Groups in Your Church* (Houston: TOUCH Publications, 1999) for a detailed explanation of how the G12 system works at the International Charismatic Mission and how 12 other church have adapted this system for their context.

[4] Yaye Dion Robert, *Cell Group Ministry: One of the Secrets of the Growth of a Church* (Tulsa, OK: Christian Works and Mission International, Inc., n.d.), 5.

Chapter 15
[1] Psalm 78:70-72.
[2] 1 John 2:12-14.
[3] 1 Thessalonians 1:5-7.
[4] 2 Corinthians 10:4-5.

Chapter 17
[1] I. Howard Marshall, *Commentary on Luke* (Grand Rapids: Eerdmans Publishing Company, 1978), 419-420.
[2] If you are not a watcher of American TV, "Mash" is a comedy from the 1970's which told the story of doctors and nurses in a battle zone during the Korean War. They treated casualties who came in wounded and were sent away patched up.

Chapter 20
[1] Contact Percept Group, Inc. 151 Kalmus Dr., Suite A104, Costa Mesa, CA, 92626. Phone: 1-800-442-6277, Fax: 714-957-1924. Website: http://www.perceptnet.com.

Chapter 22
[1] Reality Outreach can be contacted at 1-800-263-2114 or by fax at 905-646-8766.

Chapter 23
[1] Everett M. Rogers with F. Floyd Shoemaker, *Communication of Innovations: A Cultural Approach*, second edition (New York: The Free Press, 1971), 182 ff.
[2] Ibid., 131.
[3] You can download the instructions for this retreat at no cost you when you access the TOUCH Outreach Ministries Website: http://www.touchusa.org.

Index

Your Equipping Journey

The journey continues as you become a cell group leader.

CELL GROUP LEADER TRAINING
Leadership Foundations for Groups That Work

At this point, you will learn to share Christ's love with unbelievers.

Touching Hearts

Mentoring Another Christian

Soon, you'll be joined by a new believer who will rely upon you to guide him or her. Here you'll find the practical tools you'll need to mentor a new Christian.

As you walk with God, you'll find that prayer and ministry to others becomes a new lifestyle.

The Arrival Kit

TOUCHING HEARTS WEEKEND

ENCOUNTER GOD WEEKEND

Beginning the Journey

As you begin your journey, you'll find that God loves to spend time with you and if you listen, you'll hear Him.

SPIRITUAL FORMATION WEEKEND

ADDITIONAL CELL GROUP RESOURCES

THE JOURNEY GUIDE FOR NEW BELIEVERS

Launch your cell members on a journey of freedom and ministry to others! This tool helps a new believer understand his past and determine the steps leading to growth. It will guide new believers to deal honestly with their struggles and share them with those who can love them through the healing and growing process of discipleship.

THE JOURNEY GUIDE FOR GROWING CHRISTIANS

This tool is designed for growing believers in your cell groups. It will affirm how God has used them in ministry, challenge them to move forward in their Christian walk and set a workable course for their future ministry.

THE JOURNEY GUIDE FOR CELL GROUP LEADERS

This tool will help your interns and cell leaders evaluate their leadership role in your cell groups, including servanthood and ministry to others. It is an excellent assessment for group leaders who are about to take their own group. If you have seen searching for a solid way to help your leaders determine their own strengths and weaknesses and take ownership of their growth and maturity, you've found it.

COVER THE BIBLE

Interactive CD-ROM *by Ralph W. Neighbour, Jr.*
With just 5 minutes each day at your computer, you'll overview the entire Bible in one calendar year. . .

Wouldn't it be great to have a Bible scholar available at any time to help you know the background of a passage? With this comprehensive, four CD set, you will learn valuable information on every book of the Bible from a respected Bible teacher. When you use *Cover The Bible*, you will gain a strong understanding of each book before you read, helping you dig deeper into God's Word.

Features You'll Enjoy:
- Tracks multiple users. Your whole family can work at their own pace . . . even your children.
- Over 1200 illustrations, maps, and charts helping you understand the culture, customs, and location of each Bible passage.
- 26 hours of audio explanations, video clips and suggestions for further study are provided by your host, Dr. Ralph Neighbour, Jr.
- The daily sessions will complement what you learn or teach in a Bible study or Sunday School class.
- Each week ends with a puzzle or quiz you will enjoy, helping you remember what you have learned.

Minimum Hardware/Software Requirements: PC Users: 233 Mhz Pentium or faster; Windows® 95, 98, 2000, NT4; 32Mb physical Ram installed (64 preferred); 4x or faster CD Rom drive. Apple® Users: 233 Mhz Power PC or faster; OS 8.1 or higher; 32Mb physical Ram installed (64 preferred); 4x CD Rom or faster.

Order Toll-Free from TOUCH® Outreach Ministries
1-800-735-5865 • Order Online: www.touchusa.org

116865

ADDITIONAL CELL GROUP RESOURCES

THE SHEPHERD'S GUIDEBOOK

by Ralph W. Neighbour, Jr.

With over 100,000 copies in print, this tested guide will equip and train your leaders to develop community and lead people into relationship evangelism, by learning to listen to God's voice on behalf of their flock. Cell leaders will gain tools for leading a cell meeting, and learn pastoring skills that will multiply the ministry of your church. 256 pages.

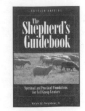

CELL GROUP LEADER TRAINING

Pick up this training and get busy. It's really that easy!

The *Trainer's Guide* leads you through each step of training. You need not be a small group expert! Just download the PowerPoint® presentations from our web site, read through the week's training, pass out a *Participant's Guide* to each leader, and walk them through the material. Practical exercises are included with each session. The hard work of preparation has been done for you.

Adapt it to fit your church calendar.

Optional formats include a two-day retreat, a one-day seminar, eight one-hour sessions or eight one and a half hour sessions. You choose the best format for your church calendar.

Everything you need to produce quality leaders.

After 20 years of training cell group leaders, we have assimilated time-tested methods for training effective leaders. This training will lay a great foundation for up-and-coming leaders and establish current leaders in effective practices that will revolutionize their groups!

Current and future leaders will learn how to:

- Prepare their hearts for leadership
- Lead an effective meeting
- Ask good questions
- Lead a group into transparent sharing
- Minister to members outside the meeting
- Reach unbelievers through cell-based relationships
- Work through the conflict stage into community
- Mentor a new leader
- Involve children in the meetings and group life

Trainer's Guide includes two bonus sections:

- A guide to facilitate *Upward, Inward, Outward, Forward*, a one-day strategic planning workshop for cell group leaders and members.
- The interview guide for the *Journey Guide for Cell Group Leaders*, a self-evaluation tool to determine what potential leaders need in order to be effective.